Matrix and line

SUNY Series in Radical Social and Political Theory

Roger S. Gottlieb, Editor

Matrix and line

Derrida and the possibilities of
postmodern social theory

Bill Martin

State University of New York Press

Published by
State University of New York Press, Albany

© 1992 State University of New York

Printed in the United States of America

For information, address State University of New York Press,
State University Plaza, Albany, N.Y., 12246

Production by M. R. Mulholland
Marketing by Dana E. Yanulavich

Library of Congress Cataloging-in-Publication Data

Martin, Bill, 1956–
     Matrix and line : Derrida and the possibilities of postmodern
social theory / Bill Martin.
          p. cm.
     Includes bibliographical references and index.
     ISBN 0-7914-1049-8 (alk. paper). — ISBN 0-7914-1050-1 (pbk. :
alk. paper)
     1. Derrida, Jacques.   2. Postmodernism.   3. Social sciences-
-Philosophy.   I. Title.
B2430.D484M37   1992
194—dc20

                                                                91-20980
                                                                CIP

10 9 8 7 6 5 4 3 2 1

For their teaching and friendship
Kathleen League
Gary Shapiro
Jacques Derrida
Donald Davidson

Contents

Preface

With this "Preface," I simply wish to give the reader, in the briefest form possible, three "keys" to the following text.

First, concerning the question of a beginning. In keeping with Derrida's arguments about origins, and with the deconstructive practice of staking out a position within a text, the analysis in this text "begins," so to speak, in the middle, in the midst of a history that is ongoing, without beginning or end. It would be wrong to think that this procedure simply reflects a decision by the author; rather, one is situated, one is never not contextualized by this history.

Second, concerning the question of intersections. The situation of this text is at the intersection of a number of ongoing debates in social theory and contemporary philosophy. Although one does not need to be an "expert" in Derrida's work (something that I do not and will never claim for myself, having realized especially at the completion of this text that my apprenticeship in that work has only begun), a basic familiarity is necessary, as is some familiarity with current discussions in social theory. I have tried to find some intersections of social theory, philosophy, and cultural criticism that, though perhaps startling at first sight, represent a realistic cartography of emerging trends. In the "Bibliography" I have marked those works that are especially significant for the present study. This system of intersections does indeed consist in main thoroughfares as well as side roads, but there is perhaps no central highway other than the open character of Derrida's work itself.

Third, concerning the question of possibility. This text, though lengthy and, at least in its fundamental intentions, systematic, is only the beginning of the opening of Derridean possibilities in social theory. In terms of the intersections just mentioned, I approached the study with an appreciation of work that has already been done in this field, as well as the sense that all of the "radical Derrideans," including myself, are still defining the field. This is an especially difficult task, given that we take it as essential that finality is something to be permanently postponed. Certainly there are other approaches to this work that could have been pursued. For example, the work that I have done here has convinced me that close readings, with an eye toward a more explicit "political thematization" and systematization of essential works such as *of Grammatology* and *Glas*, are an important part of articulating the possibilities of postmodern social theory. Although I have attended to these and many other of Derrida's texts, however, I have at this point determined that the important thing is to generate a framework in which this further articulation can be pursued. In short, I have dispatched a letter toward impossibility, in the hope of finding the possible space for a Derridean contribution to postmodern social theory.

Acknowledgments

All work within the common human project and space of intertextuality is necessarily collaborative. I wish here to thank those who
participated in various ways in the formation of this particular matrix.
To those to whom the book is dedicated I owe a debt that can only be
repaid in several installments, of which this is the first. Over the last four
years I have had many discussions concerning the project, all of which,
one way or another, have made their way into the weave. For taking the
time and energy to participate, sometimes perhaps without even knowing it, I would like to thank: Bob Antonio, Doug Atkins, Jack Bricke, Jack
Caputo, Ann Cudd, Richard De George, Martin Donougho, Jack Doody,
Janice Doores, Steve Fuller, Diana Fuss, Tony Genova, Cindi Hodges,
Greg Jay, Doug Kellner, David Krell, Rex Martin, Janet Sharistanian,
Sveta Stojanovic, Ted Vaggalis, and Jerry Wallulis. For proofreading the
text, I would like to thank Paul Schafer and Kathleen League. For
editorial assistance and encouragement I would like to thank Clay
Morgan. For having faith in a project that may seem worlds away from
his own Sartrean inclinations, I would like to especially thank Roger
Gottlieb (don't worry too much, Roger, I still believe that imagination is
power). For countless hours of philosophical discussion in often hazard-
ous circumstances (i.e., jogging in campus traffic), I would like to thank
Al Cinelli. For several years of encouragement and stimulating discussions on philosophical social theory, I would like to especially thank
George Trey. The standard disclaimer is to say that the aforementioned
are not responsible for what is presented here, but then, according to the
line that I draw out of this matrix, strictly speaking this is not true.

For kindly granting permission to reprint from their publications,
thanks to the following publishers:

From *White Noise* by Don DeLillo. Copyright © 1984, 1985 by Don
DeLillo. Used by permission of Viking Penguin, a division of Penguin
Books USA Inc.

From the essay "Heidegger's Topology of Being" by Otto Poggeler,
in Joseph J. Kockelmans, editor, *On Heidegger and Language*. Copyright
© 1972 Joseph J. Kockelmans. Used by permission of Northwestern
University Press.

From the essay "No Apocalypse, Not Now (full speed ahead,

seven missives, seven missiles)" by Jacques Derrida. Translated by Catherine Porter. *Diacritics,* v. 14, n. 2 (summer 1984), pp. 18 31. Used by permission of Johns Hopkins University Press.

From *Positions* by Jacques Derrida. Translated by Alan Bass. Copyright © 1981 by The University of Chicago. Used by permission of University of Chicago Press.

From *Margins of Philosophy* by Jacques Derrida. Translated by Alan Bass. Copyright © 1982 by The University of Chicago. Used by permission of University of Chicago Press.

From *The Book of Shares* by Edmond Jabes. Translated by Rosmarie Waldrop. Copyright © 1989 by The University of Chicago. Used by permission University of Chicago Press.

From the essay "Nietzschean Aphorism as Art and Act" by Gary Shapiro, in J. N. Mohanty, editor, *Phenomenology and the Human Sciences.* Copyright © 1985 by Martinus Nijhoff Publishers, Dordrecht. Used by permission of Kluwer Academic Publishers.

For use of the Dorothy Becker translation of the poem "Reply to the Shade of Descartes" by Anne de la Vigne. Copyright © 1986 by Dorothy Becker. From the book *The Defiant Muse: French Feminist Poems from the Middle Ages to the Present,* edited by Domna Stanton. Published by The Feminist Press at CUNY. All rights reserved.

From *The Philosophical Discourse of Modernity* by Jurgen Habermas. Translated by Frederick Lawrence. Copyright © 1987 by the Massachusetts Institute of Technology. Used by permission of MIT Press.

For the use of Richard Sieburth's translation of the poem "Mnemosyne" by Friedrich Hölderlin, from *Hymns and Fragments.* Copyright © 1984 by Princeton University Press. Used by permission of Princeton University Press.

From *Encounters between Judaism and Modern Philosophy* by Emil Fackenheim. Copyright © 1973 by Basic Books. Used by permission of Schocken Books.

1

Modalities, politics

We must avoid the temptation of supposing that what occurs today somehow pre-existed in a latent form merely waiting to be unfolded or explicated. Such thinking also conceives history as an evolutionary development and excludes crucial notions of rupture and mutation in history. My own conviction is that we must maintain two contradictory affirmations at the same time. On the one hand, we affirm the existence of ruptures in history, and on the other we affirm that these ruptures produce gaps or faults in which the most hidden and forgotten archives can emerge and constantly recur and work through history.

—Jacques Derrida[1]

The meaning of community is in danger.

In essays and longer works ranging from "The Ends of Man" to *Glas*, Jacques Derrida has been occupied with the discourse of ends, of apocalypse: the end of the book, the end of philosophy, the end of the world. What is this "occupation"? To be occupied with the end is to profess it. To profess the end, to make of oneself a professor of the end, or to be made into such a professor (to be occupied with, i.e., by the end), is also to profess against the end. Which occupation will it be? Derrida's answer is that there is no choice here; thus his strategy is an apocalyptic anti-apocalypticism. I have already announced the strategy of this study.

Humanity is on the verge of *forever* losing the sense of community, even as this sense seems to have been recreated in thousands of diffuse ways. Though the word, "community," is a commonplace of public discourse, the word is a mere trace of its former self. These are apocalyptic words, it is true. These are words that already ring with the sound of original plentitude (i.e., the idea that there was a time when the meaning of community was not in danger), loss, illusions of recovery (false messiahs) and the hint of the possibility of real recovery. For this apocalyptic tone I would readily take responsibility, if such responsibility were really possible. This remains to be seen, for the meaning of responsibility is no less in danger than the meaning of community: the fate of the former is tied to that of the latter. The apocalyptic mission I have set for this study, then, is toward the rearticulation of the meaning and (therefore) possibility of community. The strategy that I will pursue is Derridean: an anti-apocalypticism just this side of apocalypse.

What is meant by the term, "apocalypse"? The usual, of course: the end of the world in fire and cataclysm. But something more is meant as well. It has everything to do with the meaning of community that is in danger. How can "meaning" be in danger? Certainly the end of the world represents a danger to meaning, but how could the end of meaning mean a danger to the world? We have, however, only spoken thus far of a particular meaning, that of community, being in danger. How the dangerous situation of this meaning is connected to the end of the world in fire is what this study will elaborate.

On "just this side" of apocalypse is where we find ourselves. Who?

At a later point in this chapter I will introduce the larger framework that will make the profession of community possible. To "begin" with such an "introduction," however, would be to betray the discourse with which we are already occupied, and whose many layers we can only begin to differentiate by the taking of a position within the discourse. That is to say, a position must be marked out—we are already occupied with it and by it—in society.

Postsecular socialism: some words in preparation

Why focus attention on the meaning of a word? So what if "community" has lost its meaning? Is it still not true that we (who?) live in some sort of social order, a society? "Society" or "community," what difference does it make?

What then, of hearing the word, "community"? One continually hears this word. Is it spoken falsely? What would it mean to answer this last question in the affirmative? For I do answer the question this way: the notion of *Gemeinschaft* is deployed, in our modern, Western, secular societies, in a *gesellschaftliche* way.[2]

All that has been generated is a series of questions. Each of these contains at least two more questions: that is, every question must come to grips with its terms and its conditions of presentation. For example: Who or what is this "humanity" that is possibly on the verge of losing the sense of community? Is this humanity itself a community, a society, or something else? Is "it" only one thing, or is humanity a series of entities, some of which are societies and some of which are communities? If so, what then is "humanity" apart from this series—is it more than merely a biological category, if that? Under what particular historical conditions are these questions raised? At the intersection of what discourses and what kinds of discourses?

A social *theory* cannot remain on the level of undefined, albeit apocalyptic, notions. Remaining on that level assumes that the apocalyptic "energy" of these terms will somehow do the work of securing an understanding of our situation in a time or place just this side of apocalypse. This is, I think, Heidegger's strategy, which he called "thinking." That strategy must itself be interrogated, by a Derridean strategy that is occupied with thinking, but on just this side of apocalypse. Though the term does not do full justice to Derrida's project, it would not be entirely wrong to call this apocalyptic anti-apocalypticism "philosophy." The term that Derrida will use, however, is "writing," and it is very important that we come to grips with this term.[3]

A social *theory* must "ascend to the social," as Marx might have put it. The means, it could even be said, the *material* of that ascendency, is an all-important consideration. Perhaps there is an identifiable historical dialectic of community and society, but there is no transcendent *force* to this dialectic, any more than there is a transcendent energy of apocalypse, that will "propel" humanity toward a new conception and instantiation of community. There "is" only that which exists on this side of the transcendent dialectic. Derrida is also occupied with this difference.

Fake notions of community, as found either in the fascism of the first half of this century or in more recent, even more technological variants, are the last gasp of a modernity run out of steam (or fossil fuels, plutonium, etc.). The emerging world order, which I will argue is appropriately called "postmodern," is taking shape as a secular society that is structurally precluded from regenerating itself with a sense of community, try as it might. This "hyper-secular" society must therefore bleed dry those human impulses that have as their aim the reinvention of community. This reinvention depends on memory. Accordingly, the essence of hyper-secular society is the destruction of memory.

Michel Foucault (1973) has argued that "humanity" is an invention of the modern West. Thus we find in this same West, which however we have yet to define, a century of crisis rhetoric: humanity in the West is in crisis, ergo, "humanity" is in crisis.[4] What is this crisis? I will argue that it is the near-complete destruction of memory, a destruction that has its roots in modernity. This may sound like the beginnings of a "conservative" argument. Rest assured that, in conventional terms, this is not the case (this is not another "back to Burke" critique of modernity). But the question of terms is ever-present: this *is* an argument about "conservation." There may be a form of "conservatism" that appears radical in its depth. I share some sympathy for this possibility, which I find best exemplified in ordinary people who wonder at how the fabric of life can be torn up, not rewoven, for seemingly no good reason. The fabric of life can be rewoven only in appreciation of its value, but there is no appreciation without memory.[5] The damage that has been done to memory has worked through the damage of the material of memory: language and appreciation or care. The West possesses the means to make this "brain damage" worldwide, and is certainly making full use of these means. Here the dissemination of meaning is the key issue.

Are there no examples of community in the West? My argument will be that there are examples; there are community structures to be found in the *margins* of the West. One very important example would be the Christian base communities in Latin America that have encouraged and been encouraged by liberation theology. But it is very important that we grasp what is exemplified by such examples.

Repositories of memory are of course not enough in and of themselves: there is the "archive," and then there is the *opening* of the archive. This opening is necessary both for the sense of "textuality" that is central to Derrida's work, and to the existence of communities as ongoing life projects. Memory, however, is the beginning of community. Perhaps one definition of "society" (*Gesellschaft*) is: "thought" without memory. An alternative formulation might be "speech without writing." I mean these terms in the senses specified in Derrida's earlier work. Speech, that is, that takes itself to be without writing, without the mediations of language, without the atmosphere and alterity of language. (Derrida uses the term, "speech," as emblematic of a supposed immediacy; "writing," in his argot, refers to the continual insinuation of the other, by means of the principle of contextuality. These terms, as they apply to the questions taken up in this study, will be explicated further in due course.) Perhaps speech will never truly exist without writing, and perhaps this truth comprehends the repository of human possibility. This study will be concerned with the proximity of writing, in Derrida's sense of the term: the closeness or distance of humanity from the retrieval of writing. I will argue that the future possibilities for community will be postsecular, *writerly*. The distance between humanity and community may be such that the latter is not *absolutely* irretrievable (which is almost like saying, "Where there's life, there's hope"), but still a distance so great that, for all practical purposes, humanity will not be able to reinvent community. This is the danger that looms large at present.[6]

"Postsecular" is also an appropriate term here in the sense that the future possibilities of community cannot consist merely in the retrieval of pre-secular forms of community. The postsecular community for which I will attempt to provide a philosophical ground will be based, in part, on an *appreciation* of the forms of solidarity found in pre-secular communities. Such an appreciation, however, if it is not mediated by the real achievements of modernity—of secular society and Enlighten- ment—can be, in the postmodern, high-tech world, extremely dangerous.

This distinction, between a possible, postsecular community, and a social entity that is only an amalgam of secular society and pre-secular community, helps show the difference between two twentieth century social experiments that are often taken to be identical by liberal social philosophy. I refer to Hitlerian fascism and Stalinist socialism (though I hesitate to call the former an "experiment"). Nazi Germany is an earlier stage of an emerging techno-capitalist *secular* society, papered over with images of community.[7] These images were undoubtedly very sick, in that their purpose was to negate the universalistic discourse of modern secular society by an appeal to the notion of a specific "commu- nity" (in this case the artificial community of "Aryans") as a kind of messianic tribe. (The messianic imagery—German culture as the pinna- cle and savior of Western civilization—was also a kind of perverse mirror of and repository for secular universalism.) The more recent "Neo-Conservative Revolution" (Reagan, Thatcher, etc.) represents a later stage of this same secular gambit.[8]

Socialism in the Stalinist mold, on the other hand, represents an attempt to break with modernity with very little appreciation of its achievements. We might give a name to this attempt: "unenlightened socialism."[9]

That these phenomena, the social formations guided by Hitler and Stalin, were very similar in content, and somewhat in form, is a disturbing and formidably troublesome truth. But it is not a truth that either liberal politicians, or liberal social philosophers (even the more enlightened of them, e.g., John Rawls) are particularly well-equipped to analyze.[10]

In creating an unenlightened socialism, Stalin (and to some extent Lenin before him) was relying on the following set of identifications (even if they were not necessarily foregrounded in these terms): moder- nity=Enlightenment=bourgeois democracy=the discourse of rights=West-

ern secular society=capitalism. Undoubtedly the paradigmatic conception that guides unenlightened socialists is the view that all but the last
of these terms essentially add up to the last, capitalism—or that all the
other terms besides capitalism are simply the "trappings" of capitalism.
Because capitalism must be done away with (on this point I readily
agree), these other ideas and institutions must be done away with as
well—so the Stalinist argument goes. Everything hinges, however, on
whether the terms under question are linked by relations of identity or
relations of affinity or association. Clearly, there can be no argument,
other than one that is entirely formal and ahistorical, that the association
of, say, democracy, rights discourse, and capitalism is *no more than* an
"association." To a great extent these three institutions are identified
with one another, even if they are by no means identical. What is the
form and *material* of this identification? This will be a central question in
this study, because a postsecular socialism and the postsecular community can only be approached in terms that are deeply historical, terms
informed by their historicality and historical debts—debts that are
always collected.

        If the social world is to be not only interpreted, but reconfigured as
well, the material of historical identifications must be attended to. I will
argue that this will mean an emphasis, in theory and practice, on forms
of signification, especially language. Two questions will loom large in
the background of this study: 1) What are the predominant forms of
signification of modernity and postmodern secular society? 2) What
could be the forms of signification of an emerging postsecular community? Though there are many theorists and many practical experiments
that contribute to answering these questions, I propose that the work of
Jacques Derrida provides the best staging ground for their full
articulation.

The letter and the spirit

        In two very important and closely-related respects the Soviet
Union under Stalin was *not* a non-secular community. These two
respects concern the questions of science and language (and, as part of
the latter, the question of literature). Like Western societies that had
passed through the periods of Enlightenment and modernity, the Soviet
leadership was intoxicated with science, conceived as the only pathway
to everything that could legitimately be called knowledge and truth.
And, as in Western societies, the Soviet leadership sponsored a concomitant denigration of all other possible pathways to knowledge,

truth, and understanding. The form of this denigration parallels the similar privileging of "reason" over "rhetoric" in Plato, and the privileging of autonomy over heteronomy in Descartes and Kant. This positivistic repression of language is perhaps *the* major theme in Derrida's work. In the name of a radical empiricism, "science," as the royal road to knowledge, rules out the sentential in the name of a language of "propositions" that are purportedly not subject to material taint. People in and of the world, who participate in the economy of the letter, are subject to this material taint (in Chapter 5 I call it "contamination"). This is not to speak in the name of some "folk wisdom" that is "deeper" than "modern science." If what is meant by "science" is "making our ideas clear" (Peirce), then science must be measured by the faith it keeps to the entire range of human expressions and experiences. The materiality of those experiences, and the materiality of the language that discloses them, must not be sacrificed to the supposed purity of the propositional "spirit."

The privileging of the "spirit" over the "letter," which is another form of the privileging of speech over writing, is an essential Enlightenment gesture, and it is also a deeply imbedded part of the Marxism fashioned by Lenin and Stalin.[11] In order to carry through the Bolshevik consolidation of power, Lenin had to make, in Gramsci's well-known phrase, "a revolution against *Capital*." In this revolutionary struggle, Lenin (e.g., 1967) on many occasions appealed to the "spirit rather than the letter" of Marxism. This is a well-known metaphor, of course, dating at least back to its invocation by Paul in the New Testament ("The letter kills, but the spirit gives life"). Many important social endeavors (some progressive, some reactionary) have been empowered by this metaphor, all the while suppressing the irony that the suppression of the letter is founded on the letter, in this case metaphor. That is, as Nietzsche pointed out, words are taken for concepts, and thereby removed to a supposedly higher ontological status, a position from which spirit (the concept) can regulate the letter (the material word). This transposition of metaphors with concepts is called "white mythology" by Derrida (1982, 207–71). In hyper-secular society, white mythology has the effect of practically suppressing irony altogether. The cost of empowerment through the privileging of "spirit" has in some ways been too high. Often the metaphor is deployed as a means of "breaking tradition's chains" (to use another Enlightenment metaphor that also resurfaces in the "Internationale").[12] This strategic move undoubtedly has its justifications, but it can also tend to break the chain of memory, and therefore the possibility of the reconfiguration of community. These goals are part and parcel of secularism, and I will even argue that they are necessary to some extent in the longer-term project of creating a postsecular community. But how do we square these strategies and goals with Marx, Lenin, and even Stalin, who were supposedly interested in creating a post-bourgeois world?

The practical scene of Lenin's deployment of the metaphor was set by the need to catch up with the practice of the Russian situation, which had outrun Marxist theory. (Lenin stressed, correctly I think, the international dimension of the Russian situation.) Marx always stressed the primacy of practice, such that if practice seems to outrun theory, then it is theory, not practice, that has to catch up. There is a tendency in this formulation, however, to "spiritualize" practice: the attributes traditionally ascribed to speech, such as immediacy, transparency, inner assurance, and autonomy, are inscribed in practice. This positivistic gesture (and programs founded upon it) is what severs people from the basis of community, namely history and memory. Indeed, "people" are formed in the image of this gesture and this severance.

The United States represents the furthest travels of this severance, this hyper-secularism. Memory and history mean close to nothing in this setting, where plans are made to sacrifice all humanity for a certain "spirit." From Lenin to the U.S. is perhaps a long way, but from the present-day Soviet Union to the U.S. is not so far. Perhaps the same "spirit," which Lenin did not entirely escape (though at least he was trying to, after a fashion—which is a very important distinction; and it is not clear whether anyone or anything can entirely escape this "spirit," for such "escape" would probably also condemn political activity to irrelevance), motivates the matrix which both present-day superpowers belong to.

Against the spirit that motivates the existing political matrix, this study will work toward understanding the power that is inscribed in the letter: *grammatology*, as it were, as a social program. By "grammatology," I take it that Derrida means the rigorous pursuit of the question of writing and the letter, through its disruptions of the concept-metaphors that are enframed (Heidegger's term) in the name of science. Keeping in mind the apocalyptic and concretely political concerns that have been discussed thus far, the more technical side of the problems and possibilities involved in this project can now be outlined.

Elements of a Derridean social theory

Derrida's work has been broadly influential in literary criticism and philosophy. This influence is just beginning to be felt, however, in social theory. My purpose in this study is to articulate a social theory that uses Derrida's work as its methodological basis, and to demonstrate why such a social theory is needed. Derrida is not a social theorist, at least in the common understanding of the term, but his work does have profound implications for social theory, in two ways. First, this work can be deployed as the basis of a critique of contemporary social theories, especially those that are largely secular and modern in orientation. Second, on the other side of this critique, Derrida's writing can form the basis for a social theory uniquely suited to the postmodern social situation.

In each of these two stages of critique and possibility, which are in fact inseparable, Derrida's philosophy is the key to working through three complexes of problems. These are: first and foremost, problems concerning the mediations of social interaction—in particular, the interplay of structures in which meaning is generated and the larger social field that is shaped and generated by the complex of mediation/interaction/signification; second, problems concerning the nature of subjectivity, and the relation of subjectivity to human agency and responsibility; and third, problems of social relations (their configurations and possible reconfigurations), intersubjectivity, and history.

These issues, of course, are central to a large and diverse group of social theories; that is why I take them to be the issues that "yet another" social theory has to deal with. Everything hinges, however, on what sort of matrix informs the elaboration of these issues, and what sort of line leads out of this arrangement to a new theory.

Although this discussion began with some apocalyptic statements, and although the possibilities that I hope to ground in this study are indeed radical, it has already been announced that the "line" leading to a new matrix cannot go in the direction of apocalypticism, of either a Heideggerian or a Marxist sort. The way out of the current set of social predicaments can be described as the movement from secular, positivistic society to a new, postsecular conception and instantiation of community. The means for achieving this community must be in keeping with the goal. The letter that has been written one way must now be written another way. Humanity, in order to survive, must break with "society" in many important respects, but it must mediate this break through a rewriting of the social matrix, and not through an attempted leap to the spirit. For such a "leap" would run counter to the project of the reinvention of memory. The seeming moderation and conservatism of these last few statements must itself be mediated through a deeper sense of "memory," as not simply "about the past" but rather just as much about what Derrida (1989a) calls the "advent and adventure" of the future.

With Derrida's work serving as a philosophical "ground" a theory can be developed that addresses what I take to be the central problems of the contemporary social matrix. The term "ground" must be deployed with some suspicion, of course. Much of the work of this study will be taken up with the task of marking out the strategy by which the terms of social theory can be both placed "under erasure" and yet still deployed in rearticulated senses. I do believe, however, that this theory can be developed entirely out of elements taken from Derrida's text. This point is stressed in connection with two concerns.

First, my view is that Derrida's work is rigorous and argumentative and, even though it is a debatable proposition whether Derrida's work forms a "system," it is certainly "systematic" in many respects. Even though Derrida at the same time undermines systems and teases out the limits of reason (by pursuing reason to its limits, I hasten to add), it is not the wild relativism portrayed in some hasty caricatures.[13]

Second, a word or two should be said concerning Marxism. Although this study engages with Marxism especially (as opposed, that is, to liberalism or other broad categories in traditional political philosophy), this engagement is not meant as an across-the-board encounter between Derrida and Marxism.

I do not consider this study, however, to be pitched in a "post-Marxist" direction, at least not in the fashionable sense associated with a kind of euphoric or cynical postmodernism that I will criticize in Chapter 2. There is the basis in Derrida for a kind of historical materialism,[14] though one that takes as its first task the "materialization of the signifier." The notion of "marginal historical subjects" that I will outline has a more than coincidental resemblance to a certain reading of Marx's notion of the proletariat (elaborated in Chapter 4). Concerning the question of the "postmodern," a notion of historical disjuncture that owes something to Marx and Lenin is not entirely out of place. The Derridean strategy of reading against the grain might be seen as a form of immanent critique based on the materiality of the signifier. And, of course, both Marx and Derrida are well-known as readers of Hegel. Marx, then, will hardly be absent from the elements outlined here; but then, I do not think that Marx is absent from either Derrida's text or from the postmodern situation that a Derridean social theory must address.

Derrida did in fact spell out some elements of his own approach to Marxism in a well-known interview:

> . . . [W]e cannot consider Marx's, Engels's, or Lenin's texts as completely finished elaborations that are simply to be "applied" to the current situation. In saying this, I am not advocating

anything contrary to "Marxism," I am convinced of it. These texts are not to be read according to a hermeneutical or exegetical method which would seek out a finished signified beneath a textual surface. Reading is transformational. . . . But this transformation cannot be executed however one wishes. It requires protocols of reading. Why not say it bluntly: I have not yet found any that satisfy me.

No more than I have dealt with Saussure's text, or Freud's, or any other, as homogeneous volumes (the motif of homogeneity, the theological motif *par excellence*, is decidedly the one to be destroyed), I do not find the texts of Marx, Engels, or Lenin homogenous critiques. In their relationship to Hegel, for example. And the manner in which they themselves reflected and formulated the differentiated or contradictory structure of their relationship to Hegel has not seemed to me, correctly or incorrectly, sufficient. Thus I will have to analyze what I consider a heterogeneity, conceptualizing both its necessity and the rules for deciphering it; and do so by taking into account the decisive progress simultaneously accomplished by Althusser and those following him. All this poses many questions, and today I could tell you nothing not already legible in the lacunae or notes to which you alluded, at least for anyone who wishes to pursue their consequences. Above all they refer to the general economy whose traits I attempted to outline based on a reading of Bataille. It follows that if, and in the extent to which, *matter* in this general economy designates, as you said, radical alterity (I will specify: in relation to philosophical oppositions), then what I write can be considered "materialist." (Derrida 1981b, 63–64)

In marking features of a relationship between his own project and Marxism's, Derrida has set out a program for a philosophy and a social theory that, while never entirely distant from Marxism, does not at every point need to concern itself with a Marx who stands over its shoulder, keeping guard.[15]

At the same time, then, something more needs to be said about what it means for this study to be "Derridean." Though the sense of this term is best articulated in terms of the elements of Derrida's work and their specific relations to central social theoretical questions, there is also a sense in which it is not "organic" enough simply to affirm some purported homologies between passages from Derrida's text and these questions. There has to be a broader sense in which the whole approach that Derrida brings to philosophy is brought now to social theory. I have aimed to capture that sense even when it takes the study away from a more exegetical approach. With these concerns and provisos in mind, we may turn to the particular matrix in which the aforementioned elements may be arranged.

A specifically Derridean social theory must necessarily take problems of language and signification as central to understanding first subjectivity, and then social relations in their historical setting. Derrida stresses that language functions on the basis of a "system of differences" that, in principle, can unfold indefinitely. This claim can be understood as in fact nothing more than the pursuit of the programs of Frege and (especially) Saussure to their logical conclusions. Each claimed that a word only has meaning within a linguistic context. For Saussure, a word means what it means by virtue of its distinguishability from other words—its difference. The main thing that Derrida has added to this understanding is the notion that this process of differentiation is potentially endless. (Derrida has, however, a far richer understanding of what it means for a word to "differ" from other words.[16]) But this is also to claim that there is no "final" context, which claim is a particular form of anti-foundationalism. This anti-foundationalism would have very significant practical consequences, if it turns out that there is a basic relation among language, subjectivity, and social relations.

There are many diverse arguments concerning the existence of a basic relation between language and subjectivity.[17] The position I take on this question will perhaps seem extreme, though it has had its proponents (again, a diverse group): subjectivity is an *effect* of language.[18] I am less interested in pursuing this argument at great length than I am in drawing the implications that must necessarily follow if the language from which subjectivity emerges is itself not fully a "ground" in the traditional sense. (I am relieved of the former responsibility by the fact that others have already engaged in this pursuit.) Language may be supporting subjectivity, but what is supporting language?

The further ramifications of this question for social relations are clear: if subjectivity is not moored to a secure ground, then social relations would tend to be, if anything, on even less secure ground. If such conclusions were indeed the limit of a "postmodern" approach (using the term now in the loose sense popularized by Richard Rorty, in which anti-foundationalism, of whatever sort, is equated with a postmodern approach to theory), then there would be no place for social theory (or even for morality), since there would be little more than a purely existential basis for fundamental notions such as responsibility and agency. As Thomas McCarthy (an advocate of the linguistic turn in social theory, but a critic of Derridean approaches) puts it,

... if the subject is desublimated, can we really expect much more from general social "theory" than a historicist contemplation of the variety of forms of life in the *musee imaginaire* of the past; or a hermeneutic dialogue with other cultures and epochs about the common concerns of human life; or perhaps, a genealogical unmasking of any pretense to universal validity? (McCarthy 1984, viii–ix)

In other words, social theory seems in deep trouble without a grounding notion of agency or subjectivity. McCarthy, following Habermas, argues that such a notion, which cannot be grounded in a way that is intellectually defensible, is actually what has gotten social theories (and their attendant social programs) into such hot water as modernity unravels. So far so good. The Habermasians, however, argue further that an approach to language that admits of no final context cannot serve to refound a linguistically-grounded subject. On this point I disagree, at least in the case of Derrida. Much more can be argued for than mere indeterminacy on the basis of Derrida's approach to language.[19] In particular, there are two ramifications of that approach that are of prime importance for a Derridean social theory.

First, even if language is considered as an always unfolding system of mediations, the social character of language ensures that subjectivity will also have a social character. Much more will be said on that social character, and its historical dimension, in the course of this study. On the basis of understanding that subjectivity in general is rooted in language, we may assert further that the social character of language grounds the view that intersubjectivity is prior to subjectivity in the order of explanation. Already, then, there is the basis for claiming that subjectivity exists in a social matrix, and that, regardless of whether this matrix is itself "ultimately" grounded (in a foundational sense), the expressions of individual agents have significance at least as far as this matrix is concerned. Though the effects of indeterminacy and underdetermination of meaning will have to be taken into account, there is the basis for a kind of social theory, though not a theory that claims to be foundational (quite the contrary). Derrida's arguments concerning the relation of language to subjectivity, which are especially developed in *Speech and Phenomena* (1973), are compelling. However, it may be safely admitted that, if the entire thrust of these arguments was geared only toward showing the necessity for practicing social theory in the pragmatic mode, then there would already be a sufficient basis in quite a few other philosophers for moving ahead with this project. Among these would be the American pragmatists (especially Mead and

Dewey),[20] the later Wittgenstein, and the more naturalistic side of Marx. But there is another side to Derrida's approach to language that, while not necessarily detracting from this pragmatic mode (and in fact that mode will be very important in developing postmodern social theory), certainly augments that mode in a way not typical of (indeed, uncomfortable for) social theory in the pragmatic mode.

Second, then, let us turn to Derrida's problematic of "the other." Given that this problematic is found in several different forms throughout the European philosophical tradition from Hegel to Heidegger and beyond,[21] it is important that Derrida's particular contribution to the notion be attended to. Derrida's problematic is closely associated with the fact, mentioned earlier, that there is no "ultimate context." Our participation in the world through particular systems of signification is what makes subjects feel and think that there *is* such a context, but this is a kind of metaphysical illusion. Our "participation" is indeed formed in its very essence through the unfolding of language, of the material letter. In this unfolding process of the creation of participation (what Heidegger calls "disclosedness") the notion of language as a "medium" begins to break down, along with the dichotomy of subject and object that supports this notion.[22] When language is understood as the unfolding of difference,[23] we see that, in both theory and practice, the "ultimate context" is simply a horizon that recedes as we approach it. There is always the infinite "beyond" or "other." As Derrida argues in a number of studies, including *of Grammatology* and the essay, "*Differance*," this beyond is an "outside" that is also an "inside." (The inwardness of this alterity is evidenced in the movement of what Derrida calls the "trace," a point to which we will return at length.) The effect of this always-receding context is two-fold and even paradoxical: the "other" makes language *impossible*, and yet it is the "other" that "calls" us to language by continually confronting the emergent subject with possibilities. The "impossibility" of language, as a foundational enterprise in which meaning is generated in a stable process, is also, then, its possibility.[24] These categories, possibility and impossibility, are essential to this study.

The ramifications of this problematic for a Derridean social theory are encapsulated in the following set of claims, which can be set out on the basis of the framework now outlined. First, that subjectivity, in addition to having its ground in intersubjectivity, is capable of hearing and responding to the call of the "other." This I take to be the basis of responsibility, first of all social responsibility. Second, responding to this "call" is not, for Derrida, a quasi-mystical matter—as it seems to be for Heidegger. Rather, and third, it is a question of pursuing systems of signification into their "margins," to their limits, to the point where their systematicity begins to break down.[25] One way to describe this Derridean pursuit is the formulation, "reading against the grain," which would figure prominently in any discussion of history and social relations undertaken in consideration of the elements outlined here. Fourth, the problematics of (forms of) subjectivity, social relations, responsibility, and history, as reconceived in a specifically Derridean anti-foundational mode, can be distinguished from the notions that go by these names in other social theories. Fifth, these reconceived notions can be used to read against the grain of received history, to reveal a different history that will be seen to have a different trajectory than the mainstream (as opposed to the margins) of history. By "received history" I mean history that has been both created and reported from the perspective of foundational notions of subjectivity and responsibility. By a different trajectory, I mean a plurality of trajectories, *without* "outcomes." (On this latter question more will be said in the next section.) Finally, the possibility of reading against the grain will be seen as the beginning of a new practice of signification that could ground the practice of this "different history."

Wittgenstein argued for a similar possibility, namely that a new politics would require a new language—and that a new language would require a new, fundamentally different attitude toward language.[26] Where this possibility was only glimpsed by Wittgenstein (it was one of his many undeveloped insights), Derrida's work lays the foundation for the systematic justification and articulation of this possibility.[27] And, of course, it is a possibility that Derrida *practices* in his texts. While the framework just set out is in evidence in a number of Derrida's explicitly "political" writings (for instance, "No Apocalypse, Not Now," "Racism's Last Word," "The Ends of Man," etc.), it has not been fully elaborated in a social theoretical way. That is the task to which I hope this study will contribute.

Beyond the fleshing out of such an outline, a Derridean social theory must take up a number of specific problems, which I will now articulate. There is no need to claim that there is one and only one way of proceeding once we have a basic framework, but I would claim that these problems are indeed central to understanding and acting responsibly in postmodern society.

The first task in this regard is to contextualize the Derridean framework in terms of an account of the social world that it must confront. This contextualization arises from the conviction that any convincing theory of contemporary social relations must be grounded in an understanding of the nature of *contemporary* society. Despite the obviousness of this claim—which is virtually no more than a truism—it is not clear that most contemporary social theories are formulated in light of it. Ironic as it may seem, this major proviso is in many cases not even met in social commentaries that claim to be "postmodern." It is as though a style of theory that is called "postmodern" can be brought to bear on social questions that are conceived as essentially atemporal. My intuition, on the contrary, is that it is because society has entered a period, or phase, or *something* (perhaps something "out of phase," something that escapes the Hegelian sense of periodization) that is not simply "modern," but certainly *after* modernity, that a style of theorizing called "postmodern" is appropriate. In attempting to come to grips with this only half-named "something," this "postmodernity," we should both take Hegel at his word, and read against the grain of that word. That is, from Hegel we inherit both the notion of periodization that has led to the formulation of the idea of "postmodernity," and the notion of a "completion of history" that has seemingly not occurred. The understanding of postmodernity that will be developed in this study is of a "period" in which the conditions for the completion of history (in Hegel's sense) are present, but the end of history is forestalled, perhaps permanently. The sense of this impasse is captured in several of Derrida's essays, including "From Restricted to General Economy: A Hegelianism without reserve," and in a more atmospheric form in *Glas*. It remains for social theory to demonstrate how this *impasse*, which contains among its chief characteristics the suspension of received notions of subjectivity, responsibility, and praxis, is concretely the situation of contemporary society. (I am taking over this notion of "impasse" from Fredric Jameson's influential essay on postmodernism; see 1984.) What is required, then, is a "postmodern cartography." (A significant distinction can be drawn between this type of social theory, which is "postmodern" because it aims at such a cartography, and the type that claims to be "postmodern" for other reasons—not that this would in all cases be a hard and fast distinction.) This task is taken up in Chapter 2: "History past its end: outline for a postmodern cartography, taking Hegel at his word."

Within this historical contextualization (which is indeed the context of an historical impasse), the thematics of language, intersubjectivity, and responsibility can be taken up anew, in order to argue that there is a way out of the impasse. As part of that argument, however, Derridean notions of language, subjectivity, and responsibility must confront the more typical notions that are found in "modern" social theories. As a key example here, I consider the work of Jürgen Habermas. His social theory is exemplary in its comprehensiveness.[28] Furthermore, Habermas also takes the problem of language as central to the development of a contemporary social theory—and he is very attentive to what has already been marked out as the "pragmatic mode." However, Derrida and Habermas end up in two very different places in pursuit of that mode. The comparison of the two thinkers has been undertaken thus far in piecemeal fashion, in part because Derrida is not, conventionally speaking, a social theorist. What needs to be shown is that a comprehensive social theory that takes a Derridean approach to language as its methodological basis would be a fit competitor to Habermas's theory. Please be aware, reader, that there is a great deal of respect for Habermas, whom I regard as the most important social theorist writing today, embodied in this last claim—I see Habermas's theory as the one that must necessarily be taken on (and I mean these last two words in a double-edged sense).

The whole question of postmodern social theory enters in again, in two respects. First, in that Habermas, despite his pragmatic concerns, is foundational in ways to which a Derridean analysis can be specifically sensitive (here Derrida's analysis of speech act theory, carried out in the essays "Signature Event Context" and "Limited Inc" [see Derrida 1988] is very important, as this kind of language philosophy motivates Habermas's own arguments concerning communication). Second, in that Habermas is concerned to press forward "the unfinished project of modernity." At the center of that program is the rationalist paradigm that Habermas takes over from Rousseau and Kant. Here again, Derrida is especially important because, unlike some "postmodernists," he does not simply throw the rationalist "baby" out with the bathwater (to borrow an expression from Habermas). Derrida is concerned to read both with and against the grain of this Enlightenment heritage: he does not simply want to turn Reason, History, the Subject, etc., on their heads (despite what Habermas seems to think), he wants to understand how their marginal aspects both problematize and interact with, even to the point of making possible, their "central" aspects.

In this regard a useful detour can be made through the work of Donald Davidson, which provides a bridge away from the philosophy of language found in Habermas, and toward Derrida's approach to language. There are several reasons why such an engagement is practical. First, Davidson provides, in a way that is not always so clear (or, at any rate, accessible) in Derrida's work, a sense of what it means for language to have a non-foundational structure. Like Derrida, Davidson has a "minimal" conception of the sign. That is, both Derrida and Davidson take it that there is nothing essential to the sign other than its repeatability.[29] Second, Habermas has admirably attempted to break out of the analytic/continental antinomy in philosophy by engaging with analytical philosophy of language. This engagement is important for both philosophical and political (even if of a merely "institutional" sort) reasons. Habermas would have been better served, however, by a truth-conditional theory of meaning, such as Davidson's, than by a speech act theory, which actually has as a consequence the very relativism that Habermas wants very much to avoid. Third, Davidson's theory, which also has a pragmatic dimension (and is anti-foundationalist) does not recognize, at least explicitly, the problematics of otherness that I discussed earlier.[30] So that (fourth) a critique of this pragmatic alternative to Habermas's philosophy of language serves as a further basis for showing why the problematic of otherness is essential to understanding language, subjectivity, and responsibility. Finally, this comparison will also demonstrate that there are indeed different forms of anti-foundationalism, and why it is a matter of practical importance to distinguish among them. Only an anti-foundationalism of the sort that Derrida offers can allow us to gain access to the margins of history. All of these questions are taken up at length in Chapter 3: "What is at the heart of language? Habermas Davidson, Derrida."

In the midst of the matrix of language, subjectivity, and social relations that will thereby be motivated, a line can be drawn toward more straightforward "political" questions, beginning with: supposing that we do have the basis for exploring the margins of history, what will we find in those margins? Not surprisingly, I will argue that we will find marginal subjects; that is, subjects who have been written out of history, but who are also deeply inscribed in history, and into the very possibility of history, both written and lived. These subjects will be diverse, and the question of letting these others speak will therefore also be a question of radical diversity—but also a question of radical *confluence*. I shall explain. Reading against the grain in Hegel, in what I propose to call a "postmodern cartography," we can consider the Jews as exemplary marginal subjects. Hegel needs and takes what Jewish civilization had already created, namely the very notion of narrative history itself, and the basis for the concept of "civic altruism," which is found in the Jewish understanding that the relation between the human person and God is only actual insomuch as it is enacted in relationships in the human community.[31] What Hegel leaves behind are the Jews themselves. He also leaves behind the Jewish problematic of otherness, in which the Absolute can never be seen or even named—and indeed, the Absolute is always receding (the incarnation of God is always that which *will* come). This problematic is very much in evidence in Derrida (e.g., his essays, "Shibboleth," "Des Tours de Babel," and "Violence and Metaphysics: An Essay on the Thought of Emmanuel Levinas"). This simultaneous presence and absence of the Jews in Hegel can be taken as a model for reading other margins of history. On the basis of this reading, my further argument would be that these different margins, which include women, people of color, the poor, and other outcasts of history, are not reducible to one another, even if, in terms of a Derridean reading strategy, these outcasts conform to a certain model of marginality. The irreducibility of these marginalities has as a consequence the notion that a politics of the margins must depend on the possibility of confluence based on the model of marginality, rather than on a monolithic politics based on reducibility to a single, shared condition of life (as in some readings of Marx's notion of the proletariat). What unites these outcasts is, after all, their difference. The articulation of this radical diversity/radical confluence model will amount, in practical terms, to a philosophy of the new social movements. Chapter 4 articulates this philosophy, and is called, obviously enough, "Radical diversity/radical confluence."

Finally, then, we must ask what sorts of political engagements and solutions are made possible by this model. Uppermost among my concerns is the question of whether community is possible in postmodern society. This is the subject of the fifth and final chapter: "This unnameable community." The question of community can only be raised in the skeptical mode. That is, it cannot be assumed from the start that community is possible, nor can the analysis proceed on the basis of such an assumption.

Four possibilities can be raised concerning the question of community. I will outline these here, so that their attendant dangers and hopes can play a guiding role in the work of the first four chapters. Then the possibilities will be substantiated in the fifth chapter. First, there is the possibility that community is no longer possible at all, that all the social conditions that have made community possible in the past are now irreparably shattered. This is a possibility that has to be very seriously considered—no further possibilities can be considered apart from it. Second, perhaps some sort of community is possible in postmodernity itself. In setting out this possibility the responsibility of showing what sort of postmodern community is possible is incurred. Third, perhaps community will be possible again only after the impasse of postmodernity is broken. Here we incur the necessity of showing that the time after postmodernity[32] will in some sense be like the time before (and it will of course be an important question whether this would be a desirable thing). Fourth and finally, perhaps community will be possible only after the impasse of postmodernity is broken, *and* after the notion and the reality of community is recreated.

The outline that I have presented thus far points toward the fourth possibility; now it will be up to the rest of this book to clearly articulate a line toward this radical communitarian vision. The new community will be the community of radical diversity and radical confluence. This community will emerge by breaking the impasse of postmodernity and, in an interactive sense, the impasse of postmodernity will only be broken by the emergence of this community. I should clarify what I mean by the words "will" and "only" in this last sentence. I mean that either this community will emerge and the impasse of postmodernity will be broken, *or* there *will not* be a future for humanity. The outcome of this disjunctive pair—which consists in a possibility and the very negation of possibility—is far from certain. With the matrix offered here, and the contributions of others who are working in similar veins, however, I hope that we at least have the basis for some creative theoretical and practical contributions to the furtherance of human possibility.

The language of this possibility/the possibility of this language

Many present-day theories of language are careful to associate "language users" with "language communities." That broad category of theories that does not base itself in the notion of such a community can be defined as "language of thought" theories. These are especially associated with the transformational grammar of Noam Chomsky. Though there are many insights in Chomsky's system of ideas and its spinoffs in the philosophy of language (e.g., the work of Jerry Fodor, Stephen Schiffer, Fred Dretske, etc.[33]), and though I admire the political stance taken by Chomsky, this study will not be concerned very much with "language of thought" theories, for reasons that will become more clear in the third chapter. Instead, the focus will be on language theories that are based in "external relations," that is, theories that are based in the philosophy of language of Frege, Saussure, Wittgenstein, and Quine, and a fairly large and broad group of European thinkers (including Heidegger, Merleau-Ponty, Levinas, and Bataille). Perhaps the essential difference between these two broad categories of theories, "internal" and "external," is that the Chomskian theories attempt to locate meanings "in the head" (as Hilary Putnam 1987, 1988, has influentially put it), while non-Chomskian theories take it that meaning is generated through networks that are not specifically grounded in individual interior monologue.[34]

Internal theories focus more on the brain, its structure and abilities, while external theories emphasize the "mind" and language as a web or fabric of social, signifying relations—public, external, etc. At first glance, theories that emphasize the brain, as with "neurophilosophy" (an attempt to find the physical brain states that correspond to meanings; see Churchland 1986), seem more "materialistic," while theories that put language either before or on a par with thought seem either dualistic or idealistic. In analytic philosophy, a great deal of the discussion around Davidson's "anomalous monism" thesis centers on just this point. Similarly, Derrida is often accused of "linguistic idealism."[35] The question is whether there can truly be a form of materialism (and a materialist philosophy of mind and language) that is non-reductionistic.[36]

In the previous section I outlined an argument concerning what might be called the "context problem," a problem that will be present throughout this study, especially insomuch as questions of responsibility, history, social relations, as well as traditional problems of "hard philosophy"—mind, language, and metaphysics—are concerned. In brief, the context problem may be summarized in three steps, as follows. First, as mentioned, Derrida and Davidson have it that there is no essential content to the sign. (A corollary of this step is that, in principle, anything may count as a sign or even as a sentence, e.g., three chairs arranged in a particular way in a room.) The content of a sign, therefore, is provided entirely by context. Second, any given sign can function across a myriad of contexts, and there are no transcendental barriers to the movement of a sign across contexts. Third, there is no final context. With this outline of the problem in mind, let us turn to one area in the field of traditional philosophy: ontology.

The internalists would seem to have something more "solid" on their side, and therefore they seem to be more firmly materialist. The "brain" (or its genetic structure) is material, and susceptible to scientific examination; the "mind" is not material—so the story usually goes. We know where to find the brain—in an individual's *body*, surely a material place. The mind, on my reading, is just as difficult to locate materially as is language. But it cannot be taken for granted that "matter" itself is easily located. (Recall Derrida's affirmation of matter as "radical alterity.")

The question of a non-reductive materialism hinges on the acceptance of a set of terms, categories, and non-terms that are found in some analytic philosophy, much European philosophy, and especially Derrida: anomaly, the other, alterity, externality, the trace, the inexhaustible and inexhaustibility, and the impossible.[37] These terms will be rejected out of hand by those who think that materialism must necessarily be reductive or eliminative. Among these reductionists are not only certain—perhaps most—analytic philosophers, but also most Marxists (and this has some very significant political consequences). (There are also those philosophers who are idealists precisely because they reject a materialism that seems necessarily reductive.)

"There is nothing outside of context" (Derrida's clarification of his earlier "Il n'y a pas de hors-texte"; see Derrida 1988a, 136). And, there is no end to contextualization. These are facts about both the world and language, facts that allow us, compel us even, to take up an intertextual ontology. It is a basic tenet of philosophies as diverse as those of Kant, Hegel, Marx, Nietzsche, later Heidegger, Wittgenstein, and Einstein that the *relational* is real, and even perhaps *the* real. In an intertextual, relational ontology nothing is finally settled, and this seems to be a more appropriate understanding of *matter* as ultimately external.[38] (Consider Lenin's formulation: "Matter is a philosophical category—it is what is outside of consciousness," it is infinite, and infinitely divisible, and always already in motion, without temporal creation, origin, or end.[39] In this study one major theme will be the possibility of thinking such a formulation as radically as possible.)

The internalists mentioned earlier are more akin to the mechanical materialists such as Hobbes who must emphasize separation (though not in the sense of "spacing" employed by Derrida in *Speech and Phenomena* and other works) and a very narrow and behavioristic notion of consciousness.[40] It is not coincidental that, in light of this easily exhausted materialism, critical materialists have often found more to learn from idealists than from some of their supposed philosophical forerunners (Lenin again: "Better a good Hegelian than a bad Marxist").

Idealism, however, also cannot finally appreciate the inexhaustibility of the world (regardless of how the world is conceived, as material or ideal, in some sense of these words), for this kind of thinking attempts to bring the whole world under a single system of ideas and in actuality under a single consciousness.

This remark must be immediately qualified, however, on two counts. First, it is certainly the case that many Marxists have also attempted to bring the "whole world" (a paradoxical expression from the standpoint of inexhaustibility)[41] under a single system of ideas. This tendency reaches its culmination in the dialectical materialisms of Stalin and Mao. Indeed, with Mao, "contradiction" has the character of an *absolute*, and therefore of a somewhat *theological*, principle.[42] Two subthemes of some importance may be introduced here. 1) Stalin and Mao, in their search for the final monism, were simply following one basic impulse in Marxism. Mao, however, "settles" with contradiction rather than synthesis; this substitution may still prove significant in rethinking Marxism and radical social theory more generally (as in Sartre's *Critique of Dialectical Reason* and even in certain formalizations of deconstruction that stress the move from margin to center, the overturning of oppositions, etc.). 2) That the logic of an analysis propels theory in a quasi-theological direction (broadly conceived) is not a reason *per se* to abandon the analysis. Perhaps theory is entitled in the contemporary period to reject immediately any absolutist ontology. This entitlement, however, should not be employed as a security guard to keep the other out (out of a positivistic "pride," perhaps). (Derrida has convincingly argued that such police measures will always fail in any case.)

Second, perhaps the language(s) of idealism and theology is in some cases better suited to the purposes of an intertextual materialism than are certain discourses of classical or Marxist materialism. One very important "idealist," at least, takes it that "ideal Being" is not unitary. On the contrary: Heidegger speaks of "the wound in Being," which in some respects reflects the fact that the Absolute must encompass some negation that it in fact cannot encompass (which negation we may call "temporality")—and which it therefore pursues throughout eternity. That this Other is never finally captured is something that neither Hegel nor Christianity nor most forms of Marxism can comprehend. But it is this phenomenon of alterity, that is not exactly a phenomenon (all phenomena pursue it, and it leaves its trace on all phenomena), that I recommend as the motivation for a new kind of social theory.

Derrida has said that the purpose of his philosophy is to "show respect for the other," and "to let the other speak." Strictly speaking, this speech is *impossible*. That is, the other is that which *externally* strains context, and therefore we cannot comprehend its sign. But then, given that our own speech—whoever is described by the word "our" here— is marked by the trace of the other, our own speech is, strictly speaking (but also ironically speaking, which is at least a double paradox), impossible as well. Meaning never reaches its final destination or settles down, interpretation never stops, as long as there is meaning and interpretation. For meaning and interpretation to stop would mean that a final, transcendental signified had imposed itself. This signified, however, would erase not only all other signification, it would also, *and therefore* erase itself. Derrida does not identify this final transcendence with "God"—rather, he identifies it with acts and forms of anti-signification and social/cultural erasure that humans impose upon themselves and other humans. The transcendental signified is a final setting of the context and therefore a final setting of the content of signs. It is a *final solution* to the problem of meaning. These forms of anti-signification, that tend in the direction of this final setting of context, would include white supremacy, misogyny, and ultimate forms of all-erasing omnicide such as nuclear war. The transcendental signified is not, in Derrida's reading, a life-affirming thing. Another name for this transcendental signified is "the name," a thematics that will be taken up in the fourth and fifth chapters. A long passage from Derrida's "No Apocalypse, Not Now (full speed ahead, seven missiles, seven missives)" will prepare the way for the emergence of that thematics from the matrix of impossibility.

Today, in the perspective of a remainderless destruction, without mourning and without symbolicity, those who contemplate launching such a catastrophe [nuclear war] do so no doubt in the name of what is worth more in their eyes than life ("better dead than red"). On the other hand, those who want nothing to do with that catastrophe are ready to prefer any sort of life at all, life above all, as the only value worthy to be affirmed. But nuclear war—as a hypothesis, a phantasm, of total self-destruction—can only come about in the name of that which is worth more than life, that which, giving its value to life, has greater value than life. Thus it is indeed waged *in the name of.* . . . That, in any case, is the story that the warmakers always tell. But as it is in the name of something whose name, in this logic of total destruction, can no longer be borne, transmitted, inherited by anything living, that name in the name of which war would take place would be the name of nothing, it would be pure name, the "naked name." That war would be the first and the last war in the name of the name, with only the non-name of "name." It would be a war without a name, a nameless war, for it would no longer share even the name of war with other events of the same type, of the same family. Beyond all genealogy, a nameless war in the name of the name. That would be the End and the Revelation of the name itself, the Apocalypse of the Name.

You will say: but all wars are waged in the name of the name, beginning with the war between God and the sons of Shem who wanted to "make a name for themselves" and transmit it by constructing the tower of Babel. This is so, but "deterrence" had come into play among God and the Shem, the warring adversaries, and the conflict was temporarily interrupted: tradition, translation, transference have had a long respite. Absolute knowledge too. Neither God nor the sons of Shem (you know that Shem means "name" and that they bore the name "name") knew absolutely that they were confronting each other in the name of the name, and of nothing else, thus of nothing. That is why they stopped and moved on to a long compromise. We have absolute knowledge and we run the risk, precisely because of that, of not stopping. Unless it is the other way around: God and the sons of Shem having understood that a name wasn't worth it—and this would be absolute knowledge—they preferred to spend a little more time together, the time of a long colloquy with warriors in love with life, busy writing in all languages in order to make the conversation last, even if they didn't understand each other too well. (1984a, 30–31)

Among the many important points demonstrated by this passage is the way that possibility and impossibility are intertwined in Derrida's work. That matrix can be set out here, in somewhat analytical terms. Perhaps there are both good and bad senses of impossibility comparable to Hegel's "good" and "bad" infinity. "Bad impossibility" is that which ends the textual unfolding of human and other possibility, in the manner of the transcendental signified and that which aspires to its status (perhaps the most significant of such aspirants, Derrida has argued, is philosophy itself). This is the impulse, much known in human history, that would write the final chapter of the book of life and thereby end writing. This "bad impossibility" might also be called "counter-possibility." Derrida proposes that we "close the book" and "begin writing." It is not simply a matter of continuing *ad infinitum* with the "book of the world" as we have known it thus far: this would mean, for Derrida, the further instantiation of "white mythology" (the way that Western metaphysics arrests the textual processes of metaphor and figuration and seemingly gives them "substance").[43] Rather, there is an end and a beginning. The question is whether these could be conceived of in merely spatial or temporal terms, given Derrida's problematization of ends and origins. Derrida would say that there are "ruptures" that lead both to mutations and to retrievals of "the most hidden and forgotten archives." Every "line" of rupture is for Derrida (1976, 69) also a "hinge." "Good" textual impossibility draws writing out, along the path of response (Buber), toward, and in respect of, the other.

In my reading of these key terms I am especially indebted to Mark Taylor's *Altarity* (1987). I do aim, however, for a more explicitly "political" reading of these terms.

An understanding of these operations of textuality, which unfold and never stop unfolding (that is, of "dissemination," in Derrida's terminology) goes hand-in-hand with a *materialist* understanding of responsibility. This is a concept that other materialists in political theory (especially Marx and most Marxists) have had a very difficult time explaining. They want the spirit without the *Spirit* (e.g., Lukacs, Sartre), or they simply abandon collective notions altogether (e.g., recent analytical Marxists such as Jon Elster), or they even attempt to abandon any sense of the subject, whether conceived as individual or collective (e.g., Althusser—though I find this path, toward "history as a process without a subject" perhaps the most fruitful in terms of the conditional sense of subjectivity developed in Derridean terms).[44] I have suggested a reemphasis on the letter rather the spirit—for the letter contains a power that has as yet only been explored in the margins of Western culture. Even Marx and Engels have a hard time explaining, in terms of their own framework, why anyone should be a communist; that is, why anyone should be responsible to the possibility of community. In our own day this task is even far more difficult in terms of the received language and ethos of secular society.

We must be responsive to the possibilities of community because we are *called* to this responsibility. This is the claim, although it will sound extravagant at this point, that this study will ground. Even the claim (much less its justification) cannot be made in purely Marxist terms.[45]

Insomuch as metaphysics concerns closure, the intertextual ontology that has been described in these last few pages is anti-metaphysical. But this "philosophy of possibility" is not, cannot remain, and indeed does not begin as a "philosophical" pursuit, even though, of course, philosophy is a necessary and inextricable part of the matrix that forms the questions that can now be set out. To remain inside of philosophy is to remain inside of metaphysics, but there is no simple "outside" to either. The possibilities of language (philosophy's "body," after all) are the basis for and even the limit of human possibility. Fortunately, it is a shiftable limit. The further and crucial point is that understanding of the possibilities is found especially at the limit and in the *practice* of pressing and shifting the limits of signification.

These remarks are not intended as a hidden reassertion of some supposedly unproblematized distinction between theory and practice. Language is the site of both—in fact it is the exemplary site. The recognition of this site is the origin (in structuralism) of the idea of "theoretical practice." As for the political effectivity of this idea, thus far the most extensive evidence is to be found in feminist theory, in which the subject position of the theorist encourages a more integrated theoretical practice. (The question of this "subject position" is taken up in Chapter 5.) An extreme version of this idea, however, has become almost commonplace in theoretical circles: in this version, the mere fact of "writing differently" somehow "changes the world" or at least "empowers" agents of such change. Though I agree unreservedly with the *tendency* of at least the latter part of this claim, the lack of much sense of the strategic and tactical sides of the question, in the writings and proclamations of most of those advancing such claims, often makes of this position no more than a lot of huff and puff—"words about words about words," as some critics of intertextual models like to say. The scene of this kind of intertextuality is the university classroom, and it is understood that the real agents of social change are professors and students (where the professors replace the political vanguard in a parody of Leninism). The reasons that this position has been taken up by some could be analyzed at length, but a summary of the root motivations will suffice: a *certain* nostalgia for the sixties (a nostalgia for "radicalism" without rebellion against institutions and social structures, or sometimes a desire to "trump" the sixties), an underlying belief that "knowledge is power" in the pre-Foucauldian sense (i.e., a nostalgia for certain Enlightenment conceptions with little analysis of the social basis of these conceptions), a certain fear of who and what lies outside of the university—with a concomitant investment in the "idea of the university" as the basis for transforming the rest of society (again a kind of unproblematized Enlightenment nostalgia), and a certain career-oriented investment in the university that many theorists do not want to endanger through the practice of politics outside of the classroom (the ironic thing is that this is a politics that often remains unthematized even in the classroom or in the written work of many theorists).[46]

This linguistic/literary power trip attributes a kind of efficacy not so much to language, but rather, and once again, to the subject, in this case to the literary theorist or to the otherwise textually hip. This trend has as its end-point the asocial "textualism" of *Contingency, irony, and solidarity* (1989, e.g.,73–95), where Richard Rorty claims that the value of textuality (one might say, how textuality is "cashed out") is in the opening it creates for individuals to "form their vocabularies."

The central political question that this study must address is whether it is possible to tap into and unleash the communitarian possibilities of intertextuality in a non-appropriative way. In particular, here I am obviously concerned with the way that intertextual, and especially Derridean, models, which have as one central aim the disruption of "the proper," are sometimes appropriated as just another piece of intellectual property. This seems to me to be a betrayal of the real disseminative possibilities of intertextuality. There *are* gaps to be bridged, (about this, I do agree with Rorty). The fact of these gaps is indicated by the troubling but continually reaffirmed truth that there is no theory impervious to corruption, and it is especially necessary to emphasize that this corruption is always possible in the very terms of the theory in question.[47] This is what Paul de Man called an *aporia* of the text. This aporia is a logical consequence of the context problem. That is, the content of texts and their terms is never finally settled. The all-important point that Rorty misses is that aporia does not signal a gap between individual and society, or between public and private, but instead a gap that opens up in the midst of discourse that is never not communal. A certain *reading* of this aporia is in fact what creates supposedly radical distinctions between "public" and "private."[48] Though a social theory constructed in respect of the context problem,[49] its attendant aporias, and an external/intertextualist ontology can sometimes be, because of these same elements, a dangerous politics open to certain corruptions, and dangerous in ways that this study will not seek to hide, social theories that ignore these questions are in general far more dangerous. The greater danger lies in two directions: on the one hand, in the attempt to make stable and foundational that which will not fit into that mold (this attempt is the semantic ground of authoritarianism), and on the other hand, the failure to tap into the available semantic resources. On these points, much more will be said in the fourth and fifth chapters.

What remains for this chapter is to frame the possibility of an interface between a metaphysics of pure externality and socially-responsible practice aimed toward the reinvention of community.

What is/to be done?

The argument concerning impossibility (which will now be further specified) emphasizes the productivity of the horizon of possibility, which presents practitioners of interpretive activity, or what might be called "interpretive praxis," with a challenge, a call. With the aporia there is always not so much a "choice" as a "negotiation." But the negotiation does represent two "different" roads forward: toward the horizon of possibility (that is here called "impossibility") or towards counter-possibility. And yet, neither analytical nor dialectical procedures will provide a simple or straightforward path beyond the "conjuncture." Impossibility and counter-possibility are always implicated in one another, and things get still more complicated. Impossibility and counter-possibility are not transcendental categories, for two reasons. First, the context problem indicates a "pragmatic" unfolding of possibilities into the two categories of impossibility. There is nothing outside of the text—i.e., these categories of impossibility are also not outside of the text, even as they play a most significant role in generating textuality itself. For the time being, this pragmatic opening has been emphasized enough. There is, however, an important connection between this opening and the second relevant point. Notice the expression used to indicate the actual context of the seeming transcendence of impossibility: "unfolding of possibilities." Possibilities are always historical and plural.

Heidegger proposed that "Being has a history." The term that undoubtedly plays the role of Being in the post-Heideggerian, Derridean approach that I am attempting to integrate more fully with social theory, is *alterity*—what is, in Levinas's expression, "otherwise than being." Derrida has stressed that alterity, however, is not a "thing." Alterity is also not, therefore, a thing to be "played out"—either inside or outside of history. It is the call, which summons us to interpretive praxis. Even though that call is never so specific as to set out a particular political program or agenda, it is always a "we" who is(are) called—and a "we" that is formed by the call. If the "West" has not always or perhaps even very often heard this call, then this may very well be because it has not always been the "West" that is called or formed by the call.

Indeed, the call is heard in radically diverse ways, by diverse "we's" and by diverse potential "we's" that may become new sites of possibility. This diversity has often been perceived by much of the left as harmful and problematic for "the movement." But—movement toward what? There has to be *movement*—that is a necessary consequence of the framework set out thus far, of a Derridean reading of the call—but it is also a necessary consequence of the character of this call that movement will always be plural, in the form of movements. This is an effect of the undecideability of contexts, but this is a strength rather than something harmful (contrary to the standard wisdom of the left).[50]

Or: Heidegger said at one point: "Only a God can save us now." The Derridean argument is exactly to the contrary: a "God," at least in the sense that Heidegger is intending, is the last thing needed. The left also has its gods and its longing for God—it has what Heidegger and Derrida call "ontotheological" assumptions built into its theory and practice. It would be wrong to merely disdain the left for this basic human trait—one cannot help but have some sympathy for it (all humanism-bashing aside). The dissimulations of the left around this question, however, have often been very harmful. The problem is that, on the other hand, a politics without a transcendent center has only begun to be practiced or thought. This would be a politics, it is true, of the "unthought" (Heidegger).

Without a God to save us, some give up hope or commitment. There is no avoiding the fact that the material basis for hope and commitment has been systematically debilitated by counter-possibility. (Death is one, life is many.) The call remains, however, as does the letter, which is material, and there are some listeners among us.

These listeners divide into two categories: political movements and communities of resistance. The former, especially in the form of the "new social movements," work generally in a more secular framework, and there is in these movements some concern with theory "as such." Communities of resistance are more characterized by the attempt to forge a new form of life, primarily by living in a new way. In the final two chapters of this book the connection between these two categories— "sites of possibility"—will be established. Each "demands the impossible" (as a well-known sixties slogan had it: "Be reasonable—demand the impossible!"). The new social movements, especially the women's movement, the ecology movement, gay liberation movements, liberation theology, movements for popular autonomy, but also not excluding new forms of Marxist and socialist movements, are prefigurations of possible communities of radical diversity (in that respect it is essential to point out that none of these movements is monolithic; therefore, it is not entirely appropriate to refer to *the* women's movement, etc.). The communities of resistance offer models of radical confluence. The movement toward these models, however, finds itself in a hyper-secular atmosphere where even the idea of community can barely survive. Though the logic of the new social movements is drawn, practically speaking, to the prefiguration of community, this logic will not result in a set of possibility-initiating institutions and living arrangements unless the confluential logic of community is explicitly thematized. By the same token, though the logic of communities of resistance is also drawn, in a practical sense, toward respect for the other, this logic will not result in a *diverse community* unless diversity itself is also explicitly thematized and grounded. And yet the existence of these models is an extraordinarily important factor in the argument for postsecular socialism and postsecular community. This factor is important not just as a rejoinder to the usual crowd of cynics and nay-sayers. Far more important is the fact that these models serve as material grounds upon which the postsecular community will have to be built.

In a very important sense, we are only in community with those with whom we commune. *Respect* for the other does not exist unac-knowledged (or perhaps it should be put: without acknowledgement, respect for the other does not exist). Even though people are continually exemplifying the possibility of community, even in "anti-social behavior" (sometimes *especially* in behavior that has been dubbed such by the powers that be), this possibility of community, and the concomitant move to actuality, is a political movement that does not simply instantiate itself "organically."

The new social movements and the communities of resistance each exist on the margins of the West (the West that has all the same produced them). This marginality is their shared attribute. Lenin once said that the only thing the proletariat really has on its side, at least prior to the seizure of power, is truth. But "truth" is not enough. Perhaps this "formulation" will sound a bit mushy and sentimental, but, on a certain level of "analysis" (a certain level that analysis will in actuality try to deny, at least until positivism is buried conceptually and in reality), who cares what anyone "knows"? There is also the question of what someone cares about, and this quality of caring comes not from "knowing the truth," but rather from hearing the call to respect the other. Only in a society based on private property does it matter that I falsely refer to something as "my idea." A community depends on memory and language, belonging to a common narrative, "intertextuality," and here there is no room for property.[51]

The perspective offered here for social movements, then, is the direction of their truths toward shared memory and continuity, toward the possibility of community.

2

History past its end (outline for a postmodern cartography, taking Hegel at his word)

Philosophy, which once seemed obsolete, lives on because the moment to realize it was missed. The summary judgment that it had merely interpreted the world, that resignation in the face of reality had crippled it in itself, becomes a defeatism of reason after the attempt to change the world miscarried. Philosophy offers no place from which theory as such might be concretely convicted of the anachronisms it is suspected of, now as before. Perhaps it was an inadequate interpretation which promised that it would be put into practice. Theory cannot prolong the moment its critique depended on. A practice indefinitely delayed is no longer the forum for appeals against self-satisfied speculation; it is mostly the pretext used by executive authorities to choke, as vain, whatever critical thoughts the practical change would require.

—Theodor Adorno, *Negative Dialectics*

The most fashionable word today seems to be the prefix *post-*. We are living in a "postindustrial" society and admiring "postmodern art." The trendy commentators are bombarding us with futuristic images of nuclear-triggered X-ray lasers, of one-world television beamed from satellites, of robots doing our work and computers our thinking. However, if you dare ask why it is that a world changing so fantastically in so many respects must somehow be tied forever to the same forms of property and exploitation, you are dismissed as a dinosaur. On reflection, the philosophy behind this futuristic mumbo-jumbo is rather old-fashioned. Like all ruling classes, the present-day one admits the existence of history up to its own triumph, although not beyond. Post-everything means capitalism forever. There was history but time must now have a stop. Europe may still move up to the American model; the United States is, by some strange malediction, condemned to the same social state forever.

—Daniel Singer, *Is Socialism Doomed?*

With Western humanity's emergence into modernity, the conditions, in totality, are finally set for the "completion" of history. Hegel's philosophy of history is most of all a recognition of these conditions in his own day: the passage of humanity through the four cultural and spiritual levels of development (called by Hegel the "Oriental," "Greek," Roman," and "Christian" Worlds), the emergence of the modern nation state, and the instantiation of Christian universality in modern individuality (see, e.g., 1975, 124–31). Hegel does not say that history has reached its point of completion with the achievement of the Christian World; rather, the stage is set for this completion. The primary question that this chapter will raise is, What is the status of these conditions now, at the close of the twentieth century? The question is central to the problem of defining postmodernity. Taking Hegel at his word, taking his notion of historical development for granted, the aim of this chapter is to interrogate the meaning of "post" in postmodernity. In taking Hegel at his word, no more is claimed than that the pattern of development Hegel discerned in history is indicative of at least something very central to the human project. We may think of Hegel's "word" as a revelation of the *logos*, the inner logic of history and the human endeavor. The historical dialectic may be, after all, more a "projection" than a "discovery."[1] This possibility, however, does not nullify the force that the dialectic has exhibited concerning the self-understanding by humanity of the human project. In light of Hegel's philosophy of history, the following discussion will pursue three problematics that must be understood if postmodern social theory is to be situated. The first discussion concerns some available definitions of postmodernity. In the latter part of this discussion I will propose my own definition, which will remain operative for the remainder of this study. The second discussion consists in a series of questions addressed to this definition— all of these will be *Hegelian* questions. In the third and final discussion, the question of postmodern prospects and possibilities, already raised in the last part of the first chapter, will be refined in light of this Hegelian inquiry, with an eye toward the last two chapters of this study.

Postmodern, post-Hegel?

Practically all of the definitions and metaphors of postmodernity are quite self-consciously "post-Hegelian" as well. As a preamble to my own definition, I will inventory, albeit in the form of thumbnail sketches, some of these metaphors and demonstrate their "post-Hegelianism."

1. Marx: Where Hegel has the nation-state, Marx and Engels propose internationalism. The world community in Marx is still quite Hegelian. Whereas the nation-state is truly the great "individual" for Hegel, Marx sees the realization of human freedom in a transcendence of the nation that still represents the merger of myriad individuals into a larger individual entity that has outgrown its national clothes. Despite what is now conventional wisdom on this question, the later Marx may be more of a "structuralist," but he is no less Hegelian: the "human essence" that propels individuals into a solidarity has as its end the "categorical imperative to overthrow all those conditions in which man is an abased, enslaved, abandoned, contemptible being" (Marx 1964, 52) transposed into a dialectic of modes of production that generates a series of such "essences," leading to the material conditions in which the categorical imperative may be practiced. In this transposition, as in Hegel, the "spirit" of this dialectic is both something human and something other than human.[2]

2. Nietzsche: the Übermensch, or "post-man"[3] is clearly a proposed successor to the humanity that has come to fulfillment in Hegel's scheme of things. The Übermensch is not, however, a mere denial of Hegel's totalizing humanism—though it *is* that, in an important way that will be discussed further; Nietzsche, like Marx, aims for an immanent critique of the existing culture. This means that,

[L]ike Marx, Nietzsche intended to avoid a utopian view of future possibilities. This meant that he had to find the elements of a new culture contained in the present one. All real possibilities for cultural renewal must emerge from our specific situation in history.

Furthermore,

[A]lthough Nietzsche sees past and future as in some sense radically discontinuous, he does not argue for a liberation from the past but rather for a reconstitution of its resources. (Warren 1988, 161, 161)

These characterizations, provided by Mark Warren (*Nietzsche and Political Thought*) are distinctively post-Hegelian, and also very much in the spirit of a postsecular recognition of the power of the letter as historical resource. But then, Nietzsche, like Marx but quite unlike Marx, also has

his "inversion" of Hegel—the genealogical method that allows Nietzsche to read history not as progress, but rather as "error." This error is
indeed a key to historical resources, which are also resources of
cotemporaneous cultures ("other present eras," in the rubric of the
preceding chapter). "Our instincts now run back everywhere; we are
ourselves a kind of chaos" (*Beyond Good and Evil*).[4] In terms of the
modalities set out earlier, this "chaos" might be best understood as a
kind of "dance" of impossibility and counter-possibility, in which the
outcome is never certain, and concerning which "no sign from God can
help us" (*Human, All-Too-Human*).[5] No transcendental signifier (what is
a "sign from God," anyway, if not this?) will still the hermeneutic flux,
with its attendant dangers and possibilities.

3. Kierkegaard: the "leap of faith" is not simply an "alternative" to
the fulfillment of Reason in Hegel's system. Furthermore, where Hegel
leaves nothing to chance, Kierkegaard has it that ultimate concerns are
indeed a matter of that which cannot be accounted for in the economy of
Reason. These claims are well-substantiated in the final chapter, on
Kierkegaard, of Mark Taylor's *Altarity*. Note that a number of major
themes from the first chapter of this study are interwoven here as well:

> The absolutely different or wholly Other cannot be translated into
> any language. To the contrary, this altarity [Taylor's spelling of the
> word] inflicts an incurable wound upon language. Always open,
> this wound lies between the lines it (impossibly) both supports
> and undercuts. This loss of language can never be re-covered. Nor
> is it a negative that can be transferred to a positive, an absence that
> can be carried over into presence. This difference is not the
> dialectical contrary of identity; but is the difference that infinitely
> defers the eschatological movement of reappropriation. Offering
> no promise of arrival, this Other calls: "Come."

> How can one hear such a call? How can one "know" the
> Unknown? How can one communicate with that which interrupts
> communication? Perhaps, Kierkegaard re-plies, through faith—
> an exorbitant faith that takes one beyond, albeit while remaining
> within, the law of reason. A faith that is neither rational nor
> irrational, knowledgeable nor ignorant. (1987, 344)

4. Marx again, and Althusser: his "Theses on Feuerbach" arrives at
the claim that, beyond the "end of philosophy," there is "changing the
world." In fact, both the early and later works of Marx proclaim this
idea—directly in the earlier work, implicitly in the later work, in which

philosophy *as such* is rarely present. Althusser, who seemed to waver on this question, set out what seems to have been Marx's essential attitude toward philosophy in the post-*German Ideology* work:

> The XIth Thesis on Feuerbach proclaimed: "The philosophers have only interpreted the world in various ways; the point is to change it." This simple sentence seemed to promise a new philosophy, one which was no longer an *interpretation*, but rather a *transformation* of the world. Moreover, that is how it was read more than half a century later, by Labriola, and then following him, by Gramsci, both of whom defined Marxism essentially as a new philosophy, a "philosophy of praxis." Yet we have to face the fact that this prophetic sentence produced no new philosophy immediately, at any rate, no new philosophical discourse, quite the contrary, it merely initiated a long philosophical silence. (Althusser 1971, 36)

This from a well-known text of Althusser's, "Lenin and Philosophy," a text that fits in nicely (in the book with the same title) between an "Interview on Philosophy," in which Althusser argues that philosophy has no use other than as a "revolutionary weapon," and the essay entitled "Lenin before Hegel." One might expect that the thrust of the latter essay is also toward a long philosophical silence, but instead "Lenin before Hegel" is a justification, now in terms of Lenin's reading of Hegel's *Logic*, of Althusser's famous thesis that "history is a process without a subject." Despite much fashionable, "poststructualist" opinion in recent years, this notion still does some important work for us: Althusser's analysis is still a very important *via negativa* toward the reconception of agency. (One reason for bringing Althusser into the picture is as a reminder that structuralism did in fact lay some of the groundwork for poststructuralism—this point is sometimes forgotten.) Despite this trajectory, there is still in Marx's thesis some sense that what remains is for practice to realize what thought has already accomplished. My argument in the first chapter was that there is a tendency here to conceive practice in the mode of "spirit." Marx's gesture (which is all that a "thesis" can accomplish, practically or theoretically) both gropes toward post-Hegelian thought and yet also remains firmly within Hegel's orbit.

Althusser attempted to eliminate the Hegelian strain in Marx, by way of Lenin. In his formulation, a structuralist Marxism can focus on synchronic structures, as well as get on with practice (philosophy as a revolutionary weapon). While this move may be valuable as a *moment* in theory, as a guiding principle structuralism tends to dehistoricize our conceptual resources. The effects of this new positivism have been just as pernicious as older forms. I find it most helpful, in the larger theoretical landscape, to mainly think about structuralism in the context of Sartre and Merleau-Ponty on the one side, and Derrida and Foucault on the other. The point remains, however, that this resistance to Hegel remains determined by the Hegelian problematic, for what is philosophy as "practice" other than the emptying out of objective spirit into pure immanence?

5. "Multinational" and "transnational" corporations: whether blocs of capital can entirely outgrow their material underpinnings in the nation-state is the subject of intense debate, but it seems clear that to at least some very significant extent there can be forms of capitalism that transcend "narrow" nationalism and yet have nothing to do with internationalism or a world community (except in a perverse rendering of images of community).[6] The interconnections of political economy and the postmodern situation are many and diverse; the interesting thing is that these connections have only begun to be traced out. I will simply remark on one such connection: the "politics of speed" (which is at the center of Derrida's "No Apocalypse, Not Now") which makes necessary a new "cognitive map."[7] Gayatri Spivak, in a provocative talk, remarked that postmodernity began with the worldwide electronification of the stock market in 1974.[8] She would undoubtedly concede that there is more to it than that, but Spivak has a point: that is the moment when the processes that are central to the mode of production began to move at the speed of light. And that is the moment when economic processes that might trigger nuclear war also began to move, as Derrida argues, far beyond the speed of "competency."

6. Foucault: the notion that Nietzsche's "death of God" merely foreshadows a more general "death of man." For Hegel, the realization of Absolute Spirit is inextricably bound up with the coming-to-be of humanity. After the fall of the System, one can only expect the fall of humanity as well. As with Nietzsche, Foucault's observation of the fall is both a celebration and a lament. Germanic individuality falls along with Christian universality. For both Nietzsche and Foucault, this fall is mostly for the good—they identify some of the deeper problems of society with the overwhelming obtrusiveness of the Hegelian system and its subject-writ-large. The evocative passages at the conclusion of Foucault's *The Order of Things* speak of "a change in the fundamental arrangements of knowledge" that allowed "man" to appear as the object of that supposedly most fundamental of the sciences, "human" or otherwise, anthropology. But,

[a]s the archaeology of our thought easily shows, man is an invention of recent date. And one perhaps nearing its end.

If those arrangements were to disappear as they appeared, if some event of which we can at the moment do no more than sense the possibility—without knowing either what its form will be or what it promises—were to cause them to crumble, as the ground of Classical thought did, at the end of the eighteenth century, then one can certainly wager that man would be erased, like a face drawn in sand at the edge of the sea. (1987, 387)

Such a formulation, however (with which this study will implicitly disagree on two major points that will surface from time to time),[9] pays tribute in an inverted way to Hegel. "Man" may indeed have been an invention of discourse at a certain historical moment, a moment in which Hegel played a major role (Derrida 1989a, 58, reminds us, in "Psyche: Inventions of the Other," that it was Hegel's friend Schelling who first argued that "a philosopher could and should, as a philosopher, display originality by creating new forms"). But, *what an invention!* For Nietzsche there is the question of what the sea will bring in when it washes away the face of "man." This must be a question for Foucault as well, though it is not clear that he is calling for the *Übermensch*. This too is an inverted recognition of Hegel, for after the sea washes away the subject, might some ghost of the structure remain (even if it too is an "invention")?

   7. Nietzsche again: his "perspectivism," with its corollary proposition that a number of "true" perspectives can exist simultaneously. One must of course pay a great deal of attention to what is at stake in the word "true" for Nietzsche in order to appreciate the truth of perspectivism. For perspectivism is not an attempt to "deny truth"—on the contrary; rather, perspectivism simply insists that we affirm, along with "truth" (for how could we not affirm truth?), all of the things that make truth possible: power, ignorance, falsification, forgetfulness, etc. Consider what is really, after all, a somewhat typical notion of truth, that it has to do with "facts," and that the "whole truth" has to do with "all the facts." Consider, in other words, the opening propositions of Wittgenstein's *Tractatus*: "The world is all that is the case. The world is the totality of facts, not of things. The world is determined by the facts, and by their being *all* the facts" (1974, 5). Now compare this view (which admittedly starts out sounding like positivism, but in actuality ends up sounding a little more like Heidegger or Derrida) with Alexander Nehemas's cogent interpretation of Nietzsche's perspectivism:

Nietzsche's perspectivism . . . is a refusal to grade people and views along a single scale.

In order to avoid the view that the world has a determinate structure in itself, many of Nietzsche's contemporary readers have repeated his occasional claims to the effect that the world, like every text, "has no meaning behind it, but countless meanings." But I think Nietzsche was wrong to think that this ontological pluralism could support his perspectivism. An object is not indeterminate because it has many characters instead of having only one; for since each of these characters is itself determinate, this claim is not an alternative to but a particular instance of the idea that the object in question has a determinate character. Nietzsche's perspectivism denies precisely this last idea, but this denial is not, as he himself occasionally thought, equivalent to the view that the world is "infinite" in that "it may contain infinite interpretations." What must be denied instead is the more fundamental claim that there could ever be a complete theory or interpretation of anything, a view that accounts for "all" the facts; we must deny the claim that the notion of "all the facts" is sensible in the first place. (1985, 68, 64; internal refs. deleted)

This is not a merely "metaphysical" argument, as Nehemas also makes clear. Selectivity is necessary for knowledge, but the criteria of selectivity, which most often remain unthematized, are socially constituted. This claim, by now, is standard fare in postmodern arguments; the point here is to situate this perspectivism with regard to Hegel. Perspectivism, in its historicism, is most certainly post-Hegelian—its willingness to consider the situation of knowledge in its diachronic dimension, though of course with a twist: Nietzsche's history is "genealogy."[10] There are further post-Hegelian aspects to perspectivism, however, that cut against the grain of this genealogical historicism. Perspectivism implies a possible simultaneity of competing perspectives that cancels any straightforward Hegelian universalism or historical teleology. (In metaphysical terms this aspect of perspectivism might remind us of Quine's [1969] "ontological relativity"—which does not arouse the complaint against ontological pluralism issued by Nehemas—and Putnam's "internal realism" [1987].) This simultaneity is generated, historically, by the turning of historicism against itself, making historicism submit to its own principles. Nietzsche argues that this turning in on itself of historicism results in nihilism—but this is a turn that could not have been avoided.[11] Again: the course that leads humanity (*European* humanity, as Nietzsche puts it) in the direction of this nihilism may indeed be an "invention" (of Hegel, modernity, etc.), but the effects are no less real. (Put another way: humanity has simply, at the end of modernity's tether, invented itself in this nihilistic form.)

Lyotard, in his well-known and much-discussed *The Postmodern Condition*, figures the political-epistemological consequences of this historicized historicism as the scene of *agonistics*. It only remains for competing perspectives to fight it out in a context that is social but no longer historical, in light of nothing more than "the performance principle" (1984, 41–60). Lyotard takes the status of knowledge in postmodernity to be such that no grand narrative authorizes or legitimates any particular discourse. Thus, "performativity" becomes the only standard, and discourses cannot be expected to "progress," dialectically, historically, or otherwise. Whether this condition needs a cure, or simply recognition as the reality that, once invented, is the world as it ever shall be, is the major question that is the destination of these postmodern vignettes.

8. Baudrillard: the notion of the "screen," a *flattening-out* of history. It would be just as well to say, "Nietzsche again," because this point, at least at first glance, is no different in character than the ramifications just outlined under the rubric of simultaneity of perspectives and the political-epistemological effects thereof. Baudrillard, however, takes stock of this time period, especially in terms of its *televisual* character. (One might say that, in Baudrillard, Nietzsche meets Marshall McLuhan.) An unprioritized succession of images replaces an Hegelian progressive-sequential development (television replaces the novel—recall that Hegel's *Phenomenology* has sometimes been thought of as a *Bildungsroman*).[12] Douglas Kellner explains that, beyond the triumph of the synchronic over history, this succession of images

also constitutes a significant reversal of the relation between representations and reality. Previously the media were believed to mirror, reflect or represent reality, whereas now they are coming to constitute a (hyper)reality, a new media reality, "more real than real," where the "real" is subordinate to representation, thus leading ultimately to a dissolving of the real.

In this scenario, meaning itself is sucked into

a black hole of signs and information that absorbs all contents into cybernetic noise which no longer communicates meaningful mes-

sages in a process in which all content implodes into form.
(1989a, 68)

Baudrillard paints (screens?) a nuanced picture of a reality that is no less
real for having been created by an evil genius who turns out to be
Western humanity itself. Kellner, a critical theorist, traces the post-
Hegelian genealogy of this picture:

> Seen within the context of the narrative of Hegelian Marxism,
> Baudrillard brings the problematic of reification to a bizarre
> conclusion. While Hegel and Lukacs, among others, posited an
> ideal of unity and identity between subject and object as the goal of
> the overcoming of reification, by contrast with Adorno and the
> Frankfurt School, who merely wanted to preserve subjectivity and
> individuality in the face of its potential demise in the totally
> administered society, Baudrillard goes over to the other side, and
> proclaims the triumph of reification as a *fait accompli* with the
> triumph of the object over the subject. (1989a, 166–67)

(I would take issue with Kellner's description of Adorno's project as the
mere preservation of subjectivity. Adorno's critique of "identity logic,"
which we will take up in the fourth chapter, is not simply a strategic,
defensive measure, even if it seems such as refracted through Adorno's
personal pessimism.) Perhaps reification has not entirely triumphed,
but Baudrillard is surely diagnosing something fundamental about
postmodern society (that he also celebrates this diagnosis is a somewhat
different question.) The question that remains is, What is it that has not
been reified? Which is also to ask: What is sufficiently "other"? What is
its modality? These questions have already been raised; the reason for
thematizing them again at this point is to situate them in terms of the
electronic "speed race that marks every atom of our being today"
(Derrida). (The question of media will become especially significant in
the last chapter.)

    9. Difference: although this notion is extremely important in
Derrida's text, let us also give credit where credit is due, to Gilles
Deleuze, to feminism, and to differential analyses of race and ethnicity.

    Although like Derrida in many respects, Deleuze has perhaps
been more single-minded in the pursuit of a Nietzschean logic of
difference that disrupts an Hegelian, dialectical logic of identity and the
Same. Ronald Bogue argues that, while Derrida "describes a non-
linguistic dimension of *differance*," this dimension is taken into account
"only as it emerges within philosophical discourse." Bogue locates

Derrida squarely within the hermeneutic tradition. Derrida's contribution to that tradition is to show that

> *Differance*, the ground of metaphysics and of the problematic concepts that undermine metaphysics, is the logical consequence of a rigorous pursuit of Kant's transcendental critique, the result of an immanent self-critique from within the metaphysical tradition. Given the pervasiveness and resilience of metaphysics, the reinscription of problematic terms within philosophy seems the only reasonable strategy for subverting hierarchical dualisms.

Deleuze, Bogue argues, is not so interested in this hermeneutic tradition as he is in creating "science fictions,":

> He invents paradoxical concepts, which resemble such Derridean notions as *differance, pharmakon,* or originary trace, but rather than reinscribe these concepts within traditional texts, he uses them as the building blocks of an alternative world. (1989, 158–59)

Whether this difference between Derrida and Deleuze, as described by Bogue, is really so much a difference of style and focus, or one of some basic theoretical incongruities, is not as important as the question of whether or not the same sorts of post-Hegelian resources are available to social theory—for, what is social theory about if not building blocks of alternative worlds? Certainly the answer to the latter question depends on answering the former, insomuch as comparing Deleuzean and Derridean alternative worlds goes. That will be an interesting comparison to make, once we have a sense of what the latter would look like. It is only this question, however, of constructing an image of a Derridean alternative world, that will be taken up in this study. Deleuze, along with his collaborator Felix Guattari, has at least shown that there are some very significant possibilities that arise from a post-Hegelian, differential matrix.

In science fiction, of course, the future is also (and perhaps always) *now*. Likewise, the philosophy of difference also takes its impetus not only from a different set of social and discursive relations that may exist in the future, but also from the different, the others, who exist in the margins of a society officially under the regime of the Same. Though it is philosophically important and useful to admit the presence of a "generalized other," as George Herbert Mead put it, a social theory that attempts to confront the postmodern as post-Hegelian would be sorely remiss in failing to recognize the other in terms of gender and race and ethnicity. The point is to reach a certain concreteness that is not always the aim of some philosophies of alterity that remain "metaphysical" in the old sense of remaining within global categories. Some questions raised by Judith Butler, in *Gender Trouble: Feminism and the Subversion of Identity*, are instructive:

> Is it possible to identify a monolithic as well as a monologic masculinist economy that traverses the array of cultural and historical contexts in which sexual difference takes place? Is the failure to acknowledge the specific cultural operations of gender oppression itself a kind of epistemological imperialism, one which is not ameliorated by the simple elaboration of cultural "examples" of the selfsame phallogocentrism? The effort to *include* "Other" cultures as variegated amplifications of a global phallogocentrism constitutes an appropriative act that risks a repetition of the self-aggrandizing gesture of phallogocentrism, colonizing under the sign of the same those differences that might otherwise call that totalizing concept into question. (1990, 13)

These lines cannot simply be appropriated as a "motto" for the analysis presented here—they are also a warning that I, a white male theorist, must try very hard to take to heart. The test is whether or not a space for this difference, and the concrete locations of it, is opened by this text. In this respect, the simplicity of pointing to the passage just cited and saying, "the same goes for race," is rightfully undercut. The difference of gender is also the difference of "gender"—that difference that makes problematic the use of "gender" and "sex" as emblems of identity, and which therefore makes this problematizing operation a very important site for subverting identity and the politics of identity[13]—and that much "goes for" race and ethnicity as well. But we must be very careful here— and indeed Derrida warns us in this regard—that "difference" does not become simply another master concept. The fact that I must repeatedly write "race *and* ethnicity" already shows that there is something here that cannot be grasped purely through the application of master concepts, for these terms, no less than the terms "gender" and "sex," must be problematized, but in a way that does not erase their signifying potential.[14] Possibilities are always plural, I argued in the first chapter, but this is an empty claim without concrete attention to diversity. That there is a parallelism to problematics of difference should not be taken as a license to impose yet another (Hegelian) identity. (Again, this is a warning that I issue to myself as much as to anyone.) Although race/ ethnicity, gender/sex, and class are taken in this study to be key categories of social analysis, even these are not exhaustive. In this and following chapters there are still other sites of difference that this text will attempt to be open to.

10. Derrida: most important here—and therefore we will only introduce the notion at this stage of the argument—is the sense of "the ends of man." In Derrida's analysis, humanity continues—"lives on"—in full view of its "ends." Note that these are plural—indeed, these ends contain resonances of all the "ends" that are prepared for in the other nine vignettes presented.

"The Ends of Man" is also, of course, the title of a well-known essay by Derrida, an essay that deconstructs the humanism of "that last great Hegelian" (as Foucault put it), Sartre. The post-Hegelian virtue of this text that is most significant for present purposes is the fact that Derrida's analysis really is a deconstruction. That is, Derrida both criticizes, in a purely analytical sense, Sartre's "mistake" in reading Hegel, Husserl, and especially Heidegger anthropologically, and he uncovers the ontotheological presuppositions that determine and motivate the structure of this mistake. What has been missed in many analyses of this text is that Derrida is not merely reasserting a certain (non-Sartrean, to be sure) Heidegger against Sartre. This is a very important point, both politically and philosophically (at the opening of the text Derrida takes care to "date" the words that follow politically). A Heideggerian deconstruction of humanism is not Derrida's only end here—for *this* deconstruction would be no less a singular end than that posited by Kant. Kant's "end," *autonomy*, is really the humanism that Derrida's essay is most essentially concerned with—and Derrida is intent on not allowing this end, autonomy, to be simply cancelled by Heidegger's sense of the "ek-sistence of man"—"standing in the lighting of Being." For Derrida, Heidegger's "proximity" (of humanity to Being) still requires a political reading. In recognizing this, Derrida is not unlike Sartre. Derrida's political reading, however, is quite different from Sartre's:

> Is not this security of the near what is trembling today, that is, the co-belonging and co-propriety of the name of man and the name of Being, such as this co-propriety inhabits, and is inhabited by, the language of the West, such as it is buried in its *oikonomia*, such as it is inscribed and forgotten according to the history of metaphysics, and such as it is awakened also by the destruction of ontotheology? But this trembling—which can only come from a certain outside—was already requisite within the very structure that it solicits. Its margin was marked in its own (*propre*) body. In

the thinking and the language of Being, the end of man has been prescribed since always, and this prescription has never done anything but modulate the equivocality of the *end*, in the play of *telos* and death. In the reading of this play, one may take the following sequences in all its senses: the end of man is the thinking of Being, man is the end of the thinking of Being, the end of man is the end of the thinking of Being. Man, since always, is his proper end, that is, the end of his proper. Being, since always, is its proper end, that is, the end of its proper. (1982, 133–34)

Derrida proposes that "the effects of this total trembling" be read under "several very general rubrics." As it turns out, there are three of these rubrics. Most commentators have focused on the first and third of these, which concern, respectively, Heidegger and Husserl, and Heidegger and Nietzsche. The second rubric, however, concerns what Derrida calls a "strategic bet," a choice between two strategies, "from the inside" (in proximity to the "outside," from which a radical trembling comes), where "we are" (Derrida places these words within quotation marks). These are strategies for listening for the radical trembling that comes from outside. The first of these Derrida calls "Heideggerian":

To attempt an exit and a deconstruction without changing terrain, by repeating what is implicit in the founding concepts and the original problematic, by using against the edifice the instruments or stones available in the house, that is, equally, in language. Here, one risks ceaselessly confirming, consolidating, *relifting* (*relever*), at an always more certain depth, that which one allegedly deconstructs. The continuous process of making explicit, moving toward an opening, risks sinking into the autism of the closure. (1982, 135)

The second strategy, Derrida claims, "is mostly the one which dominates France today"; given that "today," in this instance, means 1968 (October, to be more specific), and that Derrida marks the date of his text in terms of the U.S. war against the people of Vietnam, the assassination of Martin Luther King, Jr., and the "events of May," it is not especially extravagant to associate this strategy with Sartre. In this strategy, the point is

[t]o decide to change terrain, in a discontinuous and irruptive fashion, by brutally placing oneself outside, and by affirming an absolute break and difference. Without mentioning all the other

forms of *trompe-l'oeil* perspective in which such a displacement can be caught, thereby inhabiting more naively and more strictly than ever the inside one declares one has deserted, the simple practice of language ceaselessly reinstates the new terrain on the oldest ground. The effects of such a reinstatement or of such a blindness could be shown in numerous precise instances.

It goes without saying that these effects do not suffice to annul the necessity for a "change of terrain." (ibid.)

What does Derrida do with these two strategies that are somewhat at odds with one another? Derrida's answer to this question may not be surprising, but the hard work of situating social theory within the problematic of his proposal has barely begun. His answer will be quoted in full because it, along with the other post-Hegelian images, must haunt any attempt by social theory to confront the postmodern world.

. . . the choice between these two forms of deconstruction cannot be simple and unique. A new writing must weave and interlace these two motifs of deconstruction. Which amounts to saying that one must speak several languages and produce several texts at once. I would like to point out especially that the style of the first deconstruction is mostly that of the Heideggerian questions, and the other is mostly the one which dominates France today. I am purposely speaking in terms of a dominant style: because there are also breaks and changes of terrain in texts of the Heideggerian type; because the "change of terrain" is far from upsetting the entire French landscape to which I am referring; because what we need, perhaps, as Nietzsche said, is a change of "style"; and if there is style, Nietzsche reminded us, it must be *plural*.(ibid.)

(If the larger part of the remainder of this study were seen simply as the unpacking of these three longer passages quoted from "The Ends of Man," that would be fair enough.)

Here our series of vignettes ends. These are surely not all the versions of the postmodern/post-Hegel matrix that one might name, but they are, as I mentioned, the versions that haunt the definition of postmodernity that I will now, finally, present.

"Postmodernity" is the continuation of history beyond its end. This definition is deceptively simple; it should be explicated at some length. The basic reasoning behind this definition goes back to the passage from Adorno that serves as an epigraph for this chapter. The references to philosophy can be replaced by references to history, which now lives on because the moment in which history might have realized its end was missed.

Where the world was once "ripe" for the culmination of history, it is now "overripe." This condition might be appropriately called the "jaded society." It is society after the sort of alienation and unhappy consciousness that could have spurred the historical process to reactivation. (It is post-existentialist society; in which existentialism becomes only a part of intellectual history and nothing like the social trend that it once was;[15] it is the age of peace signs being confused with the Mercedes Benz hood ornament). The overall shape of this jaded condition has been well-documented in much that is called "postmodern," from architecture to music to literature and philosophy. Some of these documents even celebrate this condition (it is hard to come up with that special, singular example, but Jean Baudrillard's *America* (1988) comes to mind: "Caution: Objects in this mirror may be closer than they appear!"). Others, most notably Fredric Jameson (1984), say that, like it or not, the "loss of affect" (Jameson's phrase—what I am calling the jaded society) is an undeniable part of the present condition of society. The question is whether affect, the unhappy consciousness, alienation, etc., are experiences that can be retrieved in such a way as to reactivate the historical process. This is certainly to take Hegel at his word, for we might—indeed, we must—ask at the same time if this retrieval is something to be desired. (Jameson does take Hegel at his word: the *loss* of affect that might conceivably be retrieved only makes sense in an Hegelian framework. At a later stage of this argument I will question the matrix of loss and retrieval; here I only want to suggest that what may in fact be lost, most significantly, is the ability to feel loss.)

And yet, whatever "condition" it is that society persists in after the end of history, society must in some sense live off of the *remainder* of the historical process described by Hegel. Again we have recourse to the existentialists in understanding this metaphor in a more positive light. For it was the existentialists, Kierkegaard, Nietzsche, Dostoevsky, etc., who first argued, contrary to Hegel, that the real action is not in the "mainstream" of history, but instead in history's margins. A kind of Marxist argument could be marshalled to the same point, in that Marx's first sense of the term "proletariat," apart from the actual socio-economic position of this class, is of a class that "has nothing to lose but its chains, and a world to win." That is, the proletariat is that class found in the margins. And yet it is quite undeniable that, for either the existentialist or the Marxist sense of marginality, of the remainder (of the "left out," and of the "impossible"—not a word that Marx would have used,

of course), the notion itself lives in the margins of Hegel. The existentialists and the Marxists, and after them the philosophers of marginality
and alterity such as Bataille, Adorno, Levinas, Foucault, Kristeva,
Irigaray, and Derrida, etc., all take their notion of the margin from a
reading of Hegel; against the grain, certainly, but taking Hegel at his
word.

Jaded society

This thesis concerning postmodernity may be submitted to a series
of interrogations, organized under the general, Hegelian themes of
Nature, Humanity, Reason, and Philosophy.

1. The question of nature. Hegel has it that, in the originary "state
of nature," there is no distinction to be drawn between humanity—or
what more appropriately may be called "proto-humanity"—and
nature. (A complete analysis of Hegel's investigations into the natural
settings that humanity has found itself in is not my purpose here. Given
that limitation, however, it should be added that Hegel's sense of
geography and climate is not to be underestimated; it is not wrong in
this regard to say that Hegel opened new continents within philosophy;
see 1975, 152–96.) This early humanity had not itself learned to draw the
distinction. (Hegel has it that humanity could not make the distinction
in "intemperate zones"—"neither the *torrid* nor the *cold region* can
provide a basis for human freedom or for world-historical nations"; the
presence of the sea also presents certain problems, for while the sea
encourages a certain cunning and courage, it also generates a peculiar
character not finally conducive to the generation of the higher expressions of human freedom; see 1975, 154–55, 160–61). Therefore, in
Hegelian terms, until the distinction can be drawn there is no humanity,
only a part of nature that is potentially human. In the manner of other
Enlightenment thinkers, however, Hegel maintains that this proto-
human part of nature, under the right climatic circumstances, is des-
tined sooner or later, by the fact of its peculiar hunger and its affinity
with the Absolute, to break off from nature. This proto-humanity will
sooner or later discover itself, it will draw a line between itself and
nature through the first acts of self-identification. In Chapters 4 and 5
we will consider such acts in terms of Derrida's analysis of naming in *of
Grammatology*, but that analysis should in fact begin to come into play at
this point:

To name, to give names that it will on occasion be forbidden to
pronounce, such is the originary violence of language which

consists in inscribing within a difference, in classifying, in sus-
pending the vocative absolute. (1976, 112)

This line-drawing, between humanity and nature, is called by Derrida
"arche-writing." In these acts of line-drawing begins the trajectory of
the human project from Chinese Civilization to modernity. (I explore
this question of social origins in Chapter 5.) One might wonder, then, if
in postmodernity the relationship to nature has once again become
completely one-sided and unconscious.

    In a critique of Derrida that is, to my mind, misdirected, Habermas
(1987b) refers to "the night of writing in which all cows are black."
Perhaps this image has its point after all. Again a certain brief rehearsal
of pictures is appropriate, even if only to suggest an analysis to be
carried forward in other forums. In "The Rhetoric of Temporality"
(1983) and indeed in most of his work, Paul de Man argues against an
organicism that posits an essential relation between humanity and
nature. In de Man's view, this nature is lost, and it will and should
remain lost. De Man is faithful to Hegel in his analysis: not only is there
no hope of a "return" to nature, it is not a good thing to want such a
return.[16] In a quite different vein, the televisual notions of McLuhan and
Baudrillard also suggest a permanent severance from nature that is itself
a kind of new nature, a complete "environment." The corporate world,
from MTV, which urges the viewer, in a computer-generated voice, to
"jack into the matrix" (a slogan obviously culled from William Gibson's
visionary and scary novels),[17] to AT&T's "global telecommunity," has
not only constructed this "artificial" environment; once inside the
environment of *simulacra*, there is no "outside."

    Mark, then, the fact that we are not simply lamenting the "loss of a
sense of nature." Perhaps we may lament the "loss of the sense of
loss"—a lament that is dangerously close to the abyss of infinite regress.
And yet this regress allows us to swerve away from the organicist and
indeed sometimes fascistic rhetoric of "loss," and toward a productive
aporia—impossibility.

    The contemporary matrix, however, seems like Hegel's "nature"
turned upside-down (and not by a Marxist process of inversion).

    2. The image of humanity in postmodernity. What is humanity in
this age of stasis? Two directions are suggested: either the "post-man,"
as the postmodern notion of Nietzsche's *Übermensch*; or, a turn toward
marginal subjects, in their concrete instances as women, people of the
Third World, people of color, gay people, proletarians, and others who
have been relegated to the margins of history. This either/or is the only
possible dialectic in this otherwise post-dialectical society—though it is

a vital question (an apocalyptic/anti-apocalyptic question), and by no means a certainty, whether this dialectic possesses the energy sufficient for a retrieval and reinvention of history. By another name, this is the dialectic of hyper-secular society and postsecular community.

Hegel conceives of the dimensions of humanity as freedom, reason, and self-consciousness (though these dimensions apply first of all to the concept of the nation, rather than to individuals; see 1975, 50–52). The dimensions of postmodern humanity, fortunately, are not merely the negations of these three. (The use of the term "postmodern humanity" generates a contradiction that was marked in the initial pages of this study. This contradiction will be kept in brackets for the moment.) Postmodern humanity may, however, exhibit the *dialectical* opposites of the dimensions specified by Hegel. Taking the last dimension first, there is a significant debate in postmodern philosophy and cultural criticism concerning the "end" or "death" of subjectivity.[18] Again, lines are drawn around two basic images of humanity in postmodernity. The "post-man" camp claims that the subject is dead, pure and simple, although this subject, much like Nietzsche's God, may remain in our midst as a rotting, stinking corpse for some time to come (its illusory presence, like God's, is a powerful one). A rather different view is expressed by those theorists and other writers or artists who focus on the marginal subject. Perhaps, they argue, it is only the unified, Western, male subject that is born in modernity with Descartes's *Cogito*, and that reaches its culmination in Hegel's sense of a humanity that comes to complete self-consciousness in the historical process, that is dead (in Nietzsche's sense of "dead"). Don't go around proclaiming, these theorists argue, the "death of the subject" insofar as subjects who have yet to truly live are concerned. As Nancy K. Miller puts it:

> The postmodernist decision that the Author is Dead and the subject along with him does not, I will argue, necessarily hold for women, and prematurely forecloses the question of agency for them. Because women have not had the same historical relation of identity to origin, institution, production, that men have had, they have not, I think, (collectively) felt burdened by *too much* Self, Ego, Cogito, etc. Because the female subject has juridically been excluded from the polis, hence decentered, "deroriginated," deinstitutionalized, etc., her relation to integrity and textuality, desire and authority, displays structurally important differences from that universal position. (1989, 6)

Assuming, however, that feminist and other critics of the "death of the subject" thesis do not simply wish to send previously marginalized subjects on the same modern trajectory at whose end the (hip, theoretical) white male subject now finds himself, heavy theoretical and practical burdens are thereby incurred. The question is, What does it mean to have social agency in the postmodern world? A first approximation is that this agency would not be essentially male, Western, or unified. The next step has to demonstrate that this postmodern agency is not the product of an internal self-consciousness on either a Cartesian, individualistic model, or a Kantian, intersubjective model, or an Hegelian, world-historical model; it is, instead, a *posit* of external forces. This means that the theory of the postmodern subject must deal with the question of otherness in a post-Hegelian way. That is, where Hegel was ultimately concerned to assimilate the Other (or the remainder or margin) to the Same, the postmodern theorist must allow that there is a remainder that cannot be so assimilated. (The theoretical machinery of this postmodern subject, which will be discussed under the rubric of "positionality," is set out in the next two chapters.)

Reconceiving freedom is not simply a matter of replaying the dialectic just illustrated concerning subjectivity, but this dialectic does point the way. Freedom for Hegel is more a matter of necessity than contingency. In other words, freedom serves a higher necessity, and that necessity is one of "eliminating the contingent" (1975, 26-28). Only the world-historical subject (a "that," not a "who") is truly free, and even in this singular, most special of cases the freedom is that of complete self-consciousness—*savoir absolu*, the career of which is traced in Derrida's *Glas*. This is the Enlightenment identification of freedom with knowledge, writ very large and come to life in a way inconceivable especially to Enlightenment thinkers who happen to be English. Postmodern freedom, like postmodern subjectivity, could be conceived in the margins of this necessary, world-historic movement toward the completion of the human project. In this case, postmodern freedom is the permanent delay of this completion: *Glas* being a textual example of this delaying tactic (part of a general strategy, the name of which could be *différance*, designed to forestall the war of the name, in the parlance of "No Apocalypse, Not Now," quoted in the first chapter).[19]

The postmodern counterpart to reason might then be conceived as a counter-reason that escapes the assimilating, totalizing, gesture of Hegel's historicized reason. The problem is how to keep what was gained with Hegel's historicization of reason. The solution is found in not returning to a pre-historicized reason that is perhaps, in fact, just as inaccessible to us as is "nature." Rather, the dialectical solution is to carry Hegel's program even further, to the point of historicizing Hegel's historicization itself. That this is a constant strategy of both deconstruction and the new pragmatism is well-known.[20] What is just as important is that this is in fact a kind of cabalistic strategy; we will return to this point, and its significance for Hegel, Derrida, and postsecular prospects, in the next section.

These reformulated dimensions of postmodern humanity can, in the social context in which humanity presently finds itself, be specified only as possibilities that exist simultaneously alongside other forms of counter-subjectivity, -freedom, and -reason. These hyper-secular possibilities would perhaps find their fulfillment in the total environment alluded to earlier in the discussion of nature, of the postmodern "individual." This individual would replicate the god-king of the first civilizations, but with the difference that now *each* "sovereign" individual could become such a creature. The hallmark of this individual would be the *inability* to conceive of the postsecular possibilities that might be based on countervailing forces acting within this environment.

It is unfortunate that theory has to conceive of such a predicament, that within the jaded society there lies the further possibility (counter-possibility, that is) that people could become too brain-dead to know how brain-dead they are—to put it in very crude terms. This is, however, a possibility that has to be thought in other modes than the cynical. But, at least as long as there *is* a conception of the predicament, some sense of what the danger really is, there is the possibility that other sensibilities will win out. The question will remain whether the alternative sensibilities enumerated here do not also strain too much in the direction of the dialectic that has in the past been more a part of the problem than the solution. That is to say, the problem is to reconceive the dialectic of history, but, again, in terms of a logic of alterity and margins, rather than in terms of Hegel's logic of assimilation to the Same.

For it is no longer deniable that this latter logic has its dystopian side, one that leads back to Hegel's "Orient," or, to use Max Weber's terminology, "New Egypt," and the "iron cage." Still another name for this dystopia might be the "Asiatic mode of production in the age of semiotic power." This mode of production is especially evident in the emergence of Japanese-American postmodern capitalism, in which the culture of the "East" is artificially used as the ground for the economic order of the West. (This emerging formation is perfectly depicted in William Gibson's novels.) The result is prefigured in Daniel Bell's *The End of Ideology*, the conservative implications of which Habermas (1989, Chapter One) has tried to take stock of in a progressive way. The point of presenting this dystopian picture (that is mainly evocative—the speculation attempts to name, and thereby to grope toward, what seems to be emerging) is not to claim that humanity is stuck with *this* completion of the historical project, but rather to attempt to conceive of what any realistic counter-reason will in fact have to deal with in terms of the cultural configuration that it must confront.

      3. Some distance has already been covered concerning our third theme, reason. That is, there has been an initial encounter with reason as a dimension of humanity. For Hegel, however, reason is not simply a human dimension. Rather, Reason-writ-large is also the inner logic of the dialectic of the Absolute and the human project. Is there a counter-reason here that is similar to the marginal counterpart of the human dimension of reason? Counter-reason here would have to be conceived once again in terms of that which introduces *différance* into the movement of Reason. In this sense, counter-reason is that which continually wards off the powerful human urge to give in to an overarching teleology or eschatology (which presents itself as "predetermination," "fate," or something on that order). But what is the source of that urge? To my mind it is the fear that humanity has quite rightly had for most of its existence of indeterminacy, of contingency. Now that all the elements seem to be in place for the overcoming of this contingency, especially insomuch as basic kinds of needs—for food, shelter, etc.—are concerned, why make an argument *for* contingency? At least at first glance, this would really seem to be a kind of irrationalistic counter-reason that would move in such a direction. This irrationalism would parallel the anti-subjectivity that denies the subjectivity of those who have never yet been considered as subjects—those in the margins of society. The counter-reason that makes sense as a real alternative to Reason, then, must be of a different character. It must be a counter-reason that recognizes the scope for bringing contingency under the wing of order, while at the same time carefully claiming the ground for experiment, for the conception of possibilities apart from their immediate usefulness and necessity. William Corlett makes the useful distinction between the kind of "de facto sense-making" necessary for survival, and the politics of arresting the differential flux. He assesses the cost of this latter politics:

    Those who approach politics as an imposition of form on a chaotic world can be said, after all, to have chosen order over chaos. Critics of linear time might ask instead how those who presume linear time find it possible and feel compelled to make such choices. They might wish to assess the cost of this "decision," a decision which must be forced because it can never be made. (1989, 88)

Corlett, of course, also proposes a Derridean means toward an alternative, which I fully endorse:

> . . . to avoid the pitfalls of reassurance one must make sense of the advice that a critique of the principle of hegemony, if it is to be thought radically, must insist that it is the *give* in the structures of our worlds which makes power plays possible and not the other way around. (ibid.; 90)

The ground must be claimed, in other words, for open-endedness.

4. Finally, there is the question of the role of philosophy in this postmodern reconception of possibilities. Philosophy has to be brought down several notches from the Hegelian heights (but perhaps this move would bring philosophy *up* to the concrete). But this reassessment of philosophy, its dislocation from its formerly central role in intellectual life, has been an accomplished fact for some time, and this in all the main trends in Western philosophy (analytic, continental, Marxist, etc.).

As with the antinomy of irrationalism and counter-reason, there is a bifurcation of possibilities: either the restoration of philosophy as an elite enterprise, one that once again claims to be the organ of the instantiated World Spirit (though more in terms of a socially-useful myth, akin to Plato's myth of the metals, than as a factual claim); or, the reconception of philosophy and its role along the lines of the other reconceptions suggested here. Philosophy under this latter program would consist in studies that emphasize particularities over universality (e.g., Foucault), the logic of otherness rather than assimilation to the Same (Derrida, Kristeva, Levinas, etc.), attention to the details of this post-Hegelian, jaded society rather than the sway of a supposedly timeless humanism that has indeed been lost (which would involve semiotically-sophisticated forms of cultural criticism), and a sense of how this post-history exists in both a dialectical and a differential relation to the historical project.

This last project, which might describe the parameters of postmodern philosophy as a whole, is well-served in Derrida's text, which, even where it presses the non-concept of *différance* to its limits, is not unaware of the power of dialectical notions.[21] That dialectic and *différance* exist alongside and interwoven with one another—for both are, for Derrida, forms of "weaving"[22]—in Derrida's text is the most important reason that this text is especially appropriate for analyzing postmodernity. This text is especially able to gather the post-Hegelian threads represented by the vignettes presented earlier. (This is true even for the fifth vignette, concerning multinational corporations and therefore political economy in the more ordinary sense, despite the fact that these themes are not often specifically foregrounded in Derrida's work. Gayatri Spivak and other Derrideans inclined toward Marxism have gone some way in this endeavor.)[23] With this gathering comes the possibility of showing that post-history itself has a history, even if post-history in some sense lies outside of, or is an impasse within, the historical process that created it. Derrida's materialization of the signifier creates an "impure" (or contaminated) writing that resembles the impurity of postmodern society itself. Typically, with attempts at philosophical homologies, there is an assumed symmetry of purity to purity: the purity of a monological theory that is homologous with the purity of a particular social system. In postmodern society and theory there is the danger that the impurity of one will be asymmetrical and therefore increasingly non-homologous with the other. Therefore, the ability of postmodern theory to play a role in understanding and shaping postmodern society is placed in question. A "strategic bet" is required. But Derrida would argue, I feel certain, that this is a bet that has never not been required: there are no pure theories or pure social formations. The breakthrough of contaminated theory is to foreground this impurity.

In postmodern society all of the postmodern definitions enumerated earlier exist simultaneously, though not necessarily harmoniously. The absence of nature, the contradictory images of humanity, and the possibilities of reconceived subjectivity, freedom, and reason, that co-exist with counter-possibilities of the death of the subject, the iron cage, and irrationality, all add up to the jaded society, though not in any simple arithmetic.

The Jews who bother Hegel: Intimations of the postmodern prospect

We turn, then, to an initial encounter with the complex calculus that will be required for sorting out the postmodern impasse: a mathematics in which numbers also have their letter.[24] The more hopeful prospects, for post-Hegelian humanity, are found in the margins of Hegel and, indeed, in the margins of history. These marginal prospects, it has already been noted, are in a very real sense "at home" and on familiar ground on the postmodern terrain. The wealth of marginalized historical experience that marginal subjects bring to jaded society is the key to breaking the deadlock of historical stasis.

The supreme irony is that the paradigm marginal subject is found inhabiting the margins of Hegel's text: I refer to the question of the Jews in Hegel. The Jew is the one who does not fit into the world historical scheme of things. This is a problem that occupied Hegel for his entire intellectual life. It would be the easiest thing in the world to dismiss Hegel's attempts to accommodate the Jews—to explain their persistence despite their historical obsolescence—as so much anti-Semitism, but this would be an injustice to both Hegel and to Judaism, as Emil Fackenheim has rigorously demonstrated (we will turn to his argument in a moment).

Certainly there is no harm in stating the "simple facts" of the case, for it is true that Hegel can and should be read on one level—but only one!—as a reconceptualization of Christianity and centuries of the theory and practice of Christian anti-Semitism. Judaism, however, cannot be historically obsolete in Hegel's picture in just the same way that the religions and mythologies developed by other historical cultures—the Chinese, Persians, Egyptians, Greeks, etc.—are: after all, the God of the Jews and the God of the Christians is supposedly the same God. Or, at least, the Jews were on to something, in Hegel's view, with Jehovah, though they did not have the full picture that comes only with Christianity. The Jewish God is "not yet" the authentic God; furthermore,

> The Jewish God is . . . imageless and supersensible, but a supersensible that is a mere abstraction of thought, which does not yet have within it the plenitude that makes it spirit. (1984, 331)

This "not yet" is of great importance. Judaism is not yet Christianity, but it persists all the same, in a state of disunion with God. Because the Jewish God, in Hegel's view, is merely abstract,

> there hovers, above this sphere, a grief that is not resolved, the consciousness of a fate, an unknown power, a necessity that is not cognitively understood, and with which no reconciliation takes place.

Hegel adds that this state of separation is "bound up with a particular level of self-consciousness," a level that is superceded, of course, by Christianity (ibid., 361; word order altered) Let there be no doubt that the Christian God has achieved the plenitude that the Jewish God lacks, and that the meaning of this achievement is clear for Christianity and Judaism:

> Christianity is the religion which has revealed the nature and being of God to man. Thus we know as Christians what God is;

God is no longer an unknown quantity: and if we continue to say that he is, we are not Christians. . . . Christians, then, are initiated into the mysteries of God, and this also supplies us with the key to world history. For we have here a definite knowledge of providence and its plan. It is one of the central doctrines of Christianity that providence has ruled and continues to rule the world, and that everything which happens in the world is determined by and commensurate with the divine government. This doctrine is opposed both to the idea of chance and to that of limited ends (such as the preservation of the Jewish people). (1975, 41)

The Jews, then, are a people of "limited ends." And yet they persist—and let us be clear about what the problem is here: the Jews persist as a thorn in the side of Hegel's system. For this system must, according to its own rules, do justice to every civilization: the system must show how every pre-Christian historical civilization is not only overcome, and thereby rendered obsolete, but further is sublated into the greater contours of world history. As Derrideans are wont to say, this is an economy in which every coin is accounted for. In a long argument that can only be summarized here, Emil Fackenheim, in his *Encounters between Judaism and Modern Philosophy*, demonstrates the fact that Judaism is a very special problem for Hegel, for neither can ultimately accomodate the other. It is to Hegel's credit, however, that he continually strained toward such an accommodation, in terms of "actual Jewish religious realities" which, "called into question, not some minor aspects of his thought, but nothing less than his system as a whole" (1980, 84–85). The confrontation, indeed, is between two radically different, *world-historical*, understandings. Fackenheim frames this confrontation in terms of three points about Jewish religious self-understanding:

First, like Hegel's philosophical comprehension and unlike much religious self-understanding—the Jewish religious self-understanding is itself historical: Jewish religious existence is *between* Creation (or Fall or Exodus) and the Messianic future. Second— again like Hegel's philosophical comprehension—this religious self-understanding is *world*-historical: the beginning and end of history are universal, and Jewish existence between these extremes is that of a *witness* in which the abstractions "particular" and "universal" are concretely intertwined. Third—and this is decisive—unless Jewish religious existence is to be not only *in* history but also somehow *of* it, it must sooner or later, and certainly in the modern world, relate itself not only to non-Jewish world history but also to non-Jewish ways of understanding it. But once it makes this attempt from its *own* point of view it comes face to face with the Hegelian mediation of *all* points of view from a world-historical point of view. Hegel's comprehension of world history therefore confronts the Jewish religious self-understanding with a radical challenge, and this does not vanish if Hegel's own point of view should prove to be less world-historical than he imagines. (1980, 87)

Judaism, and the Jews, are not only suppresed in Hegel as the other—that "most reprobate and abandoned" of peoples, because they "stand directly before the door of salvation" (Hegel 1977, 366)—they are problematic in being too much the same, for the Jews stand directly before the door of Hegel as well. Their crime is that they do not knock and seek entrance. What, then, are the Jews doing "out there"?

To this question a quite specific answer can be given: Judaism (my alternation between "Jews" and "Judaism" is a recognition of the problematics of identity that has not yet been thematized) is providing two notions that are of supreme importance to Hegel. First, it is to ancient Hebrew culture that we must give credit for the invention of narrative history. Second, in the conception of the relationship between humanity and God as a primarily *social* relationship, ancient Judaism provides the basis for the civic altruism that Hegel sees as necessary for the *Aufhebung* of mere liberalism and its attendent social fragmentations.[25] In Judaism, however, both of these contributions are framed in terms of a non-Christian messianism that Hegel finds not only untenable, but indeed, untouchable (Fackenheim 1980, 99).

The crux of the matter is that Jewish messianism does not seek the "key to world history," if by this "key" is meant, in Susan Handelman's appropriate terminology, the "fulfiller of signs" who provides an "escape from textuality" (1982, 83–120). Judaism does not seek a God who is a "known quantity." On the contrary, and it is this refusal to sublate alterity into a logic of the Same that Hegel cannot countenance.

Fackenheim takes the question one step further. Hegel's system, though it lives on in shadow form in Marxism and existentialism,[26] is no longer tenable as such (as a philosophical project of totalization that finds its correlate in the movement of world history, and vice-versa). The Jews and Judaism, however, live on, despite everything—meaning, even despite the attempt to make the world "Judenrein," an attempt that is one kind of culmination of Western culture. *This* historical phenomenon, this persistence—granting that, after all, an Hegelian understanding of things must remain faithful to historical phenomena, in order to discern the grand dialectic (the *Grundidee*) at work there—spurs Fackenheim to raise the following concerns:

> . . . might not Judaism challenge Hegelianism as radically as Hegelianism challenges Judaism? Hegel's philosophy mediates from an external and superior point of view between Jewish history and, respectively, the ancient Greek-Roman, medieval Catholic, and modern secular-Protestant worlds. What if, in point of historical fact, Hegel's external mediations of Jewish history with periods of world history were matched by *internal* Jewish *self-mediations in response* to the epoch-making changes which are cited by Hegel against it?
>
> This question has never been asked. It does not occur in Hegel's thought. It has not occurred to Jewish Hegelians or anti-Hegelians. Yet once it is asked, Hegel's understanding of Jewish history, his understanding of world history, and indeed his world-historical standpoint are all called into question. (1980, 88)

These questions can be translated into the rubric thus far established: What if alterity surrounds the logic of the Same? What if alterity calls for a dissemination that will not return? What if there is no "spirit" that is the destination of the (Hebrew) letter? What if the messiah only calls, but never "arrives"—so that the "I am that I am" can never be said outright? Finally, what if this non-arrival and this inability to say the name of God are indicators of the practical spaces of human possibility?

This language of alterity, however, can never be so clever as to think that it has fully escaped the logic of the same. Just as Derrida sets Sartre beside Heidegger in a strategic bet, a "double strategy," so he also sets the "Jewish" next to the "Greek." This strategy allows us to formulate a response to Fackenheim's provocation. I request the reader's indulgence in quoting once again an oft-quoted passage from Derrida, the final two paragraphs of "Violence and Metaphysics: An Essay on the Thought of Emmanuel Levinas."

> Are we Jews? Are we Greeks? We live in the difference between the Jew and the Greek, which is perhaps the unity of what is called history. We live in and of difference, that is, in *hypocrisy*, about which Levinas so profoundly says that it is "not only a base contingent defect of man, but the underlying rending of a world attached to both the philosophers and the prophets."

Are we Greeks? Are we Jews? But who, we? Are we (not a chronological, but a pre-logical question) *first* Jews or *first* Greeks? And does the strange dialogue between the Jew and the Greek, peace itself, have the form of the absolute, speculative logic of Hegel, the living logic which *reconciles* formal tautology and empirical heterology after having *thought* prophetic discourse in the preface to the *Phenomenology of Mind*? Or, on the contrary, does this peace have the form of infinite separation and of the unthinkable, unsayable transcendence of the other? To what horizon of peace does the language which asks this question belong? From whence does it draw the energy of its question? Can it account for the historical *coupling* of Judaism and Hellenism? And what is the legitimacy, what is the meaning of the *copula* in this proposition from perhaps the most Hegelian of modern novelists: "Jewgreek is greekjew. Extremes meet"? (1978, 153)

The question, then, of who or what "represents" otherness or the logic of the Same, is not uncomplicated. Each is necessarily tangled up with the other. But perhaps the question is not what we "are" or what we "were" (were we first Jews or first Greeks?), but rather what we *will* be. At the end of the day, so to speak, will we be Jews or Greeks? Fackenheim seems to ask this perfectly reasonable question. The language of it, however, is a betrayal (which Fackenheim would undoubtedly recognize), for to speak of "the end of the day" is to speak Greek. It is to speak of the letter that has arrived at its proper destination, spirit. Such is the end of possibility, the fulfillment of signs, the escape from textuality—from the text, the *Torah*, which Levinas advises us "to love more than God." Derrida takes that advice quite seriously.

Is Judaism therefore more "essential," in some "pre-logical, not chronological" sense? The simple answer is "no," because the point is not to reach either the beginning or the end of the day, but quite the contrary, "to wander without ends" ("No Apocalypse, Not Now"). Derrida, following Levinas, pursues the critique of ontology precisely through the pursuit of the *trace* that erases origins and ends.

. . . it is in the specific zone of this imprint and this trace, in the temporalization of a *lived experience* which is neither *in* the world nor in "another world," which is not more sonorous than luminous, not more *in* time than *in* space, that differences appear among the elements or rather produce them, make them emerge as such and constitute the *texts*, the chains, and the systems of traces. These chains and systems cannot be outlined except in the fabric of this trace or imprint. The unheard difference between the appearing and the appearance (between the "world" and "lived experience") is the condition of all other differences, of all other traces, and *it is already a trace. . . . The trace is in fact the absolute origin of sense in general. Which amounts to saying once again that there is no absolute origin of sense in general.* (1976, 65; emphasis in original)

In Levinas's work the pursuit of this trace leads to an originary ethics rather than to a fundamental ontology. Derrida is never quite so willing to accept this either/or of Heidegger/Levinas, or Greek/Jew, or any of a number of other formalizations (actually, instantiations) of Same/Other that we could name. The condition of life and meaning is always one of being "between." (One might say, with Edmond Jabes, "in the spaces between the pieces of the broken tablets of Moses.")[27] The "ethico-political," as Derrida prefers to put it, cannot be finally separated from the deconstruction of ontology that takes the play of presence and absence to be more essential than "essence" itself.

In the many-layered text called "Shibboleth," Derrida takes up the theme of a "pass-word" that has no external validation. A password must still grope toward the call that comes from "outside." As one might expect, Derrida has it that the Jew is in the position of this password, this *brisure* that signals both identity and difference. Although the Jew may be the very embodiment of difference, the material reminder of the letter that will not conform to Hegel's spirit, the Jew is never *simply* the other, nor is the Same—call it Christianity, or call it philosophy (as opposed to poetry)—always and only identical with itself. Discussing Marina Tsvetayeva's claim that "all the poets are Jews," Derrida argues that

[W]hat the trope comes to is locating the Jew not only *as* a poet but also *in* every man circumcised by language or led to circumcise a language. . . .

. . . a certain tropic may displace the literality of membership in the Jewish community, if one could still speak of belonging to a community to which, we are reminded, nothing belongs as its own [neither property nor essence, Derrida says earlier]. In this case, those who have undergone the *experience*—a certain concise experience—of circumcision, circumcised and circumcisers, are, in all the senses of this word, Jews.

Anyone or no one may be Jewish. No one is (not) circumcised; it is no one's circumcision. If all the poets are Jews, they are
all circumcised or circumcisers. (1986c, 340–41)

This double circumstance of circumscription is finally the condition of
postmodernity, described now such that its possibilities are as much
foregrounded as its dangers.

The question remains, however, whether a sufficient framework
has been constructed for the conduct of social theory, one in which more
concrete questions can be approached and resolved. It has to be admitted that we are not at that point yet. Instead, the account of postmodernity
given thus far is in many ways a very confusing cartography. Such a
cartography is perhaps partially excusable if the terrain that it seeks to
map is itself confused. This is indeed the case, but matters cannot be
allowed to sit with this state of affairs. Every confusion in this cartography returns, one way or another, to the question of signification. In the
later stages of this postmodern cartography we have unearthed the Jews
who make Hegel's philosophical life a bit more complicated. Their
poetry insists on an interpretation that confuses and complicates Hegel's
truth. This poetry might also be called Nietzsche, or it might be called
"materiality" or the refusal of philosophy in Marx (though we will later
discuss the Jews who bother him). Many commentators on Derrida have
only aligned him with this poetry, not seeing the space between poetry
and philosophy, and between Judaism and Hegel. It remains for this
investigation to show in more detail the meaning of this space and its
relevance for social theory. Are we "finally" circumscribed by language, or circumscribers of it? The only way to find out is to go to the
heart of this question.

3

What is at the heart of language?
Habermas, Davidson, Derrida

These same questions, developed in a more or less clear and adequate fashion, constitute at the same time the as yet hidden center of those endeavors at which contemporary "philosophy" aims for in its extreme counterpositions (Carnap, Heidegger). Today these positions are called the technological scientific view of language and the speculative hermeneutic experience of language. Both positions are determined by unfathomably diverse tasks. The first position wants to bring all thinking and speaking, even that of philosophy, within the jurisdiction of a system of signs that can be construed as a technical-logical system—to restrict all thinking and saying to being instruments of science. The second position has grown from the question of what it is to be experienced as the subject matter of philosophy's thinking and how this subject matter (Being as Being) is to be expressed. In neither position is there a question of a separate sphere of a philosophy of language (analogous to that of a philosophy of nature or of art); language is recognized as the realm within which every thinking of philosophy and every mode of thinking and saying dwell and move. To the extent that the Being of man is determined by Western tradition in such a way that man is that animal who "has language"—even man as acting being is such only as the one who "has language"—nothing less is at stake in the dispute between the two positions than the question of man and his destiny.

—Martin Heidegger, *Phanomenologie und Theologie*

Our foray into postmodern cartography yielded not one map but a series, with no single connecting line. Without such a line, it is not clear that anything approximating a postmodern *matrix* exists. In the preceding chapter the very idea of a connecting line was challenged on three levels—and these are indeed *distinct* levels that, as far as can be known at this point, are not connected, causally or otherwise. "Otherwise" is a large category, however. Taking some stock of the conceptual space that has thus far unfolded may be helpful. Recall that the motivating feature of our map is a notion of the "post-Hegelian." In fact, "post-Hegelian" also names a set of notions that may or may not be connected by something more substantial than a name.

In the first post-Hegelian map we generated a series of sketches of quite different positions that can be and are taken up in postmodernity. This activity followed the principle of the modern encyclopedia. That is, the pictures were set side by side, seemingly without any non-arbitrary principle of organization (as in an encyclopedia where "Hegel" may follow "Hedonism"). The sketches might even be said to each display a different post-Hegelianism. Is there a principle, then, to this difference? Looking ahead, to the second post-Hegelian map (the jaded society), perhaps it would serve best if we looked for something on the "surface," rather than for a depth principle. There is another reason for remaining on the surface of these sketches in searching for their principle, namely that their difference could easily be subverted by a resurgent dialectic. Whether this might be, as in earlier cases, either a "discovery" or an "invention," is not as important a question as the necessity, at this point, of disallowing an Hegelian shortcircuit of difference. Any principle of difference that is simply a "different" form of the dialectic should be avoided for now.

There is a certain compulsion, at the end of these sketches, to determine who or what has come out the "winner." Though the answer cannot be given unequivocally, it seems clear that Nietzsche comes through again and again. I do not think that this is simply a matter of the fact that I am after all the author of these sketches, and I could have made them come out any way that I wanted them to. This is not finally the case (and, truth be told, my "personal" inclination would not be toward Nietzsche). Perspectivism, then, might be taken as both the way in and the way out of these sketches. Of an earlier generation, and undoubtedly of the present generation as well—for Foucault, Derrida, Baudrillard, and Deleuze, at least, are all Nietzscheans in non-superficial respects, and even the capillary action of transnational economic articulation might be said to have a Nietzschean-Foucauldian character—Nietzsche stands as the exemplary post-Hegelian. Deleuze opens his wonderful essay, "Nomad Thought," with words that continue to ring true:

> Probably most of us fix the dawn of our modern culture in the trinity Nietzsche-Freud-Marx. And it is of little consequence that the world was unprepared for them in advance. Now, Marx and

Freud, perhaps, do represent the dawn of our culture, but Nietzsche is something entirely different: the dawn of our countercul-
ture. (1985, 142)

Perhaps it is not hard to see Nietzsche's nomad thought (a better name
for perspectivism, in my view) as the way *into* postmodernity, insomuch
as we might also see this thought as finally fragmented into the
simultaneity of competing, only partially-formed worldviews under
the near-transparent thumb of the performativity principle. But what
does Nietzsche have to do with the way out? In a penetrating analysis of
Nietzsche's deployment of the aphorism, in which philosophy done "in
the blink of the eye" shows its power as (what I've called) *interpretive
praxis*, Gary Shapiro contributes the following comments concerning
"Nomad Thought":

> Gilles Deleuze, drawing on Nietzsche's account of the foundation
> of the political state, has suggested that we ought to distinguish
> imperial and nomadic thought. An imperial political structure is
> hierarchical, bureacratic, and involves massive standardization
> and containment of spontaneity. The nomads, who have perhaps
> been displaced by the foundation or spread of empire, reject the
> imperial way of life and must adopt strategy which will allow
> them to remain free from the encroachments of empire while
> providing them the opportunity for attacks that can eventually
> destabilize the imperial machine. Imperial politics, Deleuze sug-
> gests, is bound up with imperial philosophy: the latter's insistence
> on first principles, generalizable method, and systematic form
> both echo and reinforce the demands of its political structure.
> Nomadic thought is suspicious of all this and so it cannot oppose
> philosophical imperialism with a different set of first principles,
> method and system; for if it were successful it would only lead to
> the replacement of one regime with another which is homologous
> with it. Nomadic thought must be multiple and adaptable, hunt-
> ing out the weak points and interstices of the imperial structure. It
> will not aim at a palace revolution but at what Nietzsche calls a
> "slow cure" in which old habits are gradually dismantled and
> replaced. In his aphoristic books Nietzsche seeks out those who
> are travelling actually or metaphorically, that is, those who are not
> tied to a specific place in the imperial structure. As long as
> movement of any kind is possible, those on the move can be lured
> by the nomads who constantly circle around the imperial core,
> striking when appropriate and strategically withdrawing and

regrouping. We can expect that Nietzschean aphorism will be a
source of power and an exemplary weapon in this struggle.[1]

Without forgetting about certain counter-currents within the set of
postmodern vignettes, we are approaching a principle of difference that
may serve as a key to all of our maps.
    There is a linkage here that only needs to be thematized: that
between the anti-system thrust of Nietzsche and the whole matrix of
textuality in which the notion of aphorism as an "exemplary weapon"
finds its immediate context. Once we take Nietzsche as exemplary, or as
a kind of "guide" to the construction of anti-imperialist thought that is
itself not another imperialism, there is no harm in bringing Marx back
in. Indeed, this becomes absolutely necessary—the only question is:
When will we know if we have really learned the "lesson" of Nietzsche?
The key link is the understanding of language as difference.
    A grammatological theory is needed, then, for a semiotic society.
This "theory" will finally turn out to be non-homologous with the
semiotized mode of production of advanced capitalism, and that is
exactly what will make this theory work.
    The demonstration of this practicality will take up all remaining
pages of this investigation. The framework of interpretive praxis has
been articulated to the point where a turn to what is still sometimes
called, despite Heidegger, the "philosophy of language" is the required
next step. (Later we shall see why Heidegger's point is well taken.) Here
we will find the inner logic (in actuality, the "alterior logic") of the three
maps, the logic "otherwise."

Exemplars and demarcations

    In recent years a line of demarcation has been drawn between two
exemplary thinkers, Derrida and Habermas. Habermas has entered the
fray with two chapters in his *The Philosophical Discourse of Modernity*
(1987b), to which Derrida has offered a short response in a long footnote
to the "Afterword" of the book version of *Limited Inc* (1988a). The
debate, such as it is, has been framed by the terms "modernism" and
"postmodernism," and sometimes "Enlightenment" and "post-En-
lightenment," by Habermas. Following the analysis by Ronald Bogue
presented in the second chapter, the supposed antinomy of Hegel and
hermeneutics might also describe the debate, at least as Habermas sees
it.
    These two figures, surely two of the most important thinkers of
our century, perhaps only find their real antagonism in a kind of

idealization of their respective positions. Again, this is how Habermas would have it. My intention here is to both follow out these idealizations—at a certain point an idealized version of Donald Davidson's work will enter in as well—and to provide a basis for giving a fresh start to this debate (a "debate" that has never even approached being a productive dialogue; see Ryan 1989) on the other side of these idealizations.

The terms of the modernity/postmodernity debate are not entirely satisfactory. For example, the champions of the "unfinished project of modernity" (as Habermas puts it) are often identified with "humanism," while structuralists and poststructuralists (especially Althusser, Foucault, Deleuze, Kristeva, Lyotard, Irigaray, and Derrida) are sometimes tagged with the label "anti-humanism"[2]—not an altogether happy identification after years of the inhumanism of Reagan, Thatcher, the Mitterand government's sinking of the Greenpeace Rainbow Warrior, etc. The poststructuralists (a loose group, to be sure) along with Gadamer (see 1981), occupy quite different positions in their critiques of humanism and Enlightenment ideology. The common characteristic of the "French" thinkers (not all of whom are from France, incidentally) is their problematization of the subject, such that key Enlightenment concepts such as individual freedom and autonomy seem to unravel. Derrida certainly has affinities with some "anti-humanist" currents; grammatology challenges the notion of an integrated subject, but it also links this challenge with a deep economy of Western thought. For example, in deconstructing the propriety of the "proper name," Derrida examines the earlier activities of naming in ancient Hebrew, Egyptian, and Greek cultures. Unlike Heidegger and Gadamer, however (and more like Foucault), Derrida does not take the unraveling of Enlightenment individuality (which is a practical fact, not simply a theoretical trick) to signal a return to some pre-Enlightenment organicism. The "end of man" will not issue in a simple return to pre-individualistic sensibilities. Perhaps "post-humanism," with its built-in pun, would be a better tag.

Ironically, Habermas also claims to be abandoning the philosophy of the subject. In what, then, will his humanism consist? The question is a reasonable one because Habermas still wants to talk in terms of autonomy. Autonomy of what? Is there an Enlightenment to champion without the philosophy of the subject? (At the level at which the Enlightenment project is taken over by Hegel and Marx the question is extended to worry the prospects of a grand modernist narrative.) Both Habermas and Derrida aspire to be post-Hegelian, and the path that they both take is that of thinking in terms of language rather than the subject. As mentioned in the first chapter, their respective approaches to language—and, at the heart of the matter, their understandings of what language is—are quite different. Though it may seem a roundabout approach to the confrontation, the path that I will take toward framing the differences between Habermas and Derrida must necessarily retrace some of the essential steps taken by subjectivity in modern philosophy.

Although there had been some motion in this direction already (for example, with Merleau-Ponty; see esp. 1975), no one has done more to make work in the theory of language central to social theory than Habermas. It is highly significant, in this regard, that there was talk in the late sixties and early seventies, especially around the *Tel Quel* group in France, to the effect that Marxism could progress no further until it acquired a philosophy of language (see Parker 1985, 152–55). In an interesting article, "Between Dialectics and Deconstruction," Andrew Parker raises an important challenge to this claim:

> [T]here are . . . several reasons to doubt the ultimate viability of this attempt to remedy the faults of Marxism by employing the tools of linguistics. In the first place, it is simply not self-evident that a "theory of language" is, in fact, absent from Marx's writings. Although such a theory would not, of course, find expression in any explicit or systematic form, it nevertheless might be located in the characteristic (if unpredictable) ways his texts perform *rhetorically*. We have seen above, for example, that Marx's theory of crisis can be read as an implicit theory of figuration. *Capital* is similarly not about language in an overt or sustained manner, yet in its description of the commodity form as "a social hieroglyphic," we encounter another rhetorical crux around which much of this text can be said to (un)hinge. (1985, 154)

In consideration of the many attempts that have been made by now to integrate a philosophy of language with Marxism, including those of Voloshinov/Bakhtin and other Soviet semioticians, and of Stalin in his well-known pamphlet on the "linguistics controversy" (not to mention such vigorously hybrid efforts as Coward and Ellis's *Language and Materialism*, which makes significant use of Lacan and Barthes),[3] it would be interesting to sort out the internal interactions of these newer theories in light of what Parker identifies as having already been there in Marx. Would this be another case in which Marxism turned out to be (yet again) philosophically inadequate in its original formulation? Until very recently (with the emergence of post- or non-Hegelian Marxisms), the presumed solution to this inadequacy has been to dig deeper into

Hegel. This has been the solution for Lenin, Lukacs, Adorno, Sartre, etc. (Althusser is no exception. The difference is simply that, where others shore up Marxism's inadequacies by recourse to Marx's Hegelian roots, Althusser blames many of the flaws in Marx—*humanistic flaws!*—on the traces of Hegel that Marx never fully purged from his system.)[4] This return to Hegel is found in Habermas's work as well, but with an interesting twist.

Habermas argues that the young Hegel and the young Marx faced a dilemma in grounding their theories. One horn of the dilemma for Hegel was subject-centered Reason, while one horn of the dilemma for Marx was a subject-centered practice, especially productive practice. (I argued earlier that this practice tends to become "spiritualized"; now we will see in more detail how this is the case, in terms of Cartesian subjectivity.) Habermas sets out the dilemmas of Hegel and Marx in the third chapter of *The Philosophical Discourse of Modernity*:

> The parallels between Hegel and Marx are striking. In their youth, both thinkers hold open the option of using the idea of uncoerced will formation in a communication community existing under constraints of cooperation as a model for the reconciliation of a divided bourgeois society. But later on, both forsake the use of this option, and they do so for similar reasons. Like Hegel, Marx is weighted down by the basic conceptual necessities of the philosophy of the subject. He distances himself in Hegelian fashion from the importance of the "ought" of a merely utopian socialism. Like Hegel, he thereby relies on the power of a dialectic of enlightenment: The same principle that is behind the achievements and the contradictions of modern society is also supposed to explain the transforming movement, the release of the rational potential of this society. However, Marx connects the modernization of society with an increasingly effective exploitation of natural resources and an increasingly intensive build-up of a global network of commerce and communication. This unfettering of productive forces must therefore be traced back to a principle of modernity that is grounded in the practice of a producing subject rather than in the reflection of a knowing subject. (1987b, 63)

This chapter, titled "Three Perspectives: Left Hegelians, Right Hegelians, and Nietzsche," will remain centrally important; Habermas concedes that Nietzsche represents one path away from the philosophy of the subject, but not a path that is to be endorsed. In the last part of the book, when Habermas develops his own way out of the philosophy of the subject, his alternative is specifically an alternative to Nietzsche and contemporary Nietzscheans, Derrida among them.

Leaving aside for the moment the question of Marx's modification of the philosophy of the subject from the reflective, knowing subject to the producing subject (a modification that simply traps Marx, in Habermas's view, even more within the paradigm of subjectivity),[5] the upshot of Habermas's argument is that neither the discovery of a philosophy of language supposedly embedded in classical Marxism, nor the appending of such a philosophy to Marxism will do the trick. Philosophy of language must be, for Habermas, at the core of a comprehensive, philosophically-sophisticated social theory: this philosophy must play a central, motivating role. If anything, Marx (among others, such as Weber) will have to be appended to this "theory of communicative action."

We will return to this part of the story in a moment.

Marxism is not, of course, all of social theory, although many, and probably most, twentieth century social theories owe some debt to Marxism, even if sometimes that debt is of a "negative" sort. By the same token, philosophy of language has often developed in this century somewhat apart (sometimes quite apart) from social theory, even though there are sometimes connections that can readily be drawn, as in the work of Wittgenstein, some of the Logical Positivists, and in the work of Donald Davidson and Hilary Putnam.[6] The separation of philosophy of language on the one hand, and social theory on the other, has largely resulted from the influence of a pernicious positivism (for which I blame Bertrand Russell more than anyone) that has it that separate domains of thought need not relate to one another—and that some domains of thought, such as social theory, are just not capable of the sort of systematic exposition that would allow them to interact with certain other domains, such as the philosophy of language. One reason that this line was drawn is that, for about half of this century, some parts of the philosophical world were under the spell that "logic is the soul of philosophy" (again, blame Russell). Thanks to Wittgenstein, Quine, and their successors (to my mind, especially Davidson), philosophy in the English-speaking world is finally coming out from under this conception. Once again it is possible to be a "philosopher," without having to sequester different fields from one another within the overall discipline.

Keeping this not inconsiderable part of the story in mind, it is now possible to set out concisely the outline for the rest of this chapter. In remaining with the "production paradigm" (which Habermas calls "obsolete"), Marx made a serious mistake, according to Habermas. In cutting himself off from a theory of communicative action, Marx was further cut off from a means of explaining social interaction and reproduction in a broader and non-reductive sense. The path that Hegel and Marx did choose was rooted in a philosophy of the subject that has come unraveled under the successive attacks of Nietzsche, Heidegger, Bataille, and their more recent postmodern followers—for Habermas, these would especially include Foucault and Derrida. This unraveling, however, would seem to lose its point, if there is a way to refound the project of modernity without a philosophy of the subject. In his theory of communicative action Habermas attempts such a renewal by replacing the philosophy of the subject with a philosophy of language. This, however, is purportedly what most, if not all, postmoderns are also doing, so that the major stress in this replacement has to come down to *what* philosophy of language is central in Habermas's project. We turn, then, to a closer examination of the story of language and subjectivity in modernity.

The philosophy of the subject in Hegel and Marx

The theory of the autonomous individual that had its beginnings in Descartes reached its zenith in Kant. All subsequent theories of intersubjectivity owe a fundamental debt to Kant's development of the categories of consciousness. In historicizing these categories, Hegel moved the discussion to a qualitatively different level (to say "higher" at this point would be to load the question), in fact a level where the eventual unraveling of any supposedly well-grounded autonomy or integrity became a virtual certainty. In the three "masters of suspicion," Marx, Nietzsche, and Freud, the social and linguistic elements of the individual consciousness render the subject, in Marx's famous phrase, as "the ensemble of social relations." Perhaps, as with Lenin and his definition of "matter" that we discussed in the first chapter, Marx was on to more than he knew.

What is this qualitative development—resisted so strenuously by most analytic philosophers—other than a shift from intersubjectivity to transsubjectivity? Hegel, Marx, and Freud each seem to make this shift, but not Nietzsche. This is a very important exception, which will come to bear on the differences between Habermas and Derrida. We will return to this point. The context of this confrontation is set by the transition from intersubjectivity to transsubjectivity, emblematically represented by the transition from Kant to Hegel. Both Habermas and Derrida pay a great deal of attention to the two German idealists who come between Kant and Hegel, namely Fichte and Schelling. The "philosophy of reflection" that they created seems a good place to look into the heart of language. Standing behind Fichte and Schelling is a mad poet, Hölderlin, and this is not without some significance, as we shall see.

Neither Fichte nor Schelling were satisfied with Kant's view of self-consciousness as the "transcendental unity of apperception." If such a unity may seem necessary for there to be apperception at all (that is, it is difficult to conceive of a non-ordered, non-unified consciousness that could properly be called consciousness), then it should be possible, argued Fichte and Schelling, to say something about the self itself. Intuitively, it seems that the self could be known to itself as something other and more than a mere theoretical posit. In pressing the point, both Fichte and Schelling reject the modern model of consciousness that Kant inherited from Descartes. In *Logics of Disintegration*, Peter Dews provides a useful account of this rejection of Cartesian subjectivity that is itself framed in terms of a confrontation between poststructualism and critical theory. He writes:

> Fundamentally, this theory is based on the concept of reflection: selfhood, which means self-consciousness, consists in a relation in which the subject turns back on itself and grasps its own identity with itself, in which the object is the reflection of the subject, rather than something *other than* the subject. (1987, 21)

This view contains many difficulties, perhaps chief among them the fact that the very act of reflection already presupposes a self. Thus our two post-Kantians seek an alternative grounding of self-consciousness, and their attempts form important aspects of the transition from a paradigm of intersubjectivity to one of transsubjectivity.

In brief, Fichte

> . . . attempts to avoid the contradictory implication that a subject-self pre-exists the process of reflection; both the relation and the consciousness of the identity of the related elements must be conceived of as emerging simultaneously. . . . Thus, Fichte argues that we must conceive of the self as positing itself, not in the sense that the self is the object posited, but rather in the sense that the self is nothing other than this act of positing. (ibid.)

Dews goes on to point out that this conception of the self portends a limited scope for theory: the self cannot in fact be *theoretically* grounded; rather, Fichte must make an appeal to a special form of *experience*. In

Schelling's view, this limitation of the scene of theory ironically points one toward the legitimacy of the concept of *the absolute*. Schelling develops a theory of the self, then, which not only anticipates Hegel but recapitulates Plato's theory of the forms: our individual "selves" are simply effects or emanations of an absolute self. That I (whoever "I" happens to be in any particular instance) cannot find my self in myself in any thoroughly-grounded sense has to do with the fact that humans are limited beings who experience in a limited way the self-consciousness of the absolute. (Dews 1987, 22-23)

Schelling's singular absolute subject seems a transitional point on the way to Hegel's world spirit, or so the story goes. Intersubjectivity fleshed out, under the paradigm of consciousness, requires a notion of transsubjectivity. The story could be told quite differently, however, if we find another basis for reflection in the "mirror" of signification. In a sense, the search for this mirror defines Derrida's entire reading of the history of philosophy. If consciousness must write to others and itself in the form of the letter, something different happens on the way to transsubjectivity. But this alternative tale must be stitched into the text of philosophy as we have known it thus far (that is the difference between Derrida and analytic philosophers who also seek to consider the question of subjectivity after the linguistic turn). The movement from Descartes to Kant to Hegel has set the terms for all of the discussions of the varieties of subjectivity since the time of Hegel. Our own period is no exception. We may catalogue four of these discussions as follows, in no particular order.

First, there is Marx's attempt to move back to a historicized intersubjectivity that displaces transsubjectivity by immanent critique. That is, Marx argues that a more *concrete* view of intersubjectivity, one that depends primarily on *practice* (and especially productive practice), grounds potential reworkings of mutual relations and recognitions in concrete, historical social relations. A subject that presumably stands over and above historical processes while at the same time manifesting itself in these very processes can then be dispensed with. It is well known, however, that there are elements of transsubjectivity in this account in that there is a question about what allows a potentially reworked intersubjectivity to exert its pull toward a different kind of society. Where (and what) is the space of this potentiality? What is the *measure* of its difference—what makes the reworking *better*? What is the direction of this potential? Such questions seem to beg for some sort of transcendental framework for specifying the scope of intersubjectivity. Note further that Marx's intersubjectivity does not develop the question of language,[7] so that practice becomes a kind of transcendental signified (to compare this point to the one about a shadow transsubjectivity). That is, if there are supposedly no *terms* in which practical experience is thematized, it must be that through practice our concrete subjects are entering into a kind of immediate relation—Marx's sensuous man— with the world. All this is to point out, as Habermas does, that there are two strains in Marx, regarding the question of subjectivity. One strain tends toward intersubjectivity, but Marx does not have the conceptual machinery to bring it off. This failure—which may be unavoidable, that is the rest of the story—causes Marx's intersubjectivity to slide, either toward Hegelian transsubjectivity or toward an aggregate of mere individual subjectivities that supposedly will find its pull toward social solidarity in the practical circumstances of class struggle.

Second, there is the existentialist move (or, more tendentiously, "retreat") to subjectivity in the face of an Hegelian transsubjectivity that threatens to destroy the subject in order to save it. This move is found in certain standard readings of Dostoevsky, Nietzsche, Strindberg, Kierkegaard, Heidegger, and in fact in certain expressions of Adorno and Horkheimer. Thus the insistence especially by the nineteenth-century existentialists on singular expressions of the individual, often highlighted by appeal to "extreme experience," such as the confronta-tion of the individual with his or her own finitude. From this standpoint, Hegel, Marx, and the ongoing social and technological revolutions of the nineteenth century are all in cahoots, all theorizing and concretizing the collective subject who will replace the modern individual. To put it another way, first *crush*, then "replace." Existentialism, then, is a different kind of shift to the concrete than that theorized by Marx. In fact, in their appeal to individual experience, the existentialists recapitu-late—though by quite different methods—the attempt by Fichte to conflate substantive and process-oriented conceptions of the self. (Perhaps Camus would be the only major figure who, when read closely, really fits this mold—but I am discussing a certain reading of existentialism which may in fact be entirely at odds with what the figures lopped under this heading are really about.) The methods of the existentialists themselves represent this conflation, in that the nine-teenth century thinkers often do not use "theory" to point to the space of self-experience. (Again, Gary Shapiro's "Nietzschean Aphorism as Art and Act" is an exemplary demonstration.)

Third, there is the move from intersubjectivity to subjectivity undertaken by a certain persistent strand of analytic philosophy, a move from Kant to Hume. This line of argument has it that Kant never adequately resolved the problems of the substantiality of selfhood raised by Hume. This is also a reaction to Hegel, insofar as philosophers like Bertrand Russell were initially reacting to the extreme objective idealism of the British Hegelians (esp. F. H. Bradley's doctrine of "internal relations). Hume's conception anticipates Fichte in that the former's emphasis is on a stream or procession of perceptions that cannot be said to *inhere* in a mental *substance*. Hume and Kant were both psychologists, of course, but Hume seems much closer to the empirical ideal of doing as much psychology with as little metaphysical baggage as is possible. As Barry Stroud (1977) points out, however, Hume was working with a "classical," "Newtonian" notion of ideas, in which there is a relation between ideas and perceptions that, however problematic it may be, does not involve the mind as an active force in generating ideas. This is true for all of the British Empiricists; the Humean modification was to argue that mental-physical causation could not be thoroughly grounded. What we take for causation may only be constant conjunction. The question we will raise in a moment, however, is whether some form of Humean (as opposed to Kantian) intersubjectivity is possible. The answer given by analytic philosophy since Quine is in the affirmative.

Fourth and finally, there are theories and notions of the split subject. Here we think of Hölderlin, another Nietzsche, Freud, and Heidegger. There is in all of these figures a troubled remembering, a remembering of oneself as though what is remembered is not quite oneself, nor is one quite sure who is in fact the generator of this memory. There is no better example of this *soi disant* subjectivity than the first stanza of Hölderlin's "Mnemosyne":

A sign we are, without meaning
Without pain we are and have nearly
Lost our language in foreign lands,
For when the heavens quarrel
Over humans and moons proceed
In force, the sea
Speaks out and rivers must find
Their way. But there is One,
Without doubt, who
Can change this any day. He needs
No law. The rustle of leaf and then the sway of oaks
Beside glaciers. Not everything
Is in the power of the gods. Mortals would sooner
Reach toward the abyss. With them
The echo turns. Though the time
Be long, truth
Will come to pass.[8]

I will happily allow these images to haunt this discussion; we will return to the question of "our nearly lost language."

A theme that has emerged from the discussion thus far is that, however much one might wish to "transcend" subjectivity, all of our theorists, poets, or what have you, want to find a basis for subjectivity and selfhood in whatever develops out of consideration of the problematics of intersubjectivity and/or transsubjectivity. Hölderlin represents the fragility of the "self" that remains after inter- and transsubjective designs have run their course. There is the voice of that "One," which we must be very careful not to understand simply as the voice of unity and the Same. "He needs no law." For all that there is a great deal of Christian messianism here, there is also something other.

With this somewhat superficial catalogue I only mean to show what most readers will know already, that there are problems with intersubjectivity and transsubjectivity that any philosophically-aware social theory has to confront. Philosophy of the subject in Hegel and Marx, however, has one other problem beyond a possible untenability: this philosophy has not served as a powerful basis for a continued and effective solidarity. Not that such solidarities have not played a powerful role in history—although not a continuous role, I hasten to add—but the philosophy of the subject in Hegel and Marx has been neither the political basis nor the theoretical explanation of these movements. This I take to be the more significant problem. At the very least, then, the notion of subjectivity must be rethought, and perhaps dispensed with altogether. Certainly there are theorists now arguing for all three subjectivities, and for forms of anti- and split-subjectivity, but the almost universal element that has now become the central issue in grounding forms of subjectivity is language.

Language and subjectivity after Marx

The attempt to resolve (some would say, "dissolve") the problem of subjectivity by seeking what Derrida calls the "logic of the gramme" is the most significant movement beyond the views of subjectivity held by Descartes, Kant, Hegel, Marx, and their modernist contemporaries. This project, significantly, has been taken up, for the most part, not only *after* Marx, but indeed quite *apart* from Marx. This separation has consequences for the present discussion and for the whole project of inventing postmodern social theory. What is at the heart of language is also at the heart of this project. At times, however, the pursuit of the sign seems to take us far afield from Marxism and, more significantly, of

Marxism's *raison d'etre*, the radical transformation of society. I see no alternative other than to move through this dangerous gap (the danger should not be minimized, despite the necessity of finding a means of navigation). A discussion of the philosophy of language that ignores the traditions initiated by Frege, Peirce, or Saussure makes little sense. Both Habermas and Derrida are eminently aware of this problem. Is there a fork in the road, where the pursuit of social transformation leads away from the question of language and vice-versa? In contradiction to the (most often implicit) views of many analytic philosophers, both Habermas and Derrida have answered this question in the negative.[9] For both, there *has* to be a way of getting these seemingly disparate problematics working together. Both will argue that there is indeed no point at which the problematics of language and social relations do not intertwine. The difference between them is as follows: Habermas reworks intersubjectivity in terms of what he takes to be the grounding principles of the communicative act, while Derrida's project is to materialize the signifier and to show its open-ended "logic." At the very least, Derrida thereby undermines arguments for the traditionally conceived autonomous subject. "A sign we are, without meaning. . . ." And yet, no "politics" can stop with a mere deconstruction of agency. We are therefore entitled to want great things of this materialized sign. Otherwise we might simply be better off, pragmatically speaking, with a "myth" of agency in which there is no room for questions of grounding.

Given that modern philosophy of language, as such, has developed apart from the raising of social and political concerns, we might begin to address the dangerous gap by asking how and why the turn to problems of language came about. How can the linguistic turn be situated historically? One explanation might consist in a description of the ebb and flow of central problems in Western philosophy. For example, for the ancient Greeks, ontology was central, while for the moderns epistemology comes to the fore. If these two paradigms of "first philosophy" have been displaced, what else is there left to do, other than to turn to that other term in the equation, the representations that mediate between objects and ideas? Posing the question this way also substantially broadens our field of inquiry, because such world/idea mediations may take many forms other than the "purely" linguistic. Under this picture, many thinkers might be brought within the "expressive" paradigm (see Genova 1983). (Marx would be an interesting case, because his theory concerns media and mediations perhaps more than anything else.)

There are two problems with this exceedingly grand narrative, one ontological, the other historical. First, the category of representation will not sit still as the new form of "first philosophy." Certainly, framing philosophy of language in this position provides a safe basis from which to get back into the historically-defined business of philosophy. One important strain in analytic philosophy opts for this position; perhaps the best recent representative is Michael Dummett (1978). There is another strain that is perhaps not recognized as such, however, that has it that "philosophy of language" will not, in the final analysis, fit into a neat academic pigeonhole. Language leaks, one might say (more on this in due course). At that point where language will not remain confined, the notion of language and other forms of signification and representation as "mediation" between idea and thing tends to break down. The mediation idea is certainly useful up to a point, but, pressed too far, language simply becomes the new ontology, the new metaphysics. (The question then arises, Where is the mediation in that?) For Derrida, language is ultimately not a matter of mediations (and the questions surrounding language are not questions of mediations). This is one important difference, and, for our purposes, *the* important difference between Derrida and Habermas. In analytic philosophy, some of the thinkers who seem to have grasped this issue quite well are Wittgenstein, Quine, Putnam, Rorty, and especially Davidson.[10] Davidson (1985, 185–98) has made it clear that notions of mediations, representations, or mental entities are open invitations to global scepticism.

    In historical terms, perhaps the question of language did assert itself first of all under the banner of "mediation." Furthermore, it may be that the Hegelian, as opposed to the hermeneutical, strain in European thought has tremendous difficulty in accepting language as anything other than as a "mediation." The question might be raised, then, about the sorts of ontological violence that occur when the Hegelian and the hermeneutical strains collide, as they do in Derrida's text. This is not yet, however, the historical point that I wanted to raise.

    Second, then, we would be remiss and historically arrogant were we not to ask the question, Why accept such an exceedingly grand narrative of philosophy and its supposed paradigms? Only if we stick to a fairly constrained reading of the history of philosophy do we get this picture. To cite but two large (and related) areas in which this scenario unravels, the ancient Hebrews and the medieval philosophers were very much concerned with language, the book, narrative, interpretation, etc. In literary theory especially (safely sequestered from philosophy, that is), we are reminded of this "pre-modern" concern with "postmodern" ideas practically every day, by thinkers such as Umberto Eco, Susan Handelman, and Harold Bloom.[11] But then, the Hebrews are "marginally Western," and the medieval philosophers are either equally marginal (those who are Jews or Muslims) or part of a Christian tradition in philosophy that does not fit in well with the way that philosophy is practiced in most universities these days. (We might note, as well, that surveys and curricula in "Western Civilization," except at Catholic universities, typically step rather gingerly around these areas. In order to make the three paradigm grand narrative work, philosophy's toes have to be cut to fit the shoe. (As always, in other words, there are "other present eras" that make our sense of periodization problematic.) All the same, this narrative is an accurate self-representation of modern philosophy, despite the fact—or is it, rather, *because* of the fact?—that the plot line depends on a great deal of marginalization. (The question of how such narratives are constructed is of course at the heart of Derrida's practice as a historian of philosophy.) The recognition of this process of marginalization actually makes the narrative even grander: language becomes the cultural unconscious of Western philosophy until the moment in which language begins to speak itself.

And when did that moment occur? This is where the problematics of history and ontology come together. We have already discussed, in the first chapter, this plural movement of possibilities that is organized around the fundamental aporia formed by the tension between impossibility and counter-possibility. This movement is the very structure of temporality. The debate between Foucault and Derrida, concerning Descartes and the "moment" of madness encountered on the way to self-consciousness, may be taken as instructive here. Foucault takes this moment to be a historical turning point, while Derrida takes this "moment" to be never not a part of consciousness. Foucault certainly has his point, though it might be put differently. To wit, when do we begin to notice, historically (or, as Foucault would say, genealogically, by looking backward toward the point of difference), that something new is happening with humanity's self-representation? Descartes' moment of madness does seem an historic turning-point. But then, the question might really be, as Derrida argues, not that of when madness had its "moment" in the formation of consciousness—rather, When did consciousness begin to take this moment seriously?[12] Similarly, the question is not, When did language begin to speak?—rather, When did we begin to listen? Derrida can ask this, of course, because few have listened to language as he has. And his answer here cannot be straightforward, either: it is a question of "the ear of the other" (1985a, 51). We might conjecture, however, that the ability to hear did achieve a certain critical mass in the nineteenth and twentieth centuries, resulting in the linguistic turn. That is, the question of language, as raised by Humboldt,

Herder, Locke, Rousseau, and others, came to trouble consciousness to the point where it was imperative that language be attended to.

Marxists, especially, are generally uncomfortable with this sort of narrative, because it is difficult to correlate different stages of this series of paradigms with successive historical epochs and their particular configurations of collective social subjects (i.e., classes). Furthermore, Marxism has often had difficulties with the kind of investigative philosophy (call it "hermeneutical") that attempts to ferret out the underlying assumptions of *all* those who live in a specific period and society. That languages and discourses themselves seem to constitute such "assumptions" is something that even Stalin (1952) was forced to see in the "linguistics debate" of the early fifties.

The foregoing analysis proceeds by stacking paradigms, which is largely what constitutes the postmodern condition, a situation in which the diverse materials of history are simultaneously present, but suspended in a state of impasse. The justification for painting with such a wide brush is that we are looking for those large blocks of thought that motivate and propel humanity into this polyglot but static present (this present choked with presence). We now turn to the more recent history of this impasse, still keeping to the question of the seemingly divergent paths of language and politics.

Herbert Marcuse, in a review of works by Bertrand Russell and Ludwig von Mises, exemplifies the attitude of radical social thought toward certain kinds of philosophy of language.

The debasement of cognition that is so clearly reflected in these formulations distinguishes all the general methodological utterances of modern positivism. Unable to fulfill its quest for certainty and security, positivist thought seeks refuge in tautological definitions and the fixed conventions of everyday language. It orients knowledge to the ideal of providing an adequate description of that which is. . . . In its quest for certainty and security, positivism is compelled to formalize all propositions to such an extent that they either state nothing about reality . . . or state only things in which nobody is interested and which everybody knows anyway. The propositions cannot be disputed because all controversial content has been removed. The problem of meaning and truth, on the other hand, should begin only where there is a controversial matter, one on which no agreement can possibly be arrived at by going back to the "basic propositions" of the "object language." The problems of freedom, reason, and justice cannot be discussed within a conceptual framework that centers around "basic propositions" because disagreement and the transcendence of sense-perception belong to their very essence. If meaning and truth are to be derived from statements such as "I am hot" or "this is red," then all philosophical statements are *a priori* meaningless and false. (1984, 138–39)

This passage is cited in Douglas Kellner's *Herbert Marcuse and the Crisis of Marxism* as part of a discussion of Marcuse's critique of positivism. Kellner obviously has a great deal of sympathy for Marcuse's point of view in this matter, and I cannot help but admit a fair degree of sympathy myself. The sterility of much philosophy of language in the analytic tradition coupled with that tradition's overarching rejection of social responsibility and the lack of any significant historical dimension has inspired a deep distrust on the part of engaged intellectuals. Ben Agger provides a useful summary of how the postmodern impasse is largely the product of a positivism that still refuses to reflect:

The positivist denial of positivist constitutionality is belied by the fact that positivism must discursively reconstitute itself as a principled text governing its methodological practice. In conjuring its own programmatic practice imaginatively, positivism betrays its own ontologizing representation of a world without an imagination. (1989, 119)

Much of analytic philosophy of language is still stuck in this condition, in part because of a failure, and perhaps an inherent inability, to consider its own practice in terms of both intellectual and social history.

However, an unmitigated distrust of the sorts of questions raised by analytic philosophy of language, even in its most positivistic period, may be both unwarranted and ultimately unhelpful. It is a major strength of both Habermas and Derrida that they consider the question of the "trivial," "non-controversial" aspects of language (for which some Marxists, e.g. Perry Anderson [1983], have chastised them both for making a "fetish" of discourse). In order to move closer to the language problematic that motivates their work, it may be useful to work through some of the problems with Marcuse's somewhat typical complaint, and from there toward some recent work in analytic philosophy. Some very important insights about the problem of subjectivity can be generated by pursuing this path.

Before setting out on this path, a little caveat might be issued. If there is now a certain rapprochement between certain forms of "continental" philosophy and certain forms of analytic philosophy around questions of language and society, that is not to say that analytic philosophy "anticipated" continental philosophy. On the other hand, it is perfectly right to claim that Hegel, Marx, and their successors anticipated the recent turn toward "history" (such as it is) by analytic philosophers such as Hilary Putnam and Richard Rorty. On the first question of anticipation, however, I have no problem in seeing Rorty, Putnam, and especially Davidson as kinds of "postmodern" philosophers. And, one wants to attribute this rapprochement—which has been mediated through the work of the American pragmatists by broadminded thinkers such as Joseph Margolis, Stanley Cavell, and Richard Bernstein[13]—to *something*, even if not fully to the intentions or efforts of the parties involved on either side of the continental divide. Call it the historical-linguistic *Zeitgeist* and you will not be too wide of the mark.

Language expressing itself

Let's look at Marcuse's position through the eyes of mainstream analytic philosophy. From this position the shift can be made to the way that Derrida and Habermas have thematized language.

The "quest for certainty and security" is certainly not a unique feature of logical positivism or analytic philosophy as a whole. It may be that the very fact that tautological truths at least seem secure is a feature revelatory of what may lie at the heart of any *possible* linguistic enterprise (human or otherwise). This is the "logical" part of logical positivism. (W. V. Quine, of course, makes it very difficult for positivism to allow the "facticity" of tautological truths to go unquestioned—and he is working from the "inside" of positivism.)[14] Conventionality in language may play a simliar role on the more empirical side of things. To square logical form with everyday convention is very much a Kantian project, at least in broad outline. Furthermore, to investigate the depth grammar of systems of mental representations seems hardly a "debasement of cognition." Certainly, "controversial questions" are important—though in what way they are "philosophically important" is another problem altogether—but, are we not entitled to ask how language works on the simplest, most everyday levels as in some sense preparatory to being able to raise controversial questions? What are these simple, everyday, most "trivial" workings of language? Might not the various answers given to this question be somewhat controversial (much as, e.g., answers given to questions concerning basic constituents of matter)? This preparatory work may deal with the elements of language in a static and therefore hypostasized social setting, but certainly whatever can be discovered on this plane is relevant to understanding temporal and historical dimensions of language. Or, to put it in different terms, it is valuable to look at the synchronic as well as the diachronic functioning of systems of representation. It remains to be seen, finally, whether "problems of freedom, reason, and justice" necessitate a conceptual framework that "transcends" sense-perception. Why *begin* with transcendental talk and gestures—isn't this what is to be avoided inasmuch as that is possible? If a transcendental move in the argument is seen as necessary at some point where it cannot be avoided, then at least at that point we will have a more rigorous and specific notion of what sort of "move" is necessary. To begin with transcendental assumptions about "reason," as Marcuse tends to do, may open a course of thinking that cannot be called to account by any other standard than internal consistency. And, in fact, all sorts of politically repellent schemes may possess such consistency.

Remarks such as these, if they remain concerned about the social world and do not intend a mere retreat into semantics for the sake of semantics, may be taken as a starting point for a "linguistic turn" in social theory. Of course, this is a slippery point: someone else's "semantics for semantics" may turn out to be quite useful for our social concerns. Both Habermas and Derrida maintain, significantly, that there is something in language that, shall we say, "intends" these concerns— something in language, or something that language is, that could never not intend these concerns. What that "something" is, what is at the heart of language, this is where Habermas and Derrida disagree. While Russell and some of the logical positivists seem at times to be as far away from the larger picture as one can get, this distance should not prevent social theorists from investigating what Michael Ryan (1982) calls the "metaphysics of everyday life" in terms of the structures of signification that inhabit us and that we inhabit. This last distinction, between "who inhabits what" and vice-versa, is a crucial one for present purposes.

With Hölderlin, Herder, and Nietzsche, among others, as forerunners, Heidegger and Derrida place priority on the notion that "language speaks us." The trajectory of this notion in the later Heidegger is, for the most part, well known, if not well understood. One corollary of the notion that has been repeatedly emphasized already is the priority of language over the subject, such that subjects are taken to be *posits* of systems of signification. This corollary may be said to divide into two main theses; each is true and important up to a point, but both have been presented, at times, in caricatured form by both opponents and proponents. First, there is the idea that the question of language has superceded that of the subject. The caricature has it that questions of subjectivity (and agency, consciousness, etc.) are now *passe*. Second, there is the further extension of this first thesis into the notion that language is *larger*, in a sense, than our aggregate subjectivities. If language is constitutive of these subjectivities, then, as far as subjects are concerned, language is in a real sense *autonomous*. To this idea we must say, "yes and no." The caricature is to push this autonomy toward a full-blown "linguistic idealism" (something that Derrida is often accused of). The issues attendant to these theses are central to the controversy between Derrida and Habermas.

These theses can be undoubtedly pressed to the point of absurdity. Habermas, in reaction to what are to my mind absurd caricatures of these theses, ultimately rejects both. Derrida is well known as a philosopher who pushes ideas to their limit and sometimes beyond their limit. In what follows it remains to be shown that neither of our two theses is rendered absurd by Derridean dissemination. The comparison of Derrida and Habermas must now come down to cases. The general strategy will be as follows. The question of language and subjectivity will be set out under the aegis of two basic problematics where Habermas and Derrida differ. Under the first of these, "intention and iteration," we will examine the question of linguistic foundations and the broader question of philosophical foundationalism. Here we will begin to set out the differences between two very broad trends in the philosophy of language, one represented in continental philosophy by Heidegger and in analytic philosophy by Davidson, the other represented in continental philosophy by Husserl and Habermas, and in analytic philosophy by John Searle and other speech act theorists. Furthermore, we will also begin to demarcate Derrida's contribution to and difference from the Heideggerian approach. This demarcation will permit us to see some other striking similarities between Derrida and Davidson, and further differences between these two and Habermas. The point of explicating this first problematic will be to compare an approach to language that depends, first of all, on semantics (Derrida, Davidson) with an approach that emphasizes pragmatics (Habermas). At the point of that comparison we will move to our second problematic, "poetry and communication." Once again certain Heideggerian themes will be taken up, in particular the question of language's "world-disclosiveness" as opposed to its "instrumentality." On the question of the priority of one of these two notions, Heidegger argues for the former, while Habermas argues for the latter. And therefore Habermas argues against the "leveling of the genre distinction between philosophy and literature." Here again Derrida and Davidson have some significant points of contact, especially when seen in comparison to Habermas. Derrida and Davidson both argue that the distinction between language's world-disclosive function and its pragmatic-instrumental function cannot be drawn rigorously. This argument, however, does not land us in a world of linguistic mush, as Habermas supposes, but rather allows us to rigorously set out a number of propositions concerning language and subjectivity. At this point there is perhaps a parting of the ways between Davidson and Derrida, though, I tend to think, not a necessary parting. While Davidson leaves this work at the place where its ethico-political implications begin to become explicit, he does, however, go at least a little way into this territory; that is why I say that Davidson and Derrida do not necessarily part ways at this point. Beyond that point, Derrida takes up the quite difficult work of thinking through the politics of language and the language of politics.

The reader will quite rightly expect this to be a very complex chain of reasoning. The only way to manage such a multi-layered set of arguments is once again through a methodology of exemplars and demarcations. That is, a discussion, in one movement, of theories as complex as those of Derrida, Habermas, and Davidson, not to mention Husserl, Heidegger, Searle, etc., must necessarily aim for the main thrust of their arguments. A certain degree of subtlety is thereby sacrificed. I believe, however, that a number of schematizations can be generated that will allow for a faithful representation of the parties concerned. As it is Habermas whom I am most concerned to criticize (with all due respect, as I mentioned in the first chapter), the most care must be given to the presentation of his arguments. Three of his texts in particular will guide this effort. First there is his massive *The Theory of Communicative Action*, perhaps the most important work in social theory of the post-1960 period. In addition, there are two essays from *The Philosophical Discourse of Modernity* that must be attended to, "Beyond a Temporalized Philosophy of Origins: Jacques Derrida's Critique of Phonocentrism," and "An Alternative Way out of the Philosophy of the Subject: Communicative versus Subject-Centered Reason." Other writings by Habermas will come into play also, but these are especially relevant to our purposes here.

Intention and iteration

In recent work on either side of the philosophical Atlantic in philosophy of language there is an increasing insistence on the question of *structures* in structures of signification. These structures may be considered in a quasi-architectural and certainly an architectonic sense, though perhaps without an architect or what Derrida calls a foundational "arche." (Derrida is, in John Caputo's notable expression, an "an-

archist," though a "responsible" one; see Caputo 1988). In the work of
Davidson and Putnam, for instance, one gets the sense of this structure
as something that is inhabited, as in Putnam's "internal realism". In his
provocative essay, "On the Very Idea of a Conceptual Scheme," Davidson raises the question of priority concerning mind and language: "Who
is to be master?" (1985, 184). In the end, Davidson's answer does not
accept the terms that would make a simple prioritization possible, but
he certainly does not allow that any "mind" (or "minds") could, on their
own, generate the structures that they inhabit.[15]

   In "Heidegger's Topology of Being," Otto Pöggeler sets out the
story of the assertion of structure in a way that both recapitulates what
has already been said here and that brings together the different lines of
the story in a more concentrated synthesis.

> Post-Kantian thought has asked in what medium the critical
> examination, delimitation, and legitimation of the employment of
> reason is effected. This medium was determined as language and
> history, and one thus projected a "metacritical" philosophy, using
> the question concerning language and history as a guiding clue.
> Hamann noticed that Kant's critique of reason comes to pass in the
> medium of language, but that language is historical; Herder and
> Humboldt pursued this metacritique, but the problematic gradu-
> ally changed from a philosophical one to an empirico-scientific
> one. Hegel attempts to take the modes of reason's employment
> that Kant distinguished back into the unity of a "transcendental"
> history of reason, Marx and Dilthey have certainly tried to show
> that this history, as a residue of a metaphysical semblance, is to be
> taken back into "genuine" history. Positivism conceives of the
> failure of philosophy in regard to the "genuine reality" of those
> media, namely, language and history, as something definitive.
> Heidegger, on the other hand, interprets this failure as a freeing of
> philosophy into a new mode of thought; but he says, nevertheless,
> that this new mode must appear as pseudopoetry. Is it not true
> that, at least in this way, the leading currents of contemporary
> philosophy converge, that the one current conceives as a new
> possibility what the other forbids as subterfuge? Is not the impres-
> sion of such a convergence fortified when one notices that analytic
> philosophy today is "linguistico-analytic" throughout, and that
> Heidegger, too, is of the opinion that thought should be a thought
> from language and the world as the building structure of Being's
> truth should be arranged predominantly by language as the
> "house" of Being? (in Kockelmans 1972, 128)

Although the terminology is certainly different, and there is a historical dimension hinted at here that could cause trouble at some point, I do not see why Davidson would take issue with much of this analysis. Notice that the subject does not play a motivating role on either side of the convergence.

Habermas, as has been noted, is also interested in moving away from the philosophy of the subject, but not in the way that Heidegger does. For Habermas, to move in the direction of the "language is the house of Being" thesis would be either to render the subject irrelevant or to obliterate the subject in the face of the autonomy of language. He argues, therefore, that "an alternative way out of the philosophy of the subject" must be found. We have already begun to define two broad categories of language theory, one associated with Husserl, Searle, and Habermas, the other with Heidegger, Derrida, and Davidson. These categories will march, in what follows, under the banners of "intention" and "iteration," respectively.

A theory of language is a matter of fulfilling certain conditions, explaining certain phenomena, and answering certain questions. Before examining either intentional or iterational theories, it will help to have at hand some idea of what a theory of language is about. We are after, first of all, a theory of *learnable* languages. That is, a theory of language must show how language is learnable. Of course, there are many examples of such theories, beginning with Frege's quantification logic, which shows how an infinity of expressions can be generated from finite resources, to Quine's behavioristic account of langauge acquisition in the young child, and beyond. The learnability requirement is, in fact, a way of keeping theory to the subject of *natural*, as opposed to "formal," languages.[16] It must be noted that Habermas gives some attention to this problem, while Derrida does not. Learnability, further, focuses theory on the phenomenal nature of language. On this question, of course, both Habermas and Derrida have had much to say. What, precisely, are the phenomena to be explained? In particular, we must single out two: meaning and understanding. Finally, given the direction that the learnability requirement has given to theory, we must be able to answer questions about the larger matrix of human life that language fits into. Here, as well, both Habermas and Derrida have written much.

These considerations lead theory toward the question of foundations, both linguistic and otherwise. Even in the framing of the last question there is a consideration of foundations: the question was already framed in a manner more congenial to intentional theories. Theories inspired by Heidegger would frame the question differently: the larger matrix is that of language—language is the possibility of human life (and something similar could be said of Davidson's views). In his first moves in the direction of a linguistic turn, found especially in the essay, "What is Universal Pragmatics" (in 1979), Habermas was not so worried about the consequences of foundationalism. Though he raised some questions about Chomsky's program of a universal generative grammar, the requirements that Habermas postulated for an alternative were marked by conditions that were, if anything, far more universalistic than Chomsky's. It may be, as Rick Roderick has argued, that Habermas's critique of Chomsky was somewhat misplaced, in that Chomsky did not intend to explain communication. His theory concerns syntax, not pragmatics. Habermas, in his earlier accounts of language, did not make a clear distinction between the two levels of analysis (Roderick 1986, 79) Ironically, this failure carries over, in different forms, into all of the subsequent accounts of language produced by Habermas.

The "ideal speech situation" (abbreviated as "i.s.s.") has its origins in this earlier work. At the heart of Habermas's notion of "communicative competence," the skills required for membership in a human language community, is the idea that "all speech is oriented toward the idea of truth," which "can only be analysed with regard to a consensus achieved in unrestrained and universal discourse."[17] As "ideal," the i.s.s. may seem to partake of a certain utopian transcendence, but in the period between "What is Universal Pragmatics?" and *The Theory of Communicative Action* Habermas attempts, in successive stages, to purge transcendental elements. The trick, for him, is to conduct that purge without giving up universality. Habermas makes the transition by moving from a post-Chomskian theory toward the incorporation of the speech act theory of Austin and Searle. For Habermas, this is a move that sets pragmatics firmly at the center of his project. The i.s.s. is transformed by this new direction, but not fundamentally damaged.

It is very difficult to criticize *The Theory of Communicative Action*, because it is so massive. In the opening pages of the work, Habermas tells a story, not unlike two of the stories told here, of the progressive fragmentation of philosophy and the parallel secularization of society in the modern period. "[T]he philosophical tradition, insofar as it suggests the possibility of a philosophical worldview, has become questionable. Philosophy can no longer refer to the whole of the world, of nature, of history, of society, in the sense of a totalizing knowledge" (1984, 1). This dramatic statement, however, is not the beginning of a postmodern turn for Habermas. His argument, rather, is that philosophy can no longer cover all the bases. For example (perhaps the quintessential modern example), there is no point anymore to speaking of "natural philosophy." But this does not mean that the territory formerly covered by natural philosophy no longer exists or is no longer the subject of intellectual inquiry. On the contrary, the natural sciences have now exceeded by many a light year the accomplishments of natural philosophy. The "wholes" to which Habermas refers are now the concern of specific disciplines within the natural and human sciences and the humanities. The remaining task for philosophy, its "new" role in thought, is to supply a basis by which the work of these disciplines can be coordinated and integrated. Philosophy must, in other words, supply a theory of rationality. In doing so, philosophy enters into dialogue with the other disciplines, in which the theory of rationality is both formed in light of and informs the larger work of social theory. Basing his work on this new paradigm of philosophy (how new it really is can be questioned; it seems that Marx and Weber, among others, worked with roughly the same methodology—that is why Habermas sees them as important forerunners), Habermas establishes his own "intellectual community"—the range of thinkers and subject matters that he factors into his social theory is vast. This has always been the case in Habermas's work, but nowhere more so than in *The Theory of Communicative Action*. This is not surprising, of course, because Habermas has, at this stage of his intellectual endeavors, entered into an all-out effort to achieve a grand synthesis. He is well-poised to accomplish this, as both philosopher and sociologist, in other words, as social theorist. Habermas's "community" includes a wide-ranging historical-theoretical overview of the Enlightenment, Aristotle's arguments about virtue and the good life, Freudian psychoanalysis, Hannah Arendt's analysis of power, developmental psychology, moral psychology, Chomsky, speech act theory, American pragmatism (especially Dewey and Mead), and many other elements—not to mention the background theory of the Frankfurt School. Habermas wants to weave all of these elements into a grand synthesis. Contrary to the many commentators who have recently cast so many aspersions on Habermas's designs (e.g., Ryan 1989, Huhn 1988), I find much to admire in his attempt to make use of what Western humanity has learned and created. The ironic thing is that Derrida's researches have covered much of the same territory—he is also a voracious reader, though one with a quite different perspective on how to "put it all together." Derrida rarely reads more than one or two texts at a time, and he certainly does not attempt to bring all of the texts that he reads into a single synthesis. There is something very important embodied in this fundamental difference in the two approaches to a vast body of material. We can specify that difference in the act of making plain the core conception of Habermas's synthesis.

The possibility of the ideal speech situation is grounded in the fundamental rationality of communication, its need to aspire toward a mutual understanding. This understanding, in turn, requires a normative thrust toward truth as "rational consensus." Philosophy contributes the theory of argumentation—what Habermas calls "communicative rationality"—that procedurally defines what it means to reach a rational consensus. Claims about what is true ("validity claims") must be tested in the heat of social discourse, backed by nothing more than the "unforced force of reason." Roderick's summary is cogent:

> In communication, we attempt to arrive at a rationally motivated consensus concerning both what is and what ought to be. The binding character of norms can be explained only upon the supposition that the consensus arrived at is constraint free and represents the common good. Habermas's position is basically Kantian in as much as such norms always make a claim to universality and are the product of a "rational will." However, for Habermas, the rational will is the outcome of the communication process itself. (1986, 88)

This last sentence is very important, because Habermas needs a grounding of rationality of this sort in order to provide an alternative to "subject-centered reason." This move does not work, however, for reasons that we can now begin to develop.

When I first began to describe the differences between the two approaches to language, "intentional" and "iterational," I claimed that Habermas thinks of language in primarily instrumental terms. In his more recent work on language, in *The Theory of Communicative Action* and the essay on "An Alternative Way . . . ," Habermas downplays this insistence on the instrumentality of language, arguing that this is only one part of communication. The instrumental uses of language are geared toward "success" (Habermas calls this form of communication "strategic"), while true "communicative action" aims at reaching an understanding.[18] Two very important points need to be raised here. First, regardless of whether communication is aimed at "success" (Habermas defines this "non-socially") or at "understanding," communication is the essence of language for Habermas. Second, Habermas never explains clearly why communication aimed at reaching an understanding is non-instrumental. Certainly one can imagine the universalism that makes one want to conceive a communicative realm in which instrumentality does not play a commanding role, but wishing does not make it so. Of course, we might say that "wishing" counts for something, just as the ideal speech situatation counts for something, even if it does represent an ideal that in all likelihood cannot be instantiated. (It would simply be a case of sour grapes to deny these things.) These two points are interactive: on the model of language as (fundamentally) communication, Habermas can never escape the spectre of instrumentality.

In a move that is strikingly similar to a move in the more recent work of John Rawls, Habermas allows the i.s.s. to recede in *The Theory of Communicative Action* (just as the "original position" recedes in Rawls's post-*Theory of Justice* work).[19] What comes to the fore are two model conceptions, of the "system" and the "lifeworld." Communicative rationality must carry out the central task of allowing the lifeworld, a sphere of life not dominated by instrumental reason, to flourish, insomuch as this is possible. This does not mean destroying the "system," i.e., the sphere of instrumental reason, but rather reaching the best accomodation with it. The ideal is a world in which the lifeworld guides the system, even when the system must be allowed its scope and even occasional dominance. The i.s.s. now hides out in the lifeworld, as a guiding conception for the formation of rational consensus.[20]

This conception certainly has its merits. The problem is whether it really is grounded in something other than a reworked subject-centered reason. The key notion that we have been circling around for these last several pages is *intention*. Habermas's move from Chomsky to Searle and speech act theory was motivated, from the start and throughout, by a need for intention as pragmatic ground (Habermas 1979, 45; Roderick 1986, 93). It is clear that the supposedly non-social realm of strategic action is governed by the intentions of agents. Habermas does not care to deny this. The notion of "lifeworld," however, which Habermas takes from Husserl, also has intentionality at its center, as does Searle's speech act theory (see Searle 1982, 259–76). Even a certain spreading out of the rational will, if it is still grounded in intentionality, remains a philosophy of the subject.

Like Searle, Habermas must give an account of the difference between honest and insincere intentions and their attendant utterances. How do we know that an utterance made in the context of the lifeworld really represents the better interests of that sphere? What keeps the "system" from disguising itself as the lifeworld and better working for its aims in that way? Habermas argues, certainly, that there is in fact nothing more common than this masquerade, which is the very essence of "systematically distorted communication." I am in full sympathy with the quandary, but there is really no way out of it in terms of the model of truth as rationally-achieved consensus.

The wavering between transcendent and pragmatic concerns that was evident in Habermas's failure to distinguish between the two levels of analysis in his encounter with Chomsky comes very much to the fore at this point. In order to make the conventions of language conform to a clear division between intentions aimed at truth and those not so aimed, Habermas must finally invoke a reason that is not simply constituted by the formation of the rational will in the discursive situation. Communicative rationality is based in "a wider concept of rationality connected with ancient conceptions of *logos*" (1984, 10). These conceptions are hardly to be sneered at, of course, but their ontotheological roots, which are fully present in Husserl, are not so easily dispersed. And, how is one finally to read the word, *logos*? This, certainly, is a question that is at the center of the work of both Heidegger and Derrida. Habermas's synthetic social theory can be read, I think, as an intentional gathering into the *logos*, a final homecoming of the diverse strands of Western thought.[21] *Logos* is the ur-intention that guides all human intention.

A theory that bases itself on a central notion of intentionality may not necessarily find itself in this kind of theoretical hot water. For instance, Searle's arguments may not have any need for *logos*, at least not for the purposes of grounding communication in the intentions of agents. Then again, *something* is needed, by Searle, to ground the distinction between sincere and insincere speech acts. One could always refer back to the sincerity or insincerity of the speaker's intention—that is, if one had some sort of access to this intention. Again, I am not sure whether this is a problem for Searle, insomuch as he is not interested in the historical motivation of language or the social theoretical dimensions of speech act theory. Even more to the point, it is not clear that Searle is especially worried about the philosophy of the subject; to the extent that speech acts are ahistorical, they do not tend to give rise to more troublesome notions of intersubjectivity or transsubjectivity. For Habermas and Derrida, however, such trouble cannot be avoided. The coextensive stories of language and subjectivity are not just conceptual stories, they are essential parts of the historical narrative of Western humanity as well. Neither Habermas nor Derrida would allow that one could write one's "signature" (Derrida's term) outside of history.

Habermas is right to challenge the philosophy of the subject, but it is very difficult to see how his "intellectual community" really allows him to formulate an alternative. On the contrary, a theory of communication that has intentionality at its core seems bound to emanate a theological resonance, in the gathering of intentions into a fundamental intention.[22] Furthermore, once such a theory is historically motivated, it is hard to see how the philosophy of history, which Habermas also wants to avoid, is eliminated. Again, on the contrary: Habermas seems stuck with an original intention that fulfills itself in history, ultimtely in the messianic age of the ideal speech situation.

And yet, if Habermas's pragmatic program is read in a less tendentious light, perhaps we need only admit that intentions count for something, and that, if we are ever going to turn this world in the direction of greater social justice, we have to be able to depend on something basic in social interactions that always already intends this transformation. In the midst of all the distortions of capitalism, we will have to find some basis for trusting each other, otherwise there is no possibility of social transformation.

Whether Habermas's massive formulations really add to or detract from a basic sense of "keeping faith" with humanity is a question that I will leave to the reader's judgment. "Keeping faith" is not a bad thing; "in terms of what?" is the question that has to be explored. Habermas answers this question by moving mostly within the philosophical circuit that extends from Kant to Marx (and sometimes back again). He extends that circuit with a philosophy of language that, however, never gets beyond the logic of the Same, and this precisely because Habermas never breaks with the sense of language as mediation. Language is the mediation of intentions—this results in communication. Even in "An Alternative Way out of the Philosophy of the Subject," where Habermas is at his best on these questions, and where he at times sounds not unlike Davidson or Derrida, there is this basic formulation: "We need a *theoretically constituted perspective* to be able to treat communicative action as the medium through which the lifeworld as a whole is reproduced" (1987b, 299).

In this essay Habermas is closest to Davidson and Derrida, and yet still so far away. In the remaining part of this section I want to ask whether there is an alternative to intentional theories of language and understanding. In the next section I will ask whether there is an alternative to understanding language as fundamentally communicative.

Although Habermas does not explicitly engage with Davidson's philosophy, the pursuit of the lines in philosophy of language associated with Chomsky, Austin, and Searle reflects a kind of rejection by default of the researches of Quine and post-Quinean analytic philosophy.[23] There is some significance to the fact that Davidson is not a "philosopher of language" (just as Derrida is not a "philosopher of literature"). It would be hard for Habermas to absorb Davidson's philosophy of language as something that could be detached from Davidson's larger concerns (even though the question of language is certainly central to those concerns). If Davidson cannot fit into the intellectual community that grounds the theory of communicative action, Habermas seems to say, better to leave him out. But then, better to leave everything out that does not conform to the logic of the Same. Habermas's pragmatics will not accommodate Davidson's semantics. But then, intentionality does not have a place in the heart of Davidson's semantics. We turn, then, to this critique of intentionality and Davidson's alternative way out of the philosophy of the subject.

A convenient entrance into this question is provided by a passage from Habermas's "Alternative Way" that seems quite close to Davidson:

> Insofar as speakers and hearers straightforwardly achieve a mutu-
> al understanding about something in the world, they move within
> the horizon of their common lifeworld; this remains in the back-
> ground of the participants—as an intuitively , unproblematic, and
> unanalyzable, holistic background. The speech situation is the
> segment of a lifeworld tailored to the relevant theme; it both forms
> a *context* and furnishes resources for the process of mutual under-
> standing. The lifeworld forms a horizon and at the same time
> offers store of things taken for granted in the given culture from
> which communicative participants draw consensual interpreta-
> tive patterns in their efforts at interpretation. The solidarities of
> groups integrated by values and the competences of socialized
> individuals belong, as do culturally ingrained background as-
> sumptions, to the components of the lifeworld. (1987b, 298)

If Habermas were to conceive of the lifeworld as "semantic" resource rather than as communicative resource, he would be somewhat closer to Davidson (there would still be the problem of language as "resource," which I have identified as a fundamentally instrumental conception). Habermas is worried, of course, about remaining stuck in semantics, without a way to move to the pragmatic level, therefore he begins on that level, with the communicating subject. I think that Davidson has a way to avoid this problem, as long as one is willing to give up intentionality. This way out of a puerile semantics, which is also a way out of the philosophy of the subject, can be called "triangulation." Before turning to that alternative, we might briefly summarize some of the criticisms that Davidson has of the notion of intentionality.

Davidson would not argue, of course, that there is no such thing as "intending." His claim, instead, is that there is no "intention" at the root of intending. People form "intentions," but the emphasis should be on the word "form," rather than on "intentions." Then we must necessarily attend to those elements out of which intentions are formed:

> ... acting with an intention does not require that there be any mysterious act of the will or special attitude or episode of willing. For the account needs only desires (or other pro attitudes), beliefs, and the actions themselves. There is indeed the relation between these, causal or otherwise, to be analysed, but that is not an embarrassing entity that has to be added on to the world's furniture. We would not, it is true, have shown how to *define* the concept of acting with an intention; the reduction is not definitional but ontological. But the ontological reduction, if it succeeds, is enough to answer many puzzles about the relation between the mind and the body, and to explain the possibility of autonomous action in a world of causality. (1982a, 88)

Three elements are basic to Davidson's holistic theory of meaning and action; this passage names two of them, belief and desire (or preference). The other element is meaning: in order to explain a person's actions (including her speech acts), we need to know something of her beliefs and preferences, and we need to know the meaning content of these. What we do not need to know is what a person's intentions are, if by intention we mean something different than the relationship that obtains among these elements.

Theories of language that focus on intention are looking for something that keeps people anchored to the world without denying them the possibility of self-motivated action. Intentionality seems to serve this purpose well because it both allows people to keep an eye on their environment and yet also generates the capacity for navigating through that environment. These theories seem uninterested in the question of subjectivity and its pitfalls. In fact, such theories avoid relativism precisely through the adoption of a foundational subjectivity. Intersubjectivity is, in turn, grounded in another foundational element, the "language of thought." Understanding is secured at too high a price in these theories. What is gained for the subject is lost for language. The loss for language, however, is itself a loss for the subject, which cannot form an intention apart from the web of meaning. The loss occurs in the subject's inability to generate intentions relying only on the resources of intentionality and the language of thought, unless it is claimed that the province of the latter is so extensive that it is hard to see what role is played by social interaction (see Ramberg 1989, 119–27).

Davidson's argument is that it is social interaction, especially in the form of language, that provides the anchor we need, but not in a foundational sense. The categories of mind that intentional theories still seek can be generated entirely in terms of external relations (indeed, the "mind" itself becomes an external relation in this view; see Davidson 1989c).

The conclusion of Davidson's essay, "Rational Animals," both gives a sense of these external relations and shows how far Davidson is from intentional theories:

> If I were bolted to the earth I would have no way of determining the distance from me of many objects. I would only know they were on some line drawn from me toward them. I might interact successfully with objects, but I would have no way of giving content to the question where they were. Not being bolted down, I am free to triangulate. Our sense of objectivity is the consequence of another sort of triangulation, one that requires two creatures. Each interacts with an object, but what gives each the concept of the way things are objectively is the base line formed between these creatures by language. The fact that they share a concept of truth alone makes sense of the claim that they have beliefs, that they are able to assign objects a place in the world. (in LePore and McLaughlin 1985, 480)

Intentional theories are almost always combined with a theory of reference rather than a theory of truth (that is, intentional theories define truth in terms of reference, rather than reference in terms of truth). Davidson does not think that we can legitimately come by these sorts of anchors to subjectivity and the world. (To repeat: needing or positing such anchors opens the door to scepticism.) Language of thought theorists such as J. J. Katz claim that these sorts of post-Quinean disclaimers mainly indicate an ignorance of the discoveries of Chomskyan linguistics (in Barrett and Gibson 1990). Furthermore, the Chomskyan counter-critique often points to difficulties in Quine's behaviorism (Chomsky 1975). Davidson has argued convincingly, however, that the presence or absence of a behavioristic program (which he forthrightly eschews) has no bearing on the fact that intentionality and generative grammar will not guarantee the connection of word and object (1985, 215–41). We come to be in and of the world through another path, one that gives rise to our intentions rather than originates in them. That path is an intersubjectivity that grounds subjectivity in the activity of triangulation. As Carol Rovane puts it, in "The Metaphysics of Interpretation,"

The basic idea is that one cannot recognize that one's beliefs constitute a subjective point of view on something objective, or independent of one's beliefs, except insofar as one also recognizes other subjective points of view. Hence self-conscious believers must also be self-conscious communicators, i.e., interpreters of others. If these conceptual connections traced by Davidson are allowed to stand, then one's consciousness of other points of view must be on equal footing with consciousness of one's own point of view. (in LePore 1986, 423)

We will turn to the world-disclosive aspects of language, as manifest in Davidson's philosophy, in the next section. The conclusion that can be drawn concerning intentionality is this: prior to the formation of intention there is always already a recognition of the other. This recognition may itself be distorted by an oppressively hierarchical political system, but it is this essential recognition of the other, that grounds my intention toward the other that then becomes the locus of interpretive praxis.

While Habermas does not address Davidson, he does take up Derrida's early work on Husserl and intentionality. Before turning to that confrontation, we might raise, very briefly, a simple question about Davidson. It is clear that Davidson is a strong critic of intentionalist and referential theories of meaning, but why assimilate him to the category, "iteration"? The reason is that Davidson is similar to Derrida in thinking that the subject is deployed by and in language rather than the other way around. Textuality "writes" the subject through the process of triangulation—a triangulation without end and without foundation. This is a thesis about the primacy (if that is the word) of context, rather than of "the linguistic."

Habermas is especially interested in the ways that Derrida is both like and unlike Heidegger. It might be said that this is the standard by which Habermas judges the *moral* worth of a theory, but we might do well to avoid that side of Habermas's critique. Habermas uses the comparison with Heidegger to lead into a discussion of Derrida's earlier critique of Husserl, *Speech and Phenomena, and Other Essays on Husserl's Theory of Signs* (1967). We will turn to the question of Heidegger in the next section, but we may at least indulge in a quotation that gives the tenor of Habermas's critique of Derrida:

Backed by structuralism, he can forge a direct route from Husserl's earlier philosophy of consciousness to the late Heidegger's philosophy of language. I want to test whether his grammatologically distanced conception of the history of Being avoids the objection that was raised by Heidegger against Nietzsche and that recoils upon Heidegger himself: "The Nietzschean demolition remains dogmatic and, like all reversals, a captive of that metaphysical edifice which it professes to overthrow." To anticipate my thesis: Even Derrida does not extricate himself from the constraints of the paradigm of the philosophy of the subject. His attempt to go beyond Heidegger does not escape the aporetic structure of a truth-occurrence eviscerated of all truth-as-validity. (1987b, 166–67)

Habermas finds that Derrida is trapped within the domain of the sign. Although Derrida's point of entry into the critique of the philosophy of consciousness is Husserl's distinction between the arbitrary "sign" and the linguistic "expression" that supposedly finds its meaning in an ideal connection, Habermas argues that Derrida cannot break free from the semiotic level into the domain of intersubjectivity. For Husserl, it is intentionality that ultimately bridges the gap between originary, ideal meanings, and the signs that express them in ordinary discourse. Derrida criticizes both the idea of originary meaning (which Habermas refers to as Husserl's "Platonism") and the idea of a bridge to an outside that must have already permeated the "inside" in order for a bridge to be built in the first place.[24] Habermas's worry is that Derrida then goes so far "outside," so to speak, that he can never get back to intersubjectivity or the centrality of validity claims in public discourse. Habermas summarizes his position as follows:

Against the Platonizing of meaning and against the disembodying interiorization of its linguistic expression, Derrida wants to bring out the indissoluble interweave of the intelligible with the sign-substrate of its expression, one might even say: the transcendental primacy of the sign as against the meaning. Interestingly, his reflections are not aimed at those premises of the philosophy of consciousness that make it impossible to identify language as an intersubjectively constituted intermediate domain that has a share in both the transcendental character of world-disclosure and the empirical character of the innerworldly experienceable. Derrida does not take as his point of departure that nodal point at which the philosophy of language and of consciousness branch off, that is, the point where the paradigm of linguistic philosophy separates from that of the philosophy of consciousness and renders the identity of meaning dependent upon the intersubjective practice of employing rules of meaning. Instead, Derrida follows Husserl

along the path of separating off (in terms of transcendental philosophy) every innerworldly thing from the performances of the
subject that are constitutive of the world, in order to take up the
battle against the sovereignty of ideally intuited essences within
its innermost precincts. (1987b, 171–72)

Habermas is not, for the most part, incorrect in this summary. The
problem is that he just does not see what Derrida is doing, and he
measures what he thinks that Derrida is doing by a standard that itself
can be questioned.

Derrida does argue for "the transcendental primacy of the sign,"
as Habermas has it, *against* "the meaning." Everything here hinges on
what this "transcendence against" is, and what is meant by "the
meaning." On the one hand, Derrida does not take it that there is
anything necessary for the creation of meaning other than the sign,
though "sign" is a very broad category for him. In principle, anything
might count as a sign, just as anything, e.g., the arrangement of three
chairs in a particular room, might count as a sentence for Davidson. On
the other hand, Derrida is interested in interrogating everything in
philosophy and literature that legislates against the sign. Of course
Derrida is "following Husserl"—he is always "following" someone in
the history of Western philosophy or literature. This is because it means
something that Western culture has been based on the suppression of
textuality. We have already marked that meaning in various places in
this text thus far, but in a moment we will mark it again with regard to
Habermas.

Neither Derrida nor Davidson thinks that there is a "nodal point"
at which philosophy of language and philosophy of consciousness
branch off, nor does either buy too readily into the notion of a paradigm shift (despite what some enthusiasts of Derrida's work, in a
kind of new age twist, want to attribute to that work). Furthermore,
neither Derrida nor Davidson would accept that it is the performances of the subject, pure and simple, that "constitute" the world.
These points are better addressed in the context of the next section. Suffice it to say, in preparation, that "world-disclosure" is not
a constant theme of Habermas's own arguments about language—he
only raises this term in the context of arguments with Derrida and
Heidegger.

In an insightful article on Habermas's argument with Derrida,
George Trey summarizes (while taking issue with) the political content
of Habermas's complaint:

How can a palpable notion of positive political action be constructed when the script is in a constant state of flux and the actors are
simply determinants of the "play"? Habermas considers Derrida
to be primarily concerned with textual relations. This, Habermas
suggests, results in the erroneous generalization that all structures
replicate literary texts. As such, Derrida considers everything to be
undergirded by an undifferentiated movement of forces. This
view, according to Habermas, effectively "degrades politics and
contemporary history to the status of the ontic and foreground, so
as to romp all the more, and with a greater wealth of associations,
in the sphere of the ontological and the archewriting." (1989a, 72–
73; quotation from Habermas is in 1987b, 181)

Where Habermas sees a certain freeplay of "the night of writing in
which all cows are black," Derrida sees the de-authorization of writing.
In turn, Habermas's critique may be considered a reauthorization, a
resubmission of the sign to the authority of intentionality.

Habermas's fear is that, without the connecting thread of intentionality,
there is no basis for social interaction geared toward a public sphere in
which the unforced force of reason carries the day. Intentionality, for
Habermas, is the key to pragmatics. Neither the semiotic nor the
semantic critique of semantics, Habermas thinks, will unlock that door.
On the other hand, Habermas is afraid that the critique of semantics
"from the inside" will explode the theory of the sign into a license for
"play" that knows no bounds. What is *really* going on here? I think that
the argument is really about the "autonomous" subject, which Habermas
wants to find a ground for free of the philosophy of the subject, pitted
against a "positioned" subject that must find its ground in a solidarity
that takes priority over autonomy. Unable to reject a central notion of
autonomy, Habermas grounds his autonomous subject in notions that
have the philosophy of the subject written all over them.

Habermas is not wrong to fear the dangers of the positioned
subject, however. We will consider these dangers in the rest of this
chapter and in Chapter 4—but we will also consider the unavoidablility
of positionality and the possibilities (inseparable from the dangers) that
this idea opens up for politics.

Poetry and communication

George Trey raises the provocative question of "textualizing the
lifeworld." This is a tantalizing prospect, certainly, and I would like to
follow it out in Trey's text to just the place where the trouble starts. Trey

argues that we might consider replacing Habermas's notion of lifeworld with a Derridean notion of text:

> As was the case with Habermas's lifeworld, Derrida's "text" is a loosely woven, historically structured matrix of overlapping linguistic components. Likewise, the text and the lifeworld are both fluid: shifting in compositional form with respect to factors that contribute to their fabrication. Further, both remain in the background—a quasi-transcendental foundation, although not solid ground—serving as the reserve from which textual instances or defined communicative situations are drawn. They diverge sharply, however, with respect to the relationship between the reserve and the situation or instance. Habermas ... contends that the shifting within the reserve does not effect properly defined situations. Derrida, on the contrary, claims that the "differance"— "active moving discord of different forces and of differences of forces"—of the intertextual reserve factors into every textual instance, leaving traces which seed that structure's deconstruction. Hence, the excluded other or marginalized, that which has to be politically neutralized in a defined situation or textual instance, is never quite flushed out, as the text and its instances are inseparable. (1989b, 10–11; internal references are to Derrida 1982, 20–25)

Trey notes that this move is not something that Habermas would favor, because the latter is afraid that textuality "reduces all of reality to the status of a big, self-animating book" (Habermas says as much in the last part of his essay, attributing to Derrida a kind of Jewish mysticism; Trey 1989b, 12; Habermas 1987b, 182–84). Derrida's claim, in the face of this argument about a text "pregnant with meaning, but *without specific meaning*" (Habermas 1987b, 183), is that "it is within this text, albeit in a 'highly unstable and dangerous' fashion, that responsibilities jell, political responsibilities in particular" (this is Trey 1989b, 12, quoting Derrida 1988a, 136–37).

We seem to be involved in an argument about the relationship between the specific and the general. Trey argues that Derrida's line of reasoning has a definite advantage over Habermas's on this matter:

> Habermas argues that the situations defined in specific instances of communicative action are the natural product of a language "designed" with this purpose in mind. As such, under the right definite conditions, language fulfills itself in universal validity claims. Derrida, on the other hand, claims that "there is always

something political 'in the very project of attempting to fix the context of utterances'." Such political actions attempt to bracket off spheres of meaning or truth production, marginalizing the intertextual movement that threatens them with disruption. It is not Derrida's point that attempting to contextualize spheres of discourse is wrong; he in fact notes that doing so is necessary if there is to be political "discussion." Rather, his contention is that the borders which define these contexts are never impervious to intertextual movement or difference. (1989b, 12–13; internal references to Derrida 1988a, 136)

Or, we might say, these borders are always part of a general economy that cannot fully marginalize the other, try as it might. It is the "radical trembling" that Derrida speaks of in "Differance" (which we quoted in Chapter 2) that leads, for Habermas, to a dangerous, unstable politics (Trey 1989b, 13–14). (Habermas, I might mention, has always had what seems to me a queer notion of "stability." He remarks in various places about the stability of capitalism in the twentieth century, always neglecting the fact that it has taken two world wars, the nuclear threat, and a continuing reign of terror for the Third World to maintain that "stability.")

Habermas's antidote to such instability is: 1) to reauthorize the autonomous subject by other means than the philosophy of the subject and, 2) to develop a clear sense of what the public contexts are in which the subject participates in political life. I have argued that Habermas fails in the first pursuit, autonomy without subjectivity. His reauthorization does not work in the second case either: language will not submit itself, even under threat of force, to being defined as essentially communicative.

The notion that subjectivity is an inhabitation by intersubjectivity of what comes to be a human individual, which I earlier attributed to Davidson, has further implications for the question of the situatedness of the communicating subject. If language is the basic stuff (a crude word that allows us to avoid, for the moment, the word "medium") of intersubjectivity, then we must ask how dependable language is at providing communicative contexts. The answer for Habermas is clear: language is plenty dependable for such purposes, as long as the discourse is "designed" for communicative contexts. Language understood as textuality is not so designed, however. For this reason, Habermas would keep textuality at bay. He thinks that such a maneuver is possible as long as the "genre distinction" between philosophy and literature is not "leveled." Derrida is charged with creating such a leveling. I will argue that Davidson might as well be found guilty as well. There is just one very important point that might be introduced into this hearing, however. Habermas's assumption that Derrida, or whoever, could himself effect a "leveling" of this "genre distinction" is emblematic of his whole program of understanding language as essentially communicative and indeed essentially instrumental.

For both Derrida and Davidson, there is no way to draw some fundamental distinction between signs that behave "literally" and signs that behave "metaphorically." (The "behavior" of a sign is, in line with Derrida's and Davidson's adherence to the context problem, a matter of the *situation* of a sign.) Habermas thinks that the notion of intentionality grounds such a distinction, but it is difficult to see why signs are required to submit to a regime of "pure" meaning, the meaning that supposedly exists in what one intends by a word. What seems more likely, as Jonathan Culler argues, is that Habermas begins with a project that requires a certain division among different kinds of language usage; then he systematically brackets off "deviations" from the core conception.[25] Despite the pride that Habermas takes in having dealt with analytic philosophy (he remarks at one point that Derrida has avoided this engagement, which of course is not entirely true), it is clear that there is a category of theories that he has avoided completely, namely *holistic* theories. In such theories, there is just no way for one "part" of language to be bracketed off from others, at least not *in principle*. Davidson's philosophy is perhaps the most important example of such a theory in analytic philosophy.

For Davidson, language is not essentially a medium for either expression or representation. In "On the Very Idea of a Conceptual Scheme," Davidson challenges the subject-object dichotomy that lies at the heart of the notion of language-as-medium: "this . . . dualism of scheme and content, of organizing system and something waiting to be organized, cannot be made intelligible and defensible" (1985, 189). Nor can the notion that a conceptual scheme must "fit" the world be rendered sensible. What Davidson is especially critical of is "the attempt to make sense of the metaphor of a single space within which each scheme has a position and provides a point of view" (1985, 195). The reason that Davidson finds this notion troublesome is that, if we take a natural language to be a typical candidate for "conceptual scheme" status, then we must confront the idea of an untranslateable language. Davidson does not think that there could be such a language that we could recognize as a language in the first place. That we can, by and large, translate various languages into each other indicates, for Davidson, that there is no basic incommensurability of conceptual schemes, and hence no reason to speak of such schemes at all.

This argument has been widely discussed and is not my main focus here.[26] The upshot of the argument is very important for present purposes, however. If there is no basis for an essential subject-object dichotomy, then we can further argue that there is no basis for accepting an essential "'boundary between knowing a language and knowing our way around the world generally" (Davidson, in LePore 1986, 446). This erasure of boundaries explains why Davidson is not a "philosopher of language," but it further points to the reason why Davidson thinks that "philosophers of language" do not in fact have a subject matter: "There is no such thing as a language, not if a language is anything like what many philosophers and linguists have supposed" (ibid.). In the essay from which these last two quotations are taken, "A Nice Derangement of Epitaphs," Davidson argues against the idea that language use is the application of linguistic rules (this is, of course, a basically Wittgensteinian argument, one that Habermas never really comes to terms with in discussing Wittgenstein). He especially argues against "the attempt to illuminate how we communicate by appeal to conventions." Conventions may help us keep certain domains of discourse separate, in order to facilitate certain practical ends, but they are not intrinsic to our participation in language and the world. We may wonder whether Habermas really needs to make this claim, that there really are intrinsic distinctions in language, for example between the literal and the metaphorical, or between different "genres." I think that Habermas does need distinctions of this sort to carry off his political agenda, but it is that agenda that is calling forth the distinctions, not the other way around.

Davidson's argument about metaphor is often misunderstood, so perhaps we should take a moment to consider that argument. Contrary to what many readers of "What Metaphors Mean" (1985, 245–64) seem to take home from the essay, Davidson is not positing some essential distinction between "literal" and "figurative" uses of language (again, he is rejecting the whole idea of "uses" of language, which is the larger frame for his view of metaphor). Richard Rorty makes a useful comparison between Davidson's view of language, and Nietzsche's and Derrida's. Davidson sees the distinction between the literal and the metaphorical

not as a distinction between two sorts of meaning, nor as a distinction between two sorts of interpretation, but as a distinction between familiar and unfamiliar uses of noises and marks. The literal uses of noises and marks are the uses we can handle by our old theories about what people will say under various conditions. Their metaphorical use is the sort which makes us get busy developing a new theory. (Rorty 1989a, 17)

There is no "theory" that firmly grounds, in general, the continual passage from the old to the new. In this view, "literal" language is simply that part of language that has become somewhat sedimented— keeping in mind that "literal" is itself a metaphor. By "sedimentation" is meant only that, under "normal" circumstances, members of a given language community do not argue over the usage of a particular word or phrase. For example, if I ask someone to "open the door," I am not "ordinarily" trying to provoke an interesting discussion about what this might mean. For Davidson, two points are essential here. First, there is no general theory, contrary to Habermas, of the "ordinary" circumstances of language. In this respect, Davidson is not unlike Derrida in thinking that there can be no "general science of textuality" (i.e., "grammatology"). Second, there can be no *cordon sanitaire* around the sedimented parts of language. In this he is not unlike Nietzshce (or Derrida) in thinking of "truth" as "a mobile army of metaphors."

Habermas fears the instability that might arise if language cannot be strictly regimented. Davidson and Derrida, on the other hand, see the continual rebellion of language against such regimentation as what opens up new possibilities (and yes, we can mark some of these possibilities as dangerous, once again) for the ways that we live in the world. In an interesting comparison of Davidson with Freud, Marcia Cavell suggests that metaphor might be considered the "dreamwork" of language. Metaphor is part of what allows us to take a self-critical attitude by imagining a different way of talking about the world.[27]

I will only attend very briefly to Habermas's excursus "On Leveling the Genre Distinction between Philosophy and Literature," which is purportedly a critique of Derrida. I employ this qualifier because Habermas does not quote Derrida directly in the essay, relying instead on the work of some well-known American followers of Derrida (principally Jonathan Culler), and the version of Derrida that Habermas presents is almost completely inaccurate and self-serving. (Frankly, one expects better from Habermas than this.) A brief look at some of Habermas's formulations in this piece, however, will set the stage for the encounter with Heidegger that has been looming in the background of much of this chapter.

Habermas quotes Richard Ohmann (a Marxist literary scholar) with approval: "Since the quasi-speech acts of literature are not *carrying* on the world's business—describing, urging, contracting, etc.—the reader may well attend to them in a non-pragmatic way" (1987b, 201). Having come only at the end of the day to the question of literature, provoked, as it were, by Derrida and other French thinkers, Habermas gives to this question and its supposed domain the virtue of a kind of liberation from the concerns of "real life":

> Neutralizing their binding force [of literary speech acts] releases the disempowered illocutionary acts from the pressure to decide proper to everyday communicative practice, removes them from the sphere of usual discourse, thereby empowers them for the playful creation of new worlds—or, rather, for the pure demon-stration of the world-disclosing force of innovative linguistic expressions. (ibid.)

One naturally wants to ask who is doing the "neutralizing," "remov-ing," and "empowering" (which seems more like disempowering) here. Perhaps Habermas thinks that if Derrida can "level" genre distinctions, then someone else can reauthorize them—it is all a matter of autono-mous, intentional action, after all (it is a matter of "designing" language for particular purposes and domains of life).

Having granted literature its independence, Habermas proceeds to challenge what he takes to be "the thesis of the independence of the literary work of art in Derrida's sense." The only response to this challenge is to note that Derrida has never been a defender of this thesis—to attribute it to him is simply to set up a straw man. It is not even clear that Derrida, following Roland Barthes's (1977) influential essay, "From Work to Text," would allow that there is such a thing as "the literary work of art." The thesis that Derrida has repeatedly defended concerns the understanding of language as "literary." By this he means that "literature" is that part of language that foregrounds the differential workings of language and that there is no part of language that is finally free of this "literary" quality. The attempt to achieve this "freedom" from literature is, for Derrida, the founding moment of authoritarianism.[28] All the same, pursuing Derrida's supposed literary hermeticism, Habermas argues that

> [A]n aesthetic contextualism blinds him to the fact that everyday communicative practice makes learning processes possible (thanks to built-in idealizations) in relation to which the world-disclosive

force of interpreting language has in turn to prove its worth. (1987b, 205)

Again, one wonders exactly how the "idealizations" are built in; if they are built in by a community that has the intention of making a political distinction between different, artificially distinguished (idealized) domains of language, then that is one thing—and not necessarily a bad thing. But that is not Habermas's argument. Instead, he argues that communication is the "natural" function of language, and that world-disclosure, which is a kind of "aesthetic" function, must justify itself to this essential core of linguistic activity. This is one line of argumentation in Habermas's text. Another line that sits right alongside of this one is that there is a *tension* between "normal" and "poetic" discourse:

> This *aestheticizing of language, which is purchased with the twofold denial of the proper senses of normal and poetic discourse* [Habermas's emphasis!], also explains Derrida's insensitivity toward the tension-filled polarity between the poetic-disclosive function of language and its prosaic, innerworldly functions. . . . (ibid.)

Habermas would certainly not accept as an answer to this complaint the fact that Derrida's work is about nothing other than the tensions caused by the attempt to maintain this "polarity." Be that as it may, Habermas is simply wrong to make the further claim that Derrida "permits the capacity to solve problems to disappear behind the world-creating capacity of language" (ibid.). On the contrary, and this is what Habermas cannot finally accept, the capacity to "solve problems" *appears* within the context of the world-disclosiveness of language. "Derrida" is powerless to either prevent or permit this contextualization—it is not a question of what Derrida decides to do with language versus what Habermas would prefer to do with it.

Why is it that Habermas cannot accept this view of language, in which world-disclosure can never be finally separated from problem solving? The reason is that this thesis presupposes Heidegger's argument that language is the house of Being, or at least represents a further stage in that argument. To accept the Heideggerian thesis means questioning an autonomy that is based on an intention that I cannot doubt—my own. It means questioning this intention and my ability to possess it. It means questioning "my own."

"Language is the house of Being"

In *Speech and Phenomena*, Derrida argues that

> Husserl's attempt to guarantee identity of meaning through intuitive evidence founders on his own theory of inner time consciousness. The simple presence of an object corresponds to an act of making present in time, an act, however, that is itself so temporal it continually loses its own identity in the constant experiential flux of protentions (that which is coming to pass) and retentions (that which has just passed). Insofar as the act of intuition is temporalized, presence is necessarily interwoven with absence, since the present overflows into a past that is no longer and a future that is not yet. Thus, within every act of identification there is a passive act of becoming other, or differentiation.[29]

Derrida is essentially taking issue with Husserl's Platonism, a point on which he and Habermas are not at odds. Whereas Habermas replaces that Platonism with the theory of communicative action, Derrida turns in the direction of textuality. Derrida generates this problematic not only by working through Heidegger's thinking on language, but also through an encounter with Saussure's structural linguistics. It is important that these two quite different discourses are understood to be working together in Derrida's text, for in that combination (it would not be wrong to call it a synthesis) one finds: 1) a historicization of what remains on the synchronic level for Saussure, and 2) a spatialization and therefore materialization of what remains somewhat ideal for Heidegger. As David Ingram argues, however,

> despite the structuralist substitution of writing for transcendental subjectivity, Derrida's deconstructive project remains thoroughly ensconced in a subject-based philosophy in Habermas's view. In place of Heidegger's fate of Being, one finds a retreat from public communication to an arbitrary play of signifiers, in which interpretation remains ultimately arcane: an act of private revelation, or at most, an esoteric discourse with a hidden God. (1987, 91)

Habermas is once again thinking not only of Heidegger's "God" (the only one who can save us now), but also the strain of "Jewish mysticism" that he claims to see in Derrida. When thinking of these things it is interesting that Habermas does not think of Levinas's "God," who is wholly other, who calls us to respond to the other. (Habermas mentions

Levinas in this connection, but that is not the same thing as really thinking about his problematics of alterity; see 1987b, 182.) But then, it is this dimension of Heidegger, Levinas, and Derrida that Habermas never comes close to attending to. Habermas is after an economy of discourse in which nothing is ever lost to the other, which is a view fundamentally at odds with a "Jewish" theory of language.[30] I place "Jewish" in quotation marks simply to underscore the fact that Jewish civilization and its thinkers are also not primarily "philosophers of language." These thinkers, and the civilization from which they have drawn certain lessons (never, it must be added, in a simply univocal way), *are* concerned about how to live and therefore, one might think, about "public communication" (the kind that is not just "an arbitrary play of signifiers"). I will not go so far as to say that the Jews who bother Hegel perhaps bother Habermas as well, in light of the scrupulous attention that Habermas has always paid to German-Jewish scholarship and in light of his exemplary role in the *Historikerstreit*.[31]

Undoubtedly what disturbs Habermas is what he perceives as the "mysticism" in Heidegger, Levinas, and Derrida. This is not a question that will be answered fully in this chapter, because I do not want to frame this question in terms of a response to Habermas. There is indeed a tone of religiosity (as opposed to one of "religion," which is something else) in Heidegger that I also find troublesome. But it also strikes me as fundamental that the response to the other and the regard for the other that makes of "letting the other speak" more than a formula for passivity cannot help but risk a certain "tone" (which Habermas also rightly detects in Heidegger—but my point is that, if he would really look and be open to looking, he would not find this passivity or religiosity in either Levinas or Derrida). It is Habermas, not Derrida, who would relegate this question to the "aesthetic" realm (whatever that is—it is Habermas's claim, so he can take responsibility for it) as opposed to "public communication."

We have not yet encountered Heidegger, who, for all his elitism,[32] still describes the path toward a "caring" that, for Derrida (and Levinas), must come before "claims of validity." It seems that Heidegger could not really bring this caring to bear on humanity, not always or perhaps even very often. This is a horrifying side of Heidegger, though perhaps no worse than the horrors that come into play for humanity at the point where secularism has run wild and crushed all fellow-feeling out of autonomy. In a crude and indeed inexcusable way (in his "tone" or "style"—I am trying to demonstrate why these things are not unimportant; there is even a question of "positioning" here that does bear on validity claims), this is the point that Heidegger was aiming for in his

(again, execrable) comparison of the Holocaust and the "green revolution": "Agriculture is now a motorized food industry, essentially the
same thing as the fabrication of cadavers in the gas chambers of the
extermination camps, the same thing as the blockades and the reduction
of countries to famine, the same thing as the fabrication of hydrogen
bombs."[33]
    What is this "same thing" that all of these mechanized forms (all
but one obviously an engine of death, of murder, but what about this
other one, the "motorized food industry?) supposedly have in common—or rather, that they are, in essence? In *Heidegger's Confrontation
with Modernity*, Michael Zimmerman sets for himself the extraordinarily
difficult task of sorting all of this out (he succeeds to a great degree, to
my mind).

    In this astonishing statement, Heidegger glided over the fact that
the Holocaust was a *German* phenomenon involving the slaughter
of millions of *Jews*. Instead, he chose to view the Holocaust as a
typical episode in the technological era afflicting the entire West.

    Nevertheless, in speaking of the Holocaust in the same
breath with the hydrogen bomb, Heidegger was making an important point. Mass extermination in the Nazi camps was possible
only because of developments within industrial technology. Moreover, the Nazis spoke of the Jews as if they were little more than
industrial "waste" to be disposed of as efficiently as possible.
Officials in charge of planning strategic use of nuclear weapons
must be trained to conceive of the enemy populace in wholly
abstract terms. Heidegger argued in several places that the hydrogen bomb—an instrument of mass extermination—was not the
real problem facing us. Instead, the problem is the perversion and
constriction of humanity's understanding of being itself in the
technological era. Extermination camps and hydrogen bombs,
from Heidegger's viewpoint, were both symptoms of humanity's
conception of itself and everything else as resources to be produced and consumed, created and destroyed, at will.[34]

Modern "agriculture" can be put in this category as well if it also is
guided by the ethos of "problem solving." I sympathize fully with
Habermas's difficulty in taking this lesson from one who in fact was in
some real sense a partisan of (what Derrida often calls) "the worst."
That is why I have raised this question, which is not the real question of
Heidegger that we must ultimately encounter here, at the outset, rather

than leaving it for the end (an end that never comes in many analyses). Much ink has been spilled over the question of whether Heidegger's "philosophy" was "fascist," as though the question will be resolved right there. In the discussion of community in the first chapter I already hinted that this question is not that simple, because many people are taken in by the rhetoric of community, *especially* when it is false (and, in a fully secularized world, this rhetoric can never not be somewhat "false," for, as I will argue in the last chapter, we *cannot* know for sure, situated as we are, what we are talking about when we speak of community). Studies such as Zimmerman's (and Derrida's *of Spirit* [1989b], and Philippe Lacoue-Labarthe's *La fiction du politique: Heidegger, l'art, et la politique* [1987]) forthrightly accept that Heidegger's arguments, and yes, once again, his "tone," are laced with authoritarianism. They take as a beginning point what Habermas takes as the end-point of the argument concerning Heidegger.

Or: Habermas takes this to be the penultimate point, where fascism is seen to permeate even the deep structures of Heidegger's thought. Then comes the explanation for this permeation. In Habermas's view, the problem was not that Heidegger heard the call of Being wrongly, or that he responded wrongly to this call; Heidegger's thinking is misguided in listening for this call in the first place. David Ingram provides a useful summary of the errors that Heidegger makes in listening for the call of Being, according to Habermas:

> First, by regarding the religious need for ethical community as an ontological need for Being, Heidegger depreciates the communicative praxis of the lifeworld, which he sees as a domain of objectification and self-forgetfulness. Second, the poetic thought of the philosopher that harkens to the call of Being necessarily bypasses the empirical and normative questions raised by the social sciences. . . . Third, the poetic transcendence of the ontic, of propositional truth and conceptual thought, means that the fate of Being must be left wholly undetermined, a difficulty that is compounded by Heidegger's pseudo-sacral terminology, which identifies Being with the experience of the Holy, man with the sheperd of Being, and so on. (1987, 89)

If this is indeed an accurate characterization of Heidegger and even of some of his "difficulties" (for whom?), then it might be said that Derrida is asking no more than the following questions. What can "give" (what play is there in this structure, and what openings are there) in this thinking? How much can be rewritten while maintaining the essential insight of Heidegger's problematic? We will turn to these questions momentarily, when we examine Habermas's account of Derrida's relation to Heidegger. Before turning to that account, there are two links in this chain that should be set out.

First, though we want to move, ultimately, in the direction of the dispute between Habermas and Derrida, we should not pass over in silence everything in Habermas's characterization of Heidegger. The road to Derrida, after all, does lead through Heidegger, so let us ascertain that we are indeed encountering Heidegger. I will simply raise a number of questions. What is the role of the word "religious" in Habermas's characterization? Is "the religious need for community" being affirmed here? Is Heidegger's understanding of that need or of community itself denied by Habermas? Is the need itself being questioned? Does Heidegger *necessarily* depreciate the communicative praxis of the lifeworld? Could he not instead have affirmed that praxis, but in a way that situated it in terms of the call of Being? Is Habermas saying that such a situatedness necessarily amounts to the depreciation of praxis? (I realize that this is almost a rhetorical question at this point.) Similarly, is it really the case that "empirical and normative questions raised by the social sciences" must *necessarily* be bypassed in the Heideggerian problematic? Is Heidegger's own practice our only guide on this question? Finally, to return to the beginning of this particular interrogation, is there some deeper problem, in Habermas's view, with "pseudo-sacral terminology"—the "Holy," "sheperding," "only a God can save us now," etc., than a supposed inauthenticity and an admittedly elitist, priestly attitude on Heidegger's part? Does Habermas have difficulty with the "pseudo-sacred," but not with the "sacred"? I am not asking these questions to trip Habermas up—it would really be worthwhile to know how he is approaching these issues.

I will leave this line of inquiry with only one comment, another question that reiterates something already argued in this section. In a thoroughly secular world, how could an attempt to encounter the sacred be anything but a bit "inauthentic"?

Second, let us turn once again to Davidson, for his line of thinking about language is still very much a part of the picture that I am attempting to present here. This section began by remarking on Derrida's critique of Platonism in Husserl. In the two sections previous to this one I argued that Habermas's essentially instrumental view of language linked him with a concept of intentionality that certainly has its own Platonic slant. There is a line of argument in Davidson that is also a critique of Platonism, this time the Platonism of Frege.

Frege came by his Platonism much more easily than did Husserl.

Whereas Husserl erected a rather elaborate philosophy of consciousness that was seen to contain elements of Platonism in its essential features, Frege, being at heart a logician and mathematician, simply bypassed most ordinary philosophical questions not only concerning consciousness, but also those of epistemology and metaphysics as well, and rested with a simple, self-avowed Platonist doctrine of meanings.[35] Over the years, analytic philosophy has applied much effort toward getting rid of this Platonism (or at least in testing whether Platonism can be gotten rid of). Frege himself supplied the key in his "context principle": "Only in the context of a sentence does a word have meaning."[36] In "Two Dogmas of Empiricism," W. V. Quine (1953) expands the principle: "Only in the context of a language does a sentence have meaning." What I have called the "context problem" is a further extension of this line of reasoning, carried out by Davidson and Derrida. In their extensions, the question of what it means for something to be a "language," or a "context," reaches out and blurs the boundaries among "language," "the world," "life," etc. Under this problematic, language does become (or rather, it always is) the "house of Being."

(This question, of similar genealogies leading on the one hand, from Frege, through Quine and Wittgenstein, to Davidson, and, on the other hand, from Husserl, through Heidegger, to Derrida, is of course very fascinating. A common feature at the end points is not only the critique of Platonism, but also the critique of Cartesianism. One wants to think that "something" is "going on" here, something to do with "language"—but what?)

Let us rejoin Habermas's polemic at the point where Derrida rewrites Heidegger. On the way to his analysis of Derrida's critique of Husserl's theory of signs, Habermas situates Derrida with regard to Heidegger's thinking:

> Like Heidegger, Derrida takes into consideration "the Occident in its entirety" and confronts it with its "other," which announces itself in "radical upheavals"—economically and politically (that is, manifestly) by new constellations between Europe and the Third World, metaphysically by the end of anthropocentric thought.
>
> To be sure, Derrida distances himself from Heidegger's later philosophy, especially from its network of metaphors. . . . Whereas Heidegger decks out his history-of-Being fatalism in the style of Schultze-Naumberg with its sentimental homely pictures of a preindustrial peasant counterworld, Derrida moves about instead

in the subversive world of the partisan struggle—he would even like to take the house of Being apart and, out in the open, "to dance . . . the cruel feast of which the *Genealogy of Morals* speaks."

Heidegger rests content with characterizing language globally as the house of Being; despite the privileged status accorded it, he never systematically studied language. This is where Derrida starts. A scholarly climate shaped by the structuralism of Saussure encourages him to enlist linguistics, too, in the service of the critique of metaphysics. He then redoes the step from philosophy of consciousness to philosophy of language in a methodological way and, with grammatology, opens up a field of research for analyses that could no longer have existed for Heidegger on the level of the history of Being. (1987b, 161, 162, 163)

Three levels of inquiry may be addressed to this assessment: 1) how fair is it to Heidegger (if we are interested in Derrida's development of themes from Heidegger, then once again we will want to make sure that we really are encountering Heidegger)?; 2) how fair is it to Derrida?; 3) once these questions are dealt with, where do the Heideggerian-Derridean thematics of language stand with regard to Habermas?

The question concerning Habermas's characterization of Heidegger, at least in connection with the assessment of Derrida, centers entirely around the third passage quoted just now. The unfairness of Habermas's judgment (I do not think that that judgment is only incorrect, though it is that; it is also fundamentally unfair) hinges on the fact that he claims that despite the overarching concern in all of his later work with poetry and "poetic dwelling," Heidegger "never systematically studied language." Habermas seems to presuppose that poetry is not a significant form of language, and has no real ramification for language or thinking about language. It would be interesting to compile a list of those thinkers, philosophers or otherwise, who, on Habermas's model, are not "systematically" concerned with language: perhaps the list would contain the names of Nietzsche, James Joyce, Paul de Man, Sandra Gilbert and Susan Gubar, etc. Out of some sense of fairness to Habermas and his political project, I would like to venture a guess at what his objection to Heidegger *should have been* on this score. Habermas should have argued that the credibility of the notion of "poetic dwelling" as a praxis is undermined by its seeming passivity and its seeming unconcern for that large part of humanity that does not consist in, conventionally speaking, what are called "poets." Whether Habermas could make *this* objection stick, however, is another question, especially if we grant that there may be extensions of Heideggerian problematics that Heidegger himself was uninterested in. Better then, it seems, for Habermas not to make this objection—better to sit with the ludicrous claim that Heidegger's study of language was not "systematic."

A sensitive reading of this question is provided by Werner Marx, in "The World in Another Beginning: Poetic Dwelling and the Role of the Poet." (Rather than relegate the reference to the anthology in which this essay appears to a mere footnote, it seems appropriate to enter into evidence here that the collected essays in *On Heidegger and Language*, edited by Joseph Kockelmans, attest to the fact that Heidegger's engagement with the question of language consisted in much more than the attribution of a "privileged status" to that question.) Marx quite rightly points to Heidegger's failure to consider "the interconnection between the role taken up and realized by the poet and 'poetic dwelling'." Heidegger offers only a few words on this subject, and they are inconclusive, to say the least: "the measure which the poet has already taken for [humanity] and embodied in a poetic work . . . must be 'spoken to man and communicated to him through the measure-taking of poetizing'" (in Kockelmans 1972, 246–47; slightly altered). Heidegger's failure here leads, in Marx's estimation, to an *aporia*, though one unacknowledged by Heidegger. Following this question at some length will take us to the point where Habermas should have formulated his objection.

If we pursue this thought further—which, in our opinion, does lie in Heidegger's characterization of the "role" of the poet—we find ourselves immediately in an *aporia*, which is perhaps inherent in Heidegger's "layout": in the essence of language as conceived by him. If the works of the poets find access to Saying—that is, to Saying in the form it has in withdrawal—and if they are to transform it into an essence of Saying which can be called "the poetic," then the power of affecting the granting nonhuman sphere would be attributed to the human sphere of the poem after all, which was itself granted as such by Saying: the power of affecting the "granting" sphere would be attributed to the "granted" sphere.

Heidegger has never discussed this *aporia*; moreover, he has never attempted to conceive concretely how single poetic works could totally transform Saying, in the form it has in withdrawal, into the poetic, even though the transformation of our own dwelling, which keeps becoming less and less poetic, into a poetic dwelling and the sudden arrival of the new beginning could not possibly occur before this condition had been fulfilled. (ibid.; 248)

In sum, there are certain connections that Heidegger does not make and which perhaps cannot be made. Indeed, as Calvin Schrag observes in commenting on Marx's paper, in the later work,

> on the issue of historical thinking, Heidegger is able to offer us at most only a metahistorical scheme in which the concrete experience of the historical is placed in jeopardy. A metahistorical approach seems destined to conceal the concrete solicitations of meaning within the mundane lifeworld of historical dialogue and action and, to this extent, remains impoverished. (ibid., 253)

Unlike Habermas, however, Schrag later pursued this problematic into the space of communicative praxis, rather than arguing that this space is constituted quite differently and has nothing to do with Heidegger's sense of world-disclosure (Schrag 1989, 61–62). Schrag argues that "poetic dwelling" is not enough—but it is a step on the way:

> That Heidegger's elucidation of *ethos* as a poetic dwelling carries a power of self-recognition and a profundity of vision cannot be denied. But we are of the mind that in the end he no more escapes the threat of aestheticism than did Nietzsche. Both thinkers offer us the power of the poetical so as not to die of the prosaic. But the conversations and social practices of mankind have their share of the prosaic. Concerns with the material conditions of human life, the use and abuse of power in social institutions, and distortions of communication are also features of man's dwelling on the earth. *Ethos*, we have maintained, encompasses a manifold of concerns and deliberations on the destiny of the *polis* and on man's wider sociohistorical existence. This is why the requirement of the fitting response should never be reduced to a matter of stylized comportment (Nietzsche) or poetical dwelling (Heidegger). The proper or the fitting has both a moral and an artistic posture, simultaneously solicited by the *ethos*. The new humanism will teach that man dwells rhetorically, and in this rhetorical dwelling the ethical and the aesthetical are taken up into a new relationship, in which there is a coincident cultivation of poetical perspectives and responsiveness to the socio-politico-economic needs of man. (ibid., 211–12)

We would do well to attend to Schrag's definition of a "new humanism":

In the restored portrait of man as decentered subjectivity, sketched on the terrain of communicative praxis, a new humanism begins to unfold. This new humanism no longer promises invariant definitions of a foundational subject, but instead moves about in a hermeneutical play of perspectival descriptions of the life of discourse and action. (ibid., 214)

Perhaps the most important point that might be made concerning this insertion of Schrag's well-articulated and appealing vision in the midst of this controversy over Heidegger is that Schrag's argument is not "Derridean." Certainly Schrag owes a thing or two to Derrida, as he acknowledges. The point, however, is that Schrag demonstrates that there is a way out of the Heideggerian problematic of language that does lead to an engagement with the polis and with the concerns of humanity.

Heidegger's language is at times so estranged from these concerns that it does indeed seem inhuman. Perhaps an especially acute example of this "anti-humanism" (as it came to be called in the French context) would be Heidegger's remarks on subjects such as homelessness and pain. For instance, in the "Letter on Humanism," Heidegger speaks of "a homelessness in which not only man but the essence of man stumbles aimlessly about" (1977, 218). It seems as though what we ordinarily mean by "homelessness," however, could not be further from Heidegger's thinking. John Caputo has demonstrated a similar distance with regard to Heidegger's remarks about pain, namely that "bodily" pain is simply too *gross*—it is simply not of the essence—for essential thinking (see Caputo 1990). These are and should be very troubling aspects of Heidegger's thought. Like Habermas, I would distrust implicitly any attempt to hide or ignore this side of Heidegger. And yet there is another side, a side that, although it cannot be called "humanistic" (not in the sense that Habermas would recognize, in any case, and on this point I would agree with him), does exemplify a concern for humankind—an "essential" concern. In the text just quoted we find these words:

But if man is to find his way once again into the nearness of Being he must first learn to exist in the nameless. In the same way he must recognize the seductions of the public realm as well as the impotence of the private. Before he speaks man must first let himself be claimed again by Being, taking the risk that under this claim he will seldom have much to say. Only thus will the preciousness of its essence be once more bestowed upon the word, and upon man a home for dwelling in the truth of Being.

But in the claim upon man, in the attempt to make man ready
for this claim, is there not implied a concern about man? Where
else does "care" tend but in the direction of bringing man back to
his essence? (1977, 199)

It is this kind of formulation that Derrida will rewrite in the language of
alterity. Not all Heideggerians will accept such a rewrite, because the
first thing that is deconstructed is "essence." But neither is Habermas
happier with this rewrite than he is with the "original," in large part
because he identifies the structuralist influence in Derrida as another
form of "anti-humanism." (Of course, Derrida does not accept that
there *is* an "original.")

Let us turn, then, to Habermas's characterization of Derrida's
relation to Heidegger. Derrida's approach to "confronting the Occident
in its entirety with its other" is quite different, we might even say,
radically different from Heidegger's. It can be argued without great
difficulty that Heidegger never encountered the "political other," whereas
Derrida is constantly trying to break through to a respect for this other.
Could anyone imagine, for instance, Heidegger really discussing the
Jew as the other, either before or after the Holocaust? The fact is that he
never even came close to such a discussion. In relating two kinds of
homelessness, two kinds of pain, two kinds of alterity, etc., Derrida does
indeed move "in the subversive world of the partisan struggle." On the
other hand, Derrida never merely "distances himself from Heidegger's
later philosophy, especially from its network of metaphors." Instead,
Derrida practices a very rigorous form of disruption of these metaphors,
a displacement that makes it possible to move from an essential es-
trangement within the house of Being to the kind of homelessness that
destroys real human possibilities. Finally, although Derrida does indeed draw from both Heidegger and structural linguistics, he also
draws from various other sources. Perhaps Habermas has difficulty in
recognizing Derrida's "intellectual community" (which is in large part
coextensive with Habermas's) because Derrida is not aiming at synthesis. Given that Derrida has repeatedly stressed that he is not offering a
system or "methodology," one might legitimately ask what he is doing
with such a diverse range of sources. It seems to me that the root concern
is just as political as it is with Habermas: Derrida's aim is to "let the other
speak." This aim would only be betrayed by the general strategy of
synthesis.

In completing the analysis of this chapter, then, we must outline a
Derridean rewriting of Heidegger's notion of language as the house of
Being. First, a schematization. Habermas, in the final analysis, defends

an instrumental understanding of language. Even though the communicative sphere of language is not dominated by the raw instrumentality
of language oriented toward "success," the basic model is still one of
people *deploying* language. It is a model based on an autonomy that
undergirds communication and that will hopefully triumph by shaping
communicative contexts in the direction of the ideal speech situation.
For Heidegger, "language speaks us." In this conception there is a
radical diremption of autonomy to the point where humanity is no
longer a concern in any of its material aspects. For Davidson, these
material aspects are all that there is, though he avoids any reductive
sense of materialism. This counter-reductive materialism, a position
that is anti-naturalistic (or perhaps it would be better to simply say
"non-naturalistic") at the end of the day, is not at odds with the
materialism argued for in the first chapter (indeed, Davidson loomed
large in the background of its formulation).[37] In keeping with Davidson's erasure of the line between language and life, we may say that
both Davidson and Derrida have a more systematic intertextual sense of
the relation between language and subjectivity than does Heidegger.
Language speaks the subjects who speak language that speaks the
subject, etc., etc. Already we are two steps removed from Heidegger,
first in the sense of intertextuality, and second in the sense of a
heterogeneous plurality of subjects. This latter difference necessarily
follows from the *différance* that Derrida reads in textuality. Following
this line of argument, the situation of the subject with regard to
language can be set out more comprehensively.

Heidegger's central concern was to explain the forms in which
Being makes itself manifest. The mystery at the core of this project is the
question of Being—"Why is there something rather than nothing?"
Heidegger is especially concerned that this mystery not be lost in the
matrix of validity claims. Indeed, this is a definition of "homelessness"
for Heidegger: "the abandonment of Being by beings, . . . the symptom
of oblivion of Being" (1977, 218). This notion of *unheimlichkeit* reveals an
essential dimension of the question of Being: How do we humans, as
finite beings, make our way in an infinite world? Is Heidegger not at
least a little "Jewish" in his response to this question? "Humanity must
first learn to exist in the nameless."[38] But suppose there is no return to
essence, as Derrida argues? What if there is no "home," no "Being" in
Heidegger's sense, to return to? Then humanity can never be entirely
"at home"; humanity must forever live in an "uncanny" (the typical
translation of *unheimlich*) condition. The thesis is not one of a basic
disjuncture between the world and language; following Davidson, we
may reject the supposed distinction in the first place. The question is one

of contingency in both language and the world (indeed, the same contingency). And yet, as we argued in the first chapter, this contingency—which we may once again call "impossibility"—is at the same time the locus of possibilities. It is also the locus of the counter-possibilities represented by Heidegger's political engagement. I do not say "Heidegger's politics," because I believe that the matrix of possibility/impossibility/counter-possibility *is* his "politics," more than his particular, and reactionary, development of this matrix in the concrete situation in which he found himself. That reactionary development owes a great deal to the thematics of "home" and "essence."

The contingency of beings, "homelessness," is the state of finding oneself to be a "guest." From this position, in which one might at least consider the possibility of responding to the other, because one knows in some sense what alterity is (even though one cannot name that sense, and therefore it is, as Wittgenstein rightly argued, "non-sense"), certain basic precepts of both Enlightenment thought and Marxism must be questioned. Foremost is the discourse of "mastery"—over society, over one's "self," over nature, and over the mystery of Being. To relinquish this mastery is the essence of the "Jewish mysticism" that Habermas, situated as he is between Marx and Kant, cannot recognize, much less accept.

Remainders

Two cheers can be offered to Habermas without reservation. He has set a social theoretical agenda that, like Marx's, cannot be ignored. And, he has demonstrated that the intellectual agenda of the left can be articulated with a rigor and sophistication that few conservative thinkers can match. Habermas was entirely correct in his reorientation of social theory toward the question of language. Fundamentally, then, the differences that I have marked out between Habermas and a Derridean approach to social theory have to do with a difference in political conception.

Like Habermas, Derrida is interested in the trajectory of subjectivity in modernity. The adventures of subjectivity, as played out in the philosophies of Descartes, Kant, Fichte, Schelling, Hegel, Marx, and Nietzsche are, for both Habermas and Derrida, an essential entry point into the understanding of contemporary society and culture. It would seem likely that Habermas and Derrida are also similar in thinking that the structure of language and the structure of community are linked, and therefore the fates of language and community are linked. My arguments in the first, second, and present chapters, however, problematize such a straightforward basis of comparison. For the fact is that Derrida (and Davidson) would not accept, in the final analysis, the notion of "the structure of language," especially in Habermas's sense of language as rule-governed behavior. Furthermore, Habermas, for his part, is not oriented toward community. He is a secular thinker, even if of a sort that I will conditionally endorse in the next two chapters (some further pitfalls of secularism will be specified as well).

The linkage of the "fates" of community and language lies in the fact that, for both, their conditions of possibility are also the conditions of their impossibility. This linkage, and its structuration by alterity (which is not the same thing as the possession of a "structure"), provides for what seems, in the traditional terminology, an opening to transsubjectivity. But this form of subjectivity finally gives way to something other. Habermas takes us from Descartes to Kant, while Derrida takes us from Hegel and Heidegger to Hölderlin and Nietzsche.

Davidson's role in this journey finally seems ambiguous. It is of course a matter of philosophical traditions and certain genealogical gaps that cannot be bridged by the mere comparison of concepts. The common program of what S. Pradhan calls "minimalist semantics," which links Derrida and Davidson, cannot finally encompass the larger parts of their separate texts, though the comparison does create "interesting reverberations" and the possibility of "fruitful dissemination" (1986, 77). On the synchronic level, Davidson seems ready to go quite some distance with Derrida, at least "conceptually" (by this I mean that I do not expect Davidson to take up many of the authors that Derrida is interested in). Though Davidson often traces a philosophical history of the various concepts that he discusses, it seems unlikely that he would recognize the sort of trajectory that, for both Habermas and Derrida, creates the historical motivation of a concept. As for the question of alterity, which is the final difference between Derrida and Davidson that is relevant here, there may be an opening in Davidson's text. Whether Davidson himself will pursue that opening is not the most important consideration. The encounter with Davidson is nonetheless important: first, as corroboration with Derrida on terrain that Habermas has chosen, namely analytic philosophy of language; second, as corroboration for the thesis that "something is happening with language that is also happening with society and the world," something that seems like a kind of *Zeitgeist*—this thesis is supported, in one form or another, by all three of our chief protagonists of this chapter. Neither of these points speaks to the fact that Davidson's work is fascinating, provocative, and important in its own right. In this respect, at least, this chapter does not do that work justice; I hope, however, that I will provoke a further interest in Davidson that will in some small measure atone for this failure.

In this same spirit, I beg the reader's indulgence in this discussion of language which, though it has covered much ground, historically and theoretically, is far from exhaustive. Suppose that the discussion were "exhaustive," something that in fact the subject matter renders impossible—but, just suppose. Would such a panoptic survey render, in the final analysis, a decision between two basic orientations, on the one hand an orientation to rule-governed language and secular, Enlightenment politics, and, on the other hand, an orientation to language as difference and post-secular community?

The orientation of this study is toward the possibility of a different, differential inhabitation on the border lines of language, where community is never finally secure and thus must be carefully attended to, where community must remain awake to the possibility of the non-existence which it already exists within. This is not transsubjectivity as the atmosphere of communication, though the atmospherics of alterity must, at least for the moment in which humanity finds itself, contain the possibility of communication and perhaps even enough consensus to satisfy Habermas. Intersubjectivity is as possible as language itself—and as impossible. Beyond that: a letter does not always necessarily reach its destination, and, even if the letter does "arrive," it is changed by the strangeness that it has traversed. Sender and receiver are thereby also changed.

These are conditions of community as well. And yet to finally "ground" these conditions we would have to rip the heart out of language.

4

Radical diversity/radical confluence: philosophical grounds of the new social movements

... paradoxically, invention invents nothing, when in invention the other does not come, and when nothing comes to the other or from the other. For the other is not the possible. So it would be necessary to say that the only possible invention would be the invention of the impossible. But an invention of the impossible is impossible, the other would say. Indeed. But it is the only possible invention: an invention has to declare itself to be the invention of that which did not appear to be possible; otherwise it only makes explicit a program of possibilities within the economy of the same.

It is in this paradoxical predicament that a deconstruction gets under way. Our current tiredness results from the invention of the same and from the possible, from the invention that is always possible. It is not against it but beyond it that we are trying to reinvent invention itself, another invention, or rather an invention of the other that would come, through the economy of the same, indeed while miming or repeating it, to offer a place for the other, would let the other come. I am careful to say "let it come" because if the other is precisely what is not invented, the initiative or deconstructive inventiveness can consist only in opening, in uncloseting, destabilizing foreclusionary structures so as to allow for the passage toward the other. But one does not make the other come, one lets it come by preparing for its coming.

Derrida, "Inventions of the Other"[1]

The other is not always that which is furthest away from the Same. Sometimes the other is that which is closest. It has been argued many times in recent years, mostly by literary critics, that Derrida's text is especially important for showing that the other of philosophy is litera-ture. This is certainly the case *if* by "literature" we mean the use of language such that pretensions to "pure thought" are undermined, that is, deconstructed. There are, however, two effects of this deconstruction that have not been explicitly thematized in the work of literary critics.

First, while there has been an extension of the problematics of genre to philosophy, such that philosophy may be considered "a kind of writing" (Rorty), the genre question has not been articulated *within* philosophy, except in practice, in the texts of a number of philosophers, including Derrida. This is an all-important exception, of course. The differences in approach of, for example, Habermas and Derrida, could be better understood in terms of the possibilities of genres of philosophy. For Habermas, the "genre distinction" between philosophy and literature should not be "leveled" fundamentally because philosophy is not a genre. For to say the opposite is already to attest to the literariness, in the sense specified, of philosophy, and this Habermas does not accept. Derrida not only accepts that philosophy is "literary," he further accepts that there are different genres within philosophy.[2] He often practices these different genres in the same text.

Much can and has been said about this practice. I simply want to focus on one reading of it that has not received sufficient attention. Derrida's textual strategies can be read as a critique of positivism, for it is this trend in philosophy, and in the larger intellectual sphere (including in literary studies, e.g., New Criticism), and indeed in the larger patterns of life in the West, which is most concerned to deny "literature." Positivism has it that there is one and only one road to knowledge, namely science. Derrida represents a double-turning from this thesis, and then a turning back to it. For Derrida there cannot be "one and only one" anything. And, we have been stressing that the guiding thread in Derrida's work is not "knowledge" or "truth," but rather an orientation to the other that in turn orients our approach to knowledge, truth, understanding, etc.

This justification of philosophical genres must find its way into any work in social theory that claims to take inspiration from Derrida. As I move closer to the "practical" part of the present text, this dimension of the materiality of signs, the space opened for multiple genres that do not invalidate each other, must be thematized and, more significantly, practiced.

The second effect of the deconstruction of philosophy (and, by extension, of philosophical social theory) is that we are forced to attend to the deconstruction of "pure thought" not only into "literature," but further, into all domains of the materiality of signs. The opening to history, politics, social movements, and community life structures, then, follows from the ruined transcendence (therefore the ruined counter-possibility) of philosophy.[3]

As I work in the following pages through some different genres of philosophy, I would like the following question to haunt the analysis: In order to prepare the way for the coming of the other, must philosophy be ruined?

"To verb": passing sentence on the name

The world is the world. Against certain interpretations of deconstruction or Derrida's work, I have attempted to shift the debate toward a sense of world-disclosiveness that does not run counter to the notion that we all (we persons, we practitioners of interpretive activity) drink from the same well. (There is still something of an epistemology here.) Furthermore, there is nothing wrong with calling this "well" by the name "the world." This far I go with Davidson. But this world is probably much weirder than we are entitled to infer from within a strictly Davidsonian perspective. At the very least it can be claimed that Derrida is interested in unpacking various economies to maximal effect, even if starting from minimal resources.

"The world" cannot be named, however, for there is no "name" that can *refer* to the world. The economies of the world, and its resources for naming itself, cannot be merely recuperated or capitalized within the world itself. The logical positivists were well aware of this problem, but they liked to think that it was only a problem for someone like Heidegger (see Carnap 1959). In their view, the world cannot be named, but things in the world can. Things in the world can be named and referred to.

There are some longstanding trends in the philosophy of language that take names as the most basic linguistic activity.[4] And there are similar trends in thinking about language generally.

What is this, this naming?

Citing *The German Ideology*, Jon Elster raises some interesting points about a Marxist view of the question of the name:

The basic reification of language is the process that creates nouns out of verbs: "the original roots of all words are *verbs*." When verbs are congealed into nouns, we come to speak of painters, not only of people who, among other things, also paint. This linguistic reification corresponds to the actual reification of man's capacities, so that language is no more faithful to reality when it refers to the reified activity by a reified verb such as a noun. (I note parenthetically that in Romance as well as Germanic languages the very word for *thing* ["causa," "Sache," "Ding"] originally meant *process* or *deliberation*. The word "thing" itself is a reified process!) (Elster 1985, 82; also see Erckenbrecht 1973)

Before verbs were names, were there attempts to "verb" the world? (Why speak of the "attempt"? The question may be answered with another question: Must creatures that are in and of the world attempt to find a "relationship" to it? The context problem and such applications of it as Davidson's critique of the scheme/content distinction may prove a useful guide here.)

Is the life-form of this ostensibly pre-reified world in the least bit accessible to contemporary humanity? This life-form is not "pre-secular"; rather, it is at the very least prior to the distinction between secular and sacred.

The founding act is creation ("invention"?), but creation is a process of separation, of order from chaos. This act is one of definition. But not definition by naming, rather of verbing—of course, naming *is* a verb. Naming precedes the name.

The closest we can attempt to come to this pre-reified life-form, this mythical origin that for us can never not be a myth, is in a discourse that perpetually displaces the name by revealing the arbitrariness of the name.

Strategic questions should be raised, however, about the speed at which this displacement may operate, and about the choice of targeted names.

The furthest one can go from this discourse of displacement is in a philosophy based on the notion of reference. The furthest reach of these philosophies would be the positivism of the Vienna Circle, especially their "verification principle," and the "internalist" and intentional theories discussed previously.

There are by now some well-known deconstructions of these positions. All attempts to fix reference, once and for all, depend on the acceptance of the finality of some "logic"—what Davidson (1985, 183–98) calls a "common coordinate system." Acceptance of such a system simply reinstates the scheme/content distinction. Quine's "Two Dogmas of Empiricism" and the arguments concerning on the "inscrutability of reference" were the beginning of the end of this kind of quest for correspondence in analytic philosophy.[5] There is always another logic, and no logic is set down in stone.[6] Of course, Plato was already aware of this problem, which he worries about in trying to set the relation between God and the Good (in the *Phaedrus*). Ironically, even if God sets the world's logic, then that logic is in a sense arbitrary.

An approach to language that is not centered on names ("nomocentric") already accepts this arbitrariness. In the *Genesis* story, God only creates the world by defining it. He leaves it to the world's inhabitants to name things. And thus interpretive practice begins and does not end.

But this practice had already begun, before it began. For, what is "chaos" and what is "order"? These are also arbitrary designations according to some system of naming, based in some logic. A "well-ordered" society will never readily give up its nomenclature! The names that well-ordered societies give to processes and forces that threaten "reassurance" are "chaos," "anarchy," "riot," and the like.[7]

In the *Genesis* story, God chooses "order," then immediately gives it to the inhabitants of our planet to inject a note of "chaos": they may name, by making up names (Genesis 2:19). One imagines this activity to be without closure; if God gives it to Eve and Adam to name, then surely they can rename as well. There is nothing so fundamental about a name that it cannot be changed. This open-endedness of naming makes language more an activity of verbs, and therefore an activity without an origin.

Indeed, any school of thought that takes there to be an origin has an at least secret hope for an outcome. Plato and the moderns have this in common. Modernity can be characterized as the search for clarity and distinctness: a beginning, an end, and order in the meantime. "Order" means, in this case, conformity to a single, founding principle, as in Hegel or Marx, or in twentieth century positivism. The modern source here is not only Descartes, as always, but also Luther, who bequeathed to the forces of Protestantism who were to remake much of the Western world (in the *spirit* of capitalism) a doctrine of the *clarity* of scripture. Ironically, this "clarity," an impossible (in my argot, counter-possible) and undesirable quality that is attached to a doctrine of "literal" reading, is the secular banner of the unknowingly secular movement known as Christian fundamentalism.

Origins are added on toward "the end," to justify an "end," a historical "outcome" (the "necessary" historical outcome). The origin is a supplement. Origins are always exclusionary. Are they any more dispensible, however, than metaphysics is? Derrida specifies the movement that allows "origins" to make their mark in *of Grammatology*, in terms of the trace of alterity that leaves a "pathway" in the text:

The trace is not only the disappearance of origin—within the discourse that we sustain and according to the path that we follow it means that the origin did not even disappear, that it was never constituted except reciprocally by a nonorigin, the trace, which thus becomes the origin of the origin. From then on, to wrench the concept of the trace from the classical scheme, which would derive it from a presence or from an originary nontrace and which would make of it an empirical mark, one must indeed speak of an originary trace or arche-trace. Yet we know that that concept destroys its name and that, if all begins with the trace, there is above all no originary trace. (1976, 61)

Most commentary has focused on the erasure of origins that is stressed in the last line of this passage. But, what are we to do with the injunction, "one must speak of an originary trace or arche-trace"?

Moses may have been an Egyptian, as Freud speculates, whatever that may mean (in terms of ethnicity or otherwise). At a certain point, however, Moses led the Jews across the Red Sea, and there was some sort of "origin" in this act—how could we "speak" otherwise? There may be different kinds of "speaking," however, in this case different ways of speaking of origins. Derrida does not think that it is possible to simply get "outside" of metaphysics. One aspect of this claim is that it is also not possible to dispense with talk of origins—for how else could we also speak of ruptures? Derrida's combined discussion of the originary trace that, on the one hand, destroys its name, and, on the other, must indeed be spoken of, is conceived in the context of a resistance within metaphysics. This resistance, which conceives of the writing of origins as impossible, is itself, in turn, a resistance against the counter-possible conception of originality. This is a praxis within the logic of the "concept" (in Hegel's sense), but to the limit of that logic, to the places where the other can be heard.[8]

Alfred North Whitehead, in *Process and Reality* (1978), conceived such an opening some time ago, in terms of a "language of verbs." Perhaps there was a time when this language was spoken by humans, or perhaps that myth may be useful for us as it was for Marx. A new kind of community might speak a language of verbs. In the meantime, new kinds of social movements might endeavor to displace the name, to prepare the way, to make room for the verb. These notions might serve as strategic principles, but their praxis must be further specified.

Recapitulations, thematizations, probes

The diverse threads of my exposition thus far will not conform to a single principle. But what use are they if they cannot be made to do some political work? Displacing names, proper names, and the discourse of the proper and property, these are archetypal Derridean activities. (They are preparations for "revolutions that as yet have no model"—but are they only "preparations"?)[9] To displace a name, to rename, is an empowering act. The sense of community I envision involves something further: renaming without closure. But, as already indicated, there are strategic questions involved here.

Derrida has it that a new politics requires a new language. But he has not said so much concerning the transition to this new language. My claim is that a language that is writerly, that does not privilege speech over writing, is foreshadowed by the progressive application of the "principle" of *differance*: the displacement of names, the activity of renaming, the deferral of any pretender to the throne of the final name. But, what is this "principle"? How can *differance* have or be a "principle" when it is purportedly not a concept? Just so: the principle must apply to itself also.

This displacement, this "revolution in the revolution," this "counter-finality," is the ally of impossibility against counter-possibility.

It would be extremely naive to think, however, that there is not always a power which would oppose the empowering gestures and strategies of displacement. Renaming is a dangerous task; renaming without closure, gesturing toward a language of verbs, is more dangerous still. Renaming necessarily challenges property. This is true even inside the academy, but the really difficult examples are found outside. (More and more, however, the imperialism that is outside the academy is the same imperialism that is inside—I refer to incursions of the military into the university, such that the function of the university is in no way merely "ideological"; see Derrida 1983a.)

The pursuit of interpretive praxis necessitates diversity, and vice-versa. That is, pursuing interpretation is not a gab-fest of pluralism, of the sort that we are especially used to in the United States, consisting in a few versions of the same thing, repeated ad nauseum. Renaming is not changing the channel. Interpretive praxis pursues writing as understood through many possible logics. The basis of writing is always external; therefore, writerly pursuits recognize and respect the other—for the trace of the other is what allows the Same to engage in recognition in the first place (indeed, *before* the first place).

In Chapter 3 I questioned the concept of autonomy as understood by Habermas. In the rest of this chapter I will further examine the notion of autonomy. In this examination we will also develop the notion of solidarity, which has already surfaced in various forms in the first and third chapters. One might say, with Hilary Putnam (1987), that language leaves us in solidarity in a common predicament. Another way to put this, in Davidsonian terms, is that language gives us a lot to talk about, a great deal to share, indeed the most important things, and in that sharing is a basic objectivity. Language gives us "us," and it would be quite difficult to imagine what "objectivity" or "solidarity" or "autonomy" means without this gift. But our solidarity is also our predicament: we can have an "objective" discussion of human ends, but we find no moral or political or metaphysical "calculus" in language or life—language/life, that is (see Martin 1990a). (Here we may begin to inscribe in this text, in more detail, the question of this "we." What if there were a society that did not need to be freed of the metaphysics of presence? To use such a society, perhaps an "Eastern" society, as an "example" or model would, however, itself be a return to presence, under the guise of "absence." This is precisely Derrida's point in the discussion of Chinese writing in *of Grammatology*.[10] And yet it would seem itself a kind of chauvinism to let the matter end there; more in due course). The solidarity of language/life yields a certain epistemological solidarity. This kind of talk, of course, is far afield from ordinary discussions of solidarity and its possibility in political life. But then, I did make some moves that are fairly typical, and rightly so, of social theory today: all life is "political life," and the life of politics consists in the available forms of discourse; therefore we should attempt to understand the workings of discourse in order to understand the intertwinings of life and politics. Habermas has been instrumental in setting these terms of debate, which I largely accept. My only divergence has been to argue that discourse works differently than Habermas thinks; accordingly, I attempt to draw the appropriate political conclusions. Habermas associates intentional theories of meaning with an autonomy that might give rise to solidarity under certain social conditions. I associate a Derridean understanding of language with a solidarity that awaits its more articulated political expression and which may, under certain conditions, give rise to autonomy.

One thing that should not be forgotten in this positioning of solidarity and autonomy that I argue for here, however, is that autonomy does indeed have an important role to play in the articulation of solidarity. It may even be argued, at least provisionally, that solidarity *must* await autonomy for its articulation; otherwise the dangers in the contemporary world are simply too great—especially the danger of an "iron cage" lined with microchips, where Weber and Adorno meet Foucault, Baudrillard, Marshall McLuhan, the MIT Media Lab, and William Gibson.[11]

The appropriate social conditions do exist, however, for the articulation of at least the discourse of autonomy in some parts of our planet. Like the solidarity I have thematized, this autonomy also awaits a more substantial expression. There can be no doubt, however, that it is this discourse, of autonomy, not that of solidarity, that is predominant in the West. (This is just as much the case for most political organizations, including the Polish one, that use the word "solidarity" in their names.)

This discourse of autonomy has been, undoubtedly, distorted and flattened, as Habermas claims (he also speaks, convincingly, of the "exhaustion of utopian energies"; see Habermas 1989). The flattening of the discourse *is virtually a flattening of autonomy itself*: people who do not know that they have rights, or people who speak of rights but without being able to articulate what it *means* for them to have rights, in a real sense do not have rights (if, that is, this absence of rights discourse is a general social condition). Incidentally, John Rawls, at least in his later work, depends on just this sort of claim. He is concerned about founding acts, constitutions, a continuous political discourse, and a vibrant political culture as necessary foundations for the exercise of basic rights (see Rawls, 1980, and R. Martin 1985).

The loss of these elements of modern, democratic society, however, is the inevitable outcome of a political discourse dominated by the notion of autonomy. There is a double-dialectic here. First, there is the actual trajectory of autonomy, which leads to the hollowing-out of autonomy. This is in itself a complex trajectory. The discourse of autonomy spurs the instantiation of autonomy, while the practice of autonomy leads to the impoverishment of the discourse of autonomy, which in turn leads to the fading and disappearance of the practice and its institutions. There are many liberals who, unlike Rawls, either have no sense of the possibility of autonomy's diremption (e.g., David Gauthier), or take no responsibility for it (by an analytic separation of capitalism and liberalism, e.g., Ronald Dworkin).[12] Rawls and Habermas at least grapple with the problem of anomie—the latter in great detail. The problem is that anomie derives from the predominance of the notion of autonomy itself.

Second, there is the dialectical argument that autonomy cannot save itself except by marshaling its inherent connection with solidarity—autonomy must give over its autonomy, thus it becomes provisional, in the same way that subjectivity does. In other words, autonomy cannot remain still or set up a "barricade"—there has to be a leap, to solidarity, or else autonomy itself will be lost. This is a dialectical argument of the sort offered by Mao—there is no holding still, ultimately. But why not? The answer to this question lies at the heart of the dispute between dialectic and *differance*—there is always an other, which we pursue, even unto the ends of the earth. *Differance* is what keeps the dialectical barriers of the Same from being erected permanently.

The notion of autonomy did some good work ("in its day"), and it is not something that society would do well to either dispense with or lose (contrary to certain Marxist orthodoxies that all the same depend on the notion of autonomy, whether they know it or not). That loss could occur, however, if a vibrant sense of rights continues to be replaced by mere interests (but perhaps I am romanticizing in thinking that such a sense has ever yet existed—I do not think that the answer to this question, however, affects what comes next).

Solidarity must save the day. But, what is meant, in more conventional terms, by "solidarity"? And what is *not* meant by it? Does solidarity necessarily depend on some kind of unity? Does solidarity preclude diversity? Can solidarity even entail diversity? Then, what is meant by "diversity"—does it preclude unity?

Consider the following examples.

Suppose we compare the critique of the present social order to the demolition of a building. In order to demolish the building, we need a demolition crew, consisting of different members, all with specialized tasks. Perhaps no one member understands fully all of the tasks involved. What is essential is that all crew members have as their goal the demolition of the building. This would be an example of solidarity that not only allows for, but even requires, diversity.

But the example only goes so far, and it has some troubling features. The idea that each crew member need not necessarily know how the others perform their tasks seems to duplicate the division of labor typical of capitalism. Perhaps the division in the example need not be oppressive, however. Certainly no crew member *in principle* has to know only his or her own task. And, the larger context of the division of labor in capitalism, in which workers do not even necessarily know to what *end* they work (something Adam Smith especially liked, though, in fairness, that was before workers were making nuclear weapons or working in factories that filled the air and water with carcinogens, etc.), is *necessarily* absent from this example.

The larger trouble is this: suppose our workers had to live in the building that they were planning to destroy. (The idea of destroying potential habitats in a wealthy country full of homeless people is not exactly comforting either.)

We live in this society, and we live in language. The latter certainly cannot be demolished and "replaced" in one blow. And society? But we have already questioned these distinctions, among "society," "language," and "life."

This is the well-known example of "Neurath's Boat."[13] The only way to rebuild a boat that one is at sea in, the example goes, is plank by plank. With the global interconnectedness of contemporary societies, it cannot be doubted that we are "at sea."

But, what is a "plank" in this analogy?

To extend the analogy, in recapitulation of the words that opened this study: what if an ever-increasing number of the planks in our boat are rotten and on the verge of falling apart?

Moreover: if we have to rebuild the boat, do we have to rebuild *this* boat?

Society is on the verge of losing the sense of community—but society is even on the verge of losing the sense of society. The discourse of autonomy collapses; a "rebuilt" discourse of autonomy cannot save it.

Not every form of solidarity entails diversity, and it is not clear that there has *ever* been a community that has valued diversity: these are the sorts of things that rightly frighten people about solidarity and community. No one wants to take a chance on rebuilding the boat into something that will probably be worse.[14]

Arguments concerning community and what I have called "postsecular socialism" could seem to issue in the proposal to "re-enchant" the world, according to a (by now) well-known dialectical schema, associated with German romantics such as Schiller and Hölderlin, and with certain twentieth century thinkers, especially theologians. Among these, perhaps the most interesting and relevant for our purposes is Franz Rosenzweig. His argument, in *The Star of Redemption*, is here characterized by Stephane Moses: "Originally the pagan world was an enchanted world; then science came and disenchanted the world; finally, man, by spreading revelation among the world, undertakes to make it sacred again" (Moses 1988, 188; see also Rosenzweig 1985, 220–22).

That Marx, in a way, also recapitulates this dialectic (and Engels even more forthrightly) is no secret.

Revolutions typically inscribe on their banners, "Everything Must Change!" Then, some revolutions take it that changing "everything" means a complete return to some originary state.

There has been talk for some time now of a "breakdown in language." George Steiner:

> There is a widespread intimation, though as yet only vaguely defined, of a certain exhaustion of verbal resources in modern civilization, of a brutalization and devaluation of the word in the mass-cultures and mass-politics of the age. (1982, 46)

But that is not the end of it: "Language seeks vengeance on those who cripple it" (ibid.; 31). (These words were written in the early and middle sixties.) The fate of language is not only the fate of life and society; more specifically it is the fate of values, memory, community, and history. The breakdown in the language of autonomy, one very special case in point, is the breakdown of autonomy itself. (In a moment we will turn to Descartes' attempt to ground autonomy while ignoring language.)

These schematic claims and examples depend on a certain logic, one that is well known especially in liberal political philosophy. But there is always another logic—to continually force this assertion is to struggle away from logical thought toward grammatological reading. This would be a reading that resists the flattening of discourse, and yet which at the same time is not simply attempting to restore some originary presence. The letter is what we have—what we have are some semantic resources; some forgotten but now and again "remembered" spirit will not revive the letter (nor is that the intention of this "memory" of spirit). The material of history is still to be read.

Reading diversifies, while at the same time it is always a communal, even if solitary, activity. The text is never read, finally, so we read on. Is this to say something different than, "The search for meaning is never concluded, finally, so we search on"? In the postmodern space of flattened discourses, however, the question becomes, "Why search for what will not be found?", "There is no meaning," etc. Sartre was closer to the mark with his "ethics and art of the finite" than is this postmodern cynicism.

But these are also grammatological questions, questions of language in history and history in language. These are neither mere logical questions, to be examined through endless Wittgensteinian variations on Neurath's boat,[15] nor mere invocations to return to the origin.

In the language of Habermas, this point beyond caring cancels the legitimation crisis. Are we at that point? This may be the quintessential postmodern question. This is not primarily a question of knowledge or validity claims.

Reading solidarity in the discourse of autonomy

There can be no pretense of speaking a new language today or tomorrow.[16] Our strategy, therefore, is one of displacement. The language of modern, secular society has to be rewritten from the inside. As Derrida likes to say, "from a *certain* inside." This does not mean that larger forms of displacement are not possible—sometimes it is possible to replace an entire wall rather than a single brick (but sometimes it is absolutely necessary to replace a single brick); indeed, sometimes there is no choice but to replace the entire wall in one movement (the necessity of which is something that seems incomprehensible to conservatives of the Edmund Burke type).[17] Much of Derrida's work can be seen as the rewriting of the Western philosophical canon from the inside out, in order to let the other speak. This is the essence of deconstruction.[18] A similar strategy can be applied to, or rather unfolded from within, the canon of modern political thought. I have already discussed this strategy with regard to the philosophy of the subject in Hegel and Marx. Their philosophies might be taken as combining autonomous subjects into a community of sorts, a gemeinschaftliche Gesellschaft. (In Hegel, of course, it is only at the level of the nation that a subject comes into being that can play a role in the creation of the world community; the nation is the true, modern "individual.")[19]

In a way, this characterization of Marx's vision, especially, makes him more bourgeois than John Locke or Thomas Jefferson. For they perhaps had a more communitarian understanding of property and self. But that is just to say that they had a more agrarian understanding (e.g., see Matthews 1984). This analysis is again haunted by the specter of return, which must not be fully succumbed to: pre-industrial/post-industrial. The simple strategy would be to displace the first term: agrarian society is *not* "pre-industrial"; it does not merely exhibit values that then come to fruition during the period of industrialization (on the contrary).

The notion of rights, especially, that formed during this period, necessarily entailed the idea that "I" cannot merely struggle for "my rights." The latter mean nothing, as rights, if I only struggle for my own. This is mere "interest," and even "self-interest" is meaningless, in this (anti-)context, for I have jettisoned the basis for autonomy—though I must have had this basis in the first place in order to jettison it. (The problem, then, with political philosophy based in "self-interest" is not only with the meaning of "interest," but at least as much with the meaning of "self.") Even in earlier formulations of autonomy, to be self-governing meant to take part in a political community. To be concerned with property meant to be in contact with others, with other people and, more significantly, the land.

Property consisted, in this scheme of things, in what was proper to a person by virtue of the fact that he or she had mixed labor with some part of nature (though this activity was defined, and continues to be defined, in a patriarchal way, a point to which we will return). In order to be autonomous, one had to externalize oneself: thus the kernel of solidarity in autonomy. But this kernel in fact has a dual nature. On the one hand, as I just mentioned, the autonomous person goes outside of him- or herself, in political discourse and in labor, the source of property. Thus there is a self-actualizing principle of solidarity in autonomy. But on the other hand there are the margins of autonomy, which also beckon toward solidarity. In this case, however, autonomy seems to contain a built-in principle of resistance to the other. Autonomy sets up some walls.

The margins of autonomy are of two broad, interrelated types.

First, there is the temporal margin of autonomy. That is, the discourse of autonomy arises out of a pre-secular community (but then, medieval European society was not any more "pre-secular" than it was "pre-industrial")—claims of autonomy arose in the midst of community and solidarity. That this community could no longer function in many ways is something that cannot be ignored, but this is not my focus now. The newly-emerging secular society could just as well be called "post-communal"; accordingly, there is a trace of community in secular society. It is indeed a kind of *energy* or *enchantment*, but communitarian social theorists, and here Marx is especially *not* excluded, have repeatedly made the mistake of equating this energy with *spirit*. (This is to assume what it is perhaps not right to assume, namely, that Marx is indeed a "communitarian" thinker. The arguments of G. A. Cohen on this point are telling if not completely compelling.)[20] For example, Marx's notion that the proletariat takes its poetry from the future is a good example of the kind of dialectical leap that not only moves from quantity to quality (from letter to spirit), it cancels the very material that made this leap possible. In practice this cancellation has had the consequence of further undermining the materialization of socially-transformative possibilities; debates around Marxist aesthetics, and not just in academic circles but also in the midst of broader revolutionary initiatives (e.g., the "Proletcult" debate in the Soviet Union of the 1920s), bear this out about as well as anything.[21] To put it bluntly, Marxism does not know what to do with tradition, thereby leaving this deeply important *matter* (in all senses) to be dealt with in a conservative way. Here the term "conservative" does not connote the cultural, communal continuity that is the work and aim of the conservationist. The spirit that conservatives harken back to and Marxists call forth from the future is conspicuously absent today. This absence, or exhaustion ("our current tiredness") of spirit makes it difficult for those of us who still seek the energy of spirit to understand that earlier secular theorists of community (e.g., Locke, Jefferson, Rousseau—the fact that these thinkers tried to understand community in secular terms is in fact what is at issue here) depended on this myth of spirit as a regulator of the other forces that were being set loose by secularization, especially the market.

For illustration on this point, we might inquire about the invocation of "fraternity" in the French Revolution. Was this only, as some Marxists say, a call to brotherhood in the context of the market? Undoubtedly there was always a close relationship between the democratic and the capitalist aspects of secular society, even to the point where it can be plausibly argued that at least *this* democracy will not escape the distortions impressed upon and within it by capitalism (see Bowles and Gintis 1987). Perhaps brotherhood and the market are two sides of the same coin (though it is hard to imagine the invocation of universal brotherhood in, say, Beethoven's Ninth Symphony, as simply a "reflection" of emerging capitalist social relations). The issue is still more complex.

Consider the gendered, patriarchal form of democracy and autonomy that arises in the secular period, perhaps most easily seen in the denial of the existence of women's labor (including, most obviously, the labor in childbirth).[22] This patriarchy is the remnant of a community that predates capitalism and that has adapted itself to capitalism. This adaptation works both ways, however, something that feminist historical research has convincingly argued against orthodox Marxism (e.g., see Delphy 1977, and Hartsock 1985). "Fraternity," in the sense of the term put forward in the French Revolution, is both inseparable from this ancient patriarchy and at the same time representative of the trace of a communal life-form in which values are not merely the expression of individual interests. Thus "fraternity" gives some sense of community in emerging secular society, but at the same time it does not provide a model for the rethought community that this analysis is attempting to imagine. Indeed, as Derrida (1988b, 642–44) argues in "The Politics of Friendship," this form of fraternal community is based upon the exclusion of the very idea that women could form communities or even participate in friendship. In a moment we will turn to the idea that it is precisely in this margin where the possibilities for community are to be found. (We should not fail to mark at this point, however, the recent feminist work that has established this margin as precisely temporal. I refer to recent research concerning the status of women in medieval society—what was until recently called the "dark ages," in part out of patriarchal motivation.)[23]

We should experiment however, by asking why fraternity does not provide a model for rethought community. It is not enough, after all, to argue simply that the idea of *extending* fraternity to include sisterhood is merely a secular idea, the further point along the path of bourgeois society at which the discourse of rights becomes more inclusive (no thanks to fraternity itself, however). After all, if fraternity represents in some respects the trace of community in society, and if this trace is then articulated in such a way as to give community a better prospect for re-emergence, then what is the problem? Not only some Rawlsian liberals but, more significantly, liberal feminists, take the possibility of such an articulation as the cornerstone of their theorizing and activism.[24]

Indeed, there would be no problem, if fraternity were capable of giving rise to a diverse community (which notion has yet to be defined, but we are laying the groundwork). Patriarchy has always provided for a kind of community, and indeed it is the kind of community held out as a prospect to men especially in desperate times (see Theweleit 1987). How might we define this community in terms of the philosophical framework set out thus far? Again, to recapitulate, two connections stand out. First, what real and new possibilities would be opened by rehearsing, once again and after so many repetitions, the discourse of patriarchy, as though it could be expanded? How would this discourse call the subject out, to a recognition and respect for the other? In this regard, patriarchy is a discourse of counter-possibility, and not only because of its exhaustion (which is real enough)—rather, also, because patriarchy only cares to re-establish its own subjectivity again and again. Furthermore, as Derrida (1988b, 638–40) argues in the essay on friendship, this fraternity cannot articulate the dimension of responsi-bility that is essential for recognition of the other. Second, and not unrelated to this first point, the discourse of the subject has itself always been patriarchal (as Luce Irigaray claims) and accordingly has left its mark on the discourse of autonomy. We will return to this question in the second section following this one.

Note that there is nothing about the analysis presented thus far that shows that all forms of "community" are good, for this is not something that can be shown. "Community" sounds like a nice, fuzzy, user-friendly word, which is of course why the media and politicians often use it to describe the military (the "defense community"), or secret police (the "intelligence community"), etc. I use the example of patriarchal fraternity in order to confront this issue head-on. Communities allow people to create shared meanings, values, and ways of life, but the fact of this sharing does not, in and of itself, tell us whether what is shared is any good or not (a further analysis of what it means to "share" or "commune," however, will give some useful indications). On my model, it still has to be admitted that the Ku Klux Klan, neo-Nazis, etc., are "communities" of a sort. There is still some way to go in showing why there is another sense of community that is truly postsecular.

And yet, to bring this pursuit of the temporal margins of autonomy to a provisional conclusion, not every trace of some pre-existing community is so marked by counter-possibility. Some of these traces might indeed be resources for the reinvention of community. In the previous example the substance of the other margin of autonomy has already been alluded to.

Second, then, there are marginal subjects. These are subjects that, in their assertions of "autonomy," under present conditions, must transcend autonomy and by their positionality in the social matrix must draw a line toward solidarity.

Others at the well

Marginal subjects are impossible. They do not exist. But it is very important to specify the matrix in which these non-existent subjects fail to appear. We are often reminded that the "universal" discourse of the "rights of man" promulgated by Enlightenment thinkers and revolutionaries was never so universal as all that. Out of this recognition two strategies have emerged, one based on inclusion, the other on difference and diversity. In order to make the case for the second strategy, it is necessary to point out the fatal flaw in the first.

The universalism of the Enlightenment was indeed universal, if one looks at the matter in the following way. Everyone who conforms to a certain universal model can participate in the universal rights of man. No one is excluded in principle from conforming to this model. What more could anyone ask? It is not the fault of the champions of this universalism that so many people (bodies?) fall into spaces between the lines of universalism, because of gender, color, nationality, sexual orientation, religion, etc. In other words, how can universalism do any better? (It is not unlike the problem of the canon.) Inclusionism works according to this same logic. In actuality it should be called "exclusionism."

But we have yet to specify how the unity in community is different and better than that in Enlightenment universalism. The answer to this question, however, is that by and large community is *not* better than universalism on this score (though it may be better on other points that have some sort of compensating effect). *Only* a diverse community presents a real alternative to secular society.

There is a great deal of talk about community these days. Most of this talk is trapped in a secular logic. Most of the rest of this talk is framed by the logic of return, restoration, and organicism. A well-known example would be Alisdair MacIntyre's recent work. As William Corlett (1989, 47–63) puts it, MacIntyre wants to return to a previous Paris, that of Aquinas. There is a troubling, even terrifying, and frankly offensive logic to his proposals. Like other people who talk about community, MacIntyre is after a forthright acceptance of the contextual basis for creating meaning in our lives. I am in favor of that too, though in a different way: the context is never *finally* set. Most communitarians will not accept this aspect of the context problem and its implications (they may talk in some way about community being "open-ended," but usually in some rather unspecified and ungrounded way). In practical terms, the problem with MacIntyre's proposals can be put bluntly: we have already heard too much from those whose empire MacIntyre seeks to restore. Hasn't the One True Church already had its day in the sun? I don't mean to sound so nasty about this, and I say this with all due respect for those progressive and radical Catholics who themselves fight the logic of exclusion (the wrath of which they thereby incur). Of course it is not a question of "Catholics"—because there is certainly a world of difference between Pope John Paul II and William F. Buckley on the one side, and Leonardo Boff, Camillo Torres, Johannes B. Metz, and Gustavo Gutierrez on the other (see Hennelly 1990). The point is simply that some forms of community, precisely those forms that are pre-secular, exact too high a price. The unfortunate thing is that the logic of secularism may force society in that direction.[25]

MacIntyre (1984, 1988) undoubtedly offers a critique of the problems of modernity that is subtle and in many respects true. His proposals, however, represent a somewhat desperate clutching for some unifying force, *any* unifying force (not that he has arrived at the One True Church by accident, of course). This turn places him in the company, as Corlett argues, of other contemporary (Leo) Straussians, whose sub-Nietzschean cures are worse than the disease.

It is time, instead, to give the other a turn—or, better, it is time to turn to the other. Like some Marxists and other radicals, I am proposing a two-stage strategy, with the proviso that the second stage, diverse community, is not the "final" stage—because the point is to continually

postpone finality. Displacement is the transition to an age of displacement and postponement: the "Post-Age" (Gregory Ulmer).

There are some general prescriptions or steps for turning to the
other, for this transitional movement. The key problem is developing a
strategy that creates a space in which the other can speak. The meaning
of this Derridean prescription is itself complex. Significantly, this strategy differs from major tenets of Marxism *and* "post-Marxism." Marxist
strategies often depend on speaking *for* the other (Sartre's analysis of the
way that the Soviet Union degenerated, under Stalin, into a "dictatorship *for* the proletariat" is very important here),[26] even in the case of the
"mass line" (Mao). Some post-Marxist strategies, notably some influenced by Foucault, reacting negatively to the presumptions involved in
speaking for the other, put forward the idea that no one must speak for
any group other than his or her own (see, e.g., Poster 1984). In particular,
the idea is that intellectuals, "organic" or otherwise, must not attempt to
speak for the proletariat or "the oppressed" more generally. At most,
this line of argument goes, intellectuals may only speak for themselves.
(I wish to bracket two major concerns: 1)how much this is actually a
Foucauldian strategy; 2) the fact that among intellectuals there are
indeed some—not enough!—women, people of color, people of
working-class origins, etc.)

I must admit no small measure of sympathy for at least the
motivation of this line of reasoning. When Marx said that "the proletariat must emancipate itself, no one must try to do this for them," he
enunciated an important principle, the betrayal of which (especially by
Stalin) has had grievous consequences. Marx's proviso might well be
extended to the semantic and semiotic resources of the margins of
history. That is, there is a material difference between letting the
proletariat speak its emancipation and attempting to speak it for them.

But that difference is not always so easily figured: it all turns on the
words, "letting" or "to let," etc. What does it mean to "*let* the other
speak"? Is it a question of keeping silent? That is part of the truth, if
understood strategically.[27] But it is important that this silence be defined
and understood, because it is an *active* silence. In the discourse of
Enlightenment universalism, marginal subjects do not exist, therefore
they cannot speak. But these subjects cannot speak because they do not
exist, and therefore their voices cannot be heard. "Marginal subjects" is
an oxymoron, a name for the nameless—but also perhaps for the yet-to-
be-named. The important thing here is that "letting the other speak"
does not exactly mean "letting marginal subjects speak"—for these
subjects do not exist.

"Now, wait a minute!", any right-thinking interlocutor should feel entitled to say—"Are you saying that down through the history of Western civilization there have not been those who have been pressed into the margins of patriarchy, the dominant economic order, the "West," Christianity, etc?" In other words, what about the non-male, the non-European, the non-Christian, etc.?

This is an instance of the question of the "inside" and "outside" of history, which Derrida analyzes under the rubric of "the writing lesson" in *of Grammatology*. Derrida is concerned with Claude Levi-Strauss's argument that there are cultures without writing, which are therefore "without history." The introduction of writing into such cultures, a moment in which "a passage was effected from a stage where nothing had sense to another where everything did," initiates a turn from a Rousseauian state of nature to the exploitation of man by man. As Levi-Strauss puts it, "the primary function of writing, as a means of communication, is to facilitate the enslavement of other human beings." Derrida's analysis of this argument is aimed at showing that there never was such a "moment" in which writing is "introduced," or in which writing has its origin. Such a conceptualization of writing (or of "exploitation") is, for Derrida, part and parcel of the dream of origins that is an essential part of the metaphysics of presence (Derrida calls Levi-Strauss's story of the writing lesson the best example of such a metaphysics).[28]

I raise this question, the analysis of which by Derrida is well known, simply as a prelude to raising the further question: Is there an outside of history for human subjects any more than there is an outside of Being for beings? And what is otherwise than being? This is a senseless question, as any positivist will tell you. For there is no sense to the copula in this question. The world is the world.[29]

Not everything always works according to economies of scale—which is one reason why Nietzsche and Freud are just as important in coming to grips with the postmodern universe of discourse as Marx. That is, there is a mixture of economies at work, all of which owe something to the three just named (as in the case with every one of the postmodern vignettes set out in Chapter 2), and it is not clear that a single logic of expenditure and return governs all economies. The semantic resources of language and the alterity that marks these resources are as dependent on recognition as they are on work. Or: recognition and "letting" must somehow enter into circulation with our other activities of value-creation (i.e., work). But this is a dangerous supplement: "letting" displaces, transforms, transfigures. Following Derrida's (1978, 251–77) analysis of Bataille's "general economy," in which Hegel is "put out of work," Jean-Luc Nancy (1986, esp.175–98) speaks of the *desoeuvrement* of community. (Maurice Blanchot [1988] has also contributed to this discussion.) I simply wish to remark on the role that "letting" plays in unraveling (a possible translation of *desoeuvrement*) the economy of the Same. (". . . if the other is precisely what is not invented, the initiative or deconstructive inventiveness can consist only in opening, in uncloseting, destabilizing foreclusionary structures so as to allow for the passage toward the other." Counterpose "counter-finality" to "foreclusionary structures.")

We all, in some sense, drink from the same well. The qualifier, paradoxically, is not so much concerned with this "well"—which is indeed language, the resource that allows us, *lets* us, be human—rather, with the "we all." For who is at the well? Do we see the woman, the Black, the Jew? "As such"? We like to say that "of course we do, because we are all in the same community." But most of us are not in any community at all. (Then again, who is the "we" who claims this?)

All that I have been pressing toward is the idea that the semantics of community may still be here, in the form of writing in the margins, the letter smothered by the spirit. This way of identifying the margins of history has as part of its motivation the avoidance of Enlightenment-style inclusionism—"we have been autonomous, now you can be too." I distrust this form of "recognition," for it simply attempts a displacement that will not serve well in the long run and perhaps not so well in the short run (though I find it incumbent on my theory not to ignore the short run, which is why I am postponing the question of community as such and working through the transitional strategy of displacement). That is, the self-narrowing, counter-possible discourse of autonomy is itself attempting to keep alive its counter-possibility by finding new subjects. (The analogy to a capitalism that keeps itself alive by adopting certain "socialist" measures is not inappropriate here.) That it "finds" these new subjects by in a sense creating them, by giving names to the nameless, is part of the ingeniousness of the strategy. My counter-proposal is to keep alive the impossibility of marginal subjects.

Do you have your "own name"—do you have autonomy—if that name is granted according to a singular logic? This ownership of the name seems at best, as Derrida and de Man (e.g., "Autobiography as De-Facement" 1984) have argued, a legal fiction, at worst a trap, a prison. In the classical discourse, especially of Locke, my "autonomy" is similar to a deed to myself that God has given me *on loan*. Without God as guarantor, the self-imposed prison of autonomy generates a kind of "liberal totalitarianism."[30] No other will ever speak by the workings of that logic, except in the case of its deconstruction. We will turn to the possibility of this deconstruction in the next section.

Some particular points of strategy can be summarized.

1) No other can speak in the language of the Same. The enforce-
ment of this language (sometimes by straightforwardly authoritarian,
even fascistic measures, i.e., "English only" laws, sometimes by what
Marcuse called "repressive tolerance") is a way of keeping the other
silent—and of admitting the possibility (in fact the counter-possibility)
of the other only if the other submits to the logic of the Same. "Letting
the other speak" therefore means actively resisting the predominance of
the Same and its identity-logic (Adorno). This also means resisting
translation in the very name of that "tower of Babel" which "exhibits an
incompletion, the impossibility of finishing, of totalizing, of saturating,
of completing something on the order of edification, architectural
construction, system and architectonics" (Derrida 1985b, 165).

   2) No language of the Same is truly solid or monolithic; the
language of the Same, however, attempts to destroy its own semantic
resources in the name of sameness, in the name of the Name. As long as
language is language, there are resources that will not be depleted. (But,
to repeat something said in the first chapter, this is tantamount, in the
scheme of things set out here, to saying, "Where there's life there's
hope," but there is no guarantee that there will be life.) Language
replenishes itself in working around and through its aporias, its gaps. A
general strategy of displacement, with the aim of letting the other speak,
seeks to recognize these gaps and open them further. This recognition
could take the form of historical scholarship—I think of Gilbert and
Gubar's *The Madwoman in the Attic* (1979) as exemplary here, as well as
more theoretical work that helps us understand the material nature of
aporia and its possibilities (e.g., Paul de Man)—but it could also take
other forms, all of them active forms of letting.

   3) To pursue this point in a slightly different direction, there is the
question of a *clearing*. What happens to the voice of the other when it
must struggle to be heard in the context (or anti-context) of the
deafening roar of the same? A space must be opened up, but not just any
space. Heidegger is the obvious reference here (some scholars even
claim that the idea of the clearing is Heidegger's one great, original
idea). That being the case, I prefer to consider Houston Baker's notion of
a "sounding field." Baker, a critical theorist whose main interest is Afro-
American literature, is of course not explicitly concerned to supplement
or corroborate Heidegger. Instead, Baker is after a development of
Stephen Henderson's notion of the "Soul Field": "the complex galaxy of
personal, social, institutional, historical, religious, and mythical meanings that affect everything we say or do as Black people sharing a
common heritage" (Baker 1984, 79). This is a notion not at all points
radically at odds with Heidegger, but there is a wealth of human feeling

and experience in the "Soul Field" that is almost completely lacking in Heidegger (it is no news that Heidegger didn't have "soul"). Baker's modification is to open the semantic dimensions of the Soul Field—he plays a role here analgous to Derrida's relation to Heidegger. There is another similarity to Derrida: Baker is also concerned with "*Geschlecht,*" in this case with the "Blackness of Blackness". In particular, Baker traces out the appearance of a certain "vernacular," which all the same advances masked (curiously enough, Descartes' motto—"I advance masked"), in the form of minstrelsy: "to ensure survival, to operate changes, to acquire necessary resources for continuance, and to cure a sick world" (Baker 1987, 47). Baker's insistence on *soundings* of Afro-American culture, *vernacular* expressions, is not a gesture toward essentialism or an uncomplicated ("simple," in the philosophical sense of a homogenous substantiality) autonomy that sets itself apart from community. On the contrary. Baker's favorite instance of a vernacular sounding in the Soul Field is the blues:

> . . . Afro-American culture is a complex, reflexive enterprise which finds its proper figuration in blues conceived as a matrix. A matrix is a womb, a network, fossil-bearing rock, a rocky trace of a gemstone's removal, a principal metal in an alloy, a mat or plate for producing print or photograph records. The matrix is a point of ceaseless input and output, a web of intersecting, crisscrossing impulses always in productive transit. American blues constitute such a vibrant network. They are what Jacques Derrida might describe as the "always already" of Afro-American culture. They are the multiplex, enabling *script* in which Afro-American cultural discourse is inscribed. (1984, 3–4)

Baker is very close here to the situated and problematized form of autonomy that we will explore in the next section under the rubric of positionality. The further importance of the sounding field for present purposes is that it demonstrates well the fact that a shift away from simple autonomy, which no Afro-American is privileged to claim, does not in the least bit detract from the specificity of the experience of a people, a community in the margins. Indeed, this shift is necessary in order that a clearing can be created in which the other can speak.

4) If we promise not to leave aside the specificity that Baker reminds us of, the productive transit at the crossings, the railroad crossings that inspire blues people (Amiri Baraka) from Robert Johnson to Muddy Waters to Cecil Taylor to Koko Taylor (there is indeed a specificity in marking the names, which, Derrida reminds us, resist and

even confound translation), perhaps we may also still move to a more general approach to the question of autonomy. We typically take the word "autonomy" to refer to a principle of self-governance. That is a difficult principle to ground. Classical theorists of autonomy, from Locke to Kant, ultimately appeal to a principle of solidarity as a ground. None of us invents our "reasons," after all, except in light of some Principle of Reason, or (to be less grandiose about it) logic, that is generally independent of our individual thought-processes. The shift from autonomy to mere interests and individuality, typical of late-modern and postmodern societies, finds its precursor in Hobbes, who is enjoying great popularity among some liberal political philosophers of late. But Hobbes too has his other side, one that makes him more a precursor of Nietzsche. This other side is not well-represented by contemporary Hobbesians. Be that as it may, the point is that an autonomy which has become mere interest has destroyed itself in order to save itself (the reference to U.S. "strategy" in Vietnam is intentional). But there is an additional question of the subject involved with autonomy. To be autonomous means both to give the law and the *name* unto oneself. Unless we can freeze our "selves" for eternity, none of us can name ourselves. The inclination to even want to is an effect of counter-possibility, a striving toward finality and presence. None of us decides on our own name, much less our own "vocabulary" (contrary to Rorty, 1989). To have a name is to have a place in discourse, and none of us can create that place on our own (although the very idea of the "name" is a pretense toward this self-designated place). Why do we feel it necessary to think that we can both name ourselves and have that name for eternity? These are dangerous, counter-possible impulses, with dangerous consequences. (People die for these impulses, and kill for them as well.) Therefore, what is needed is a politics that does not *fundamentally* rely on a notion or theory of the subject.

    5) There has emerged, in the past twenty years especially, an array of new social movements based in part on the idea of naming marginal subjects. Such movements have one foot in the present, in a notion of inclusive autonomy, and one in the future, in their emphasis on the new and the marginalized. For sure, transitional politics must necessarily have this orientation. Perhaps it would be helpful to have a third foot in the past (or a foot in the past rather than in the "present"), in the sense that whatever depth there is in the present can only be fathomed through an insistence on history and memory. Capitalism is a "presentist" system and ideology, both in its economics and its notion of autonomy. The opposition between "conservatives" (and neo-conservatives) and radicals should be deconstructed in part by the mere fact that those

identified with conservatism generally could not give a damn about history or "the past," or even tradition (except in the Burkean sense of blind adherence). Transitional political strategies, however, must pay close attention to their movement and direction, or else they degenerate into lame reformism and are recuperated by the metaphysics of presence. The key question is whether a philosophy of the new social movements can be systematically articulated that avoids falling into an Enlightenment philosophy of the subject without planting both (or all three) feet in a future with no material or ideological connection with the present. In other words, other textual connections must be articulated that allow us to write a fundamental dependence on the philosophy of autonomy and the subject out of the narratives of postmodern society.

6) Finally, then, there is the question of destination. A transitional politics is worthless without some sense of what the transition is to. And yet, I have associated the notions of "destiny" or historical "outcome" with counter-possibility. The sense of impossibility developed in this study, the work of alterity in language, and the question of diversity are all factors that militate against any standard notion of political destination.

This is also, certainly, a remark about historical self-consciousness, which is displaced in the same movement that displaces the autonomous name. Where does this leave the interrelated questions of a diverse community and the transition there? I will attempt to answer this question by developing themes four and five in the final three parts of this chapter, while devoting the final chapter to the sixth theme.

Sisterhood: from autonomy to positionality

A large part of feminist theory is concerned with the question of the subject. In some respects, feminism has been a form of deconstruction *avant la lettre* in raising the notion of a matrix of positionality. Feminist arguments about the subject rarely, if ever, simply leave the subject shattered and abandoned as some poststructuralist theories do. Rather, feminist analyses typically reconstitute subjectivity, but in a conditional sense that we will specify further. (There is an "unmaking and making," as Gayatri Spivak (in 1987) puts it in a provocative article on Virginia Woolf; see also Martin 1989a.) This reconstitution might be best understood under two imperatives that exist in a contentious and troubling relationship with one another.

First, feminism does not only critique the notion of a unified self, it moves the question to a different terrain. It is no longer simply a matter of "who" you are; rather it is a question of *positionality*. Perhaps *"Where are you?"* would be the more pertinent question under this rubric—and, Where are you going?/What is happening at this moveable site? Still more to the point, it is also a question of place in the sense of "neighborhood," one's *surroundings*, one's possibility of community (a possibility that is made extremely difficult in the neighborhood of postmodernity), one's possibility of being "at home." The first imperative, therefore, of a non-essentialistic politics is the move toward positionality. In moving from subjectivity to positionality, feminism prepares the ground for a second imperative.

That is, as an explicitly political discourse and movement, feminism must have access to some form of social agency. A new form of agency becomes necessary not only, or mainly, in light of poststructuralist criticisms of the traditional conception of the self-conscious subject, though these criticisms are certainly a motivation toward reconceiving agency. More significant, however, is the actual decomposition of autonomy and the poverty of the inclusionary model.

Without an intellectually defensible, politically powerful alternative, the traditional conception of subjectivity will hold its ground—it is not simply a "conception," after all, but a form of life that is deeply insinuated into the fabric of modern and postmodern society. Therefore, much more needs to be said about positionality and its challenge to subjectivity. I propose to move this agenda through three closely-related problematics: 1) a further articulation of the question of positionality; 2) an examination of a founding moment of modern, Western subjectivity and a feminist deconstruction that was contemporaneous with that moment; 3) a discussion of different kinds of deconstructions of the subject and their political import.

We begin with a consideration of the perils of positionality. What does it mean to be a girl or a boy or a woman or a man? These finally become fully-legitimated questions once the terrain is shifted from subjectivity to positionality. Not that their legitimacy has never been a matter of self-assertion before—on the contrary. Rather, the conditionality of these terms has finally come home to roost as a displacement of selfhood. However, while subjectivity has its pitfalls, so does its displacement/replacement by positionality. If the foremost problem with subjectivity is its unreflective claim to self-assertion (i.e., autonomy), a claim that intends to subvert all mediations of gender, language, history, etc., the most troubling aspect of positionality is that it tends to give way entirely to "other-assertion." That is, as Spivak has suggested, one's subject position is something that is always designated by others.[31] This may be even more true than Professor Spivak realizes; that is, there is the whole dimension of the relation of *others*, writ small, to the Other, i.e., alterity. This is the surrounding framework of the particular analysis we are pursuing here, the positioning of positionality that follows from the context problem. And yet it is the particular that politically enables the analysis of positionality (recall that I have taken a vow to attend to this particularity).

My reading of the question of positionality is that it is a matter of the threads (lines) of the fabric (matrix) of social relations. One is reminded, too, of Lyotard's (1984) figure of the self as a "nodal point" of criss-crossing media. Because the others who are designating a position for me are also themselves placed by others, and because the media of the matrix in which "I" form an always moving line are multi-dimensional, "my position" is never a settled question. Quite the opposite, it can be a most *unsettling* question (one of "opening, uncloseting, destabilizing foreclusionary structures"). For that reason, however, the notion of positionality is essential for a transformative politics, assuming that politics is about unsettling some things.

Consider the question of "re-reading as a woman" that has in recent years served as a strategically important model in academia. This question would seem to have everything to do with positionality, and yet we have to be very careful, *politically careful and responsible*, with this slippery notion. "The educator must himself be educated." One very significant value of recent feminist research, essentially related to the problematics of positionality in its entirety, is that it questions the position of the theorist her- or himself. Especially the latter, the educator *himself*. Let us be honest, then: "re-reading as a woman" is not something that I, a "male" theorist, can rightfully and responsibly claim to be able to do (the moral and political resonances of the term are intended).[32] And yet, one very important upshot of the idea of positionality is that the educator himself can indeed be "educated," by being positioned differently. But this cannot be a question of "positioning myself," or of my "decision" to "re-read as a woman."[33]

There are two important and obvious reference points here: Derrida's *Spurs: Nietzsche's Styles*,[34] and the question of "men in feminism." In the former case the criticism has ranged from Gayatri Spivak's mostly friendly critique ("Displacement and the Discourse of Woman," 1983) to sharp denunciations, in terms of what Kelly Oliver (1988) calls "the poststructuralist attempt to do away with women." Spivak's criticism focuses on the fact that a philosophical concept of "woman," which is then deployed as a figure of *differance*, has nothing of the experience of *women*. As Diana Fuss puts it, "... positing woman as a figure of displacement risks, in its effects, continually displacing real material women" (1989, 14). Fuss does an excellent job of setting out both the possibilities and dangers of positionality:

> For a male subject to speak as a woman can be radically de-essentializing; the transgression suggests that "woman" is a social space which any sexed subject can fill. But because Derrida never specifies *which* woman he speaks as (a French bourgeois woman, an Anglo-American lesbian, and so on), the strategy to speak as a woman is simultaneously re-essentializing. The risk lies in the difficult negotiation between these apparently contradictory effects.[35]

Exactly so: the possibilities and the dangers are not finally separable. Nor are they, as Fuss recognizes, avoidable.

Barbara Johnson (1987, 2) has a neat way of summing this question up with specific reference to Derrida's "position": positioning oneself *philosophically* as a woman (as Derrida claims for Nietzsche and perhaps for himself) is not at all the same thing as being *politically* positioned as a woman. To put it bluntly, just because a male philosopher has "positioned himself as a woman" does not mean, for example, that he has to worry about being sexually assaulted if he walks across town or campus at night.

But then, this is not a limitation on the concept of positionality, if we take it that subject position is always designated externally. Undoubtedly the distinction between "philosophical" and "'political" positions deconstructs itself (a fact of which Johnson is certainly aware), but it is a question, as Fuss maintains, of a difficult negotiation, or strategy.

And yet none of these perils of positionality redeem the traditional view of the subject, to which we now turn in one of its founding moments. I previously argued that the crux of the debate between Derrida and Foucault on the *cogito* was the question not of invention, but rather of recognition, of the replacement of God by the sovereign human subject. This replacement "begins" with Luther as much as with Descartes. But then, it also "begins" with Augustine's "invention" of himself in autobiography. There is always a time before the "beginning," but there are also moments when the Red Sea is crossed and at least something "new" is recognized. Such is the case with the Cartesian *cogito*.

This passage from divine to human sovereignty repeats one of the essential gestures of Western metaphysics, the reduction of body to mind. It is a matter of utmost necessity, in the ancient and the modern reductions, that there be no remainder. This elimination of matter from the economy of spirit is just as much at work in California body cults, which are, in the final analysis, cults of personality and accumulation to a center that is not so much absent as it is filmic or televisual— Baudrillard's "screen."

Let us attend, albeit schematically, to the earlier motion of this reduction of body to mind. For Plato there is a hierarchy of form over content such that the latter is considered merely mimetic and therefore secondary and dispensable. In this telling of the mind/body story, the body has no role in demonstrating the powers of mind. With Descartes things are different: though self-assertion is an act of mind, the internal mechanism of this assertion is itself a mimesis of the body. Specifically, Descartes employs the suggestive devices of the "mind's eye" and the "inner light." An enduring image from the days of Descartes (and Locke) is that of a little person in the mind (the homunculus), sitting before a screen on which is displayed images from the external world (or memory, imagination, etc.). This internal body is not recognized as internalized, however: the mind's eye is taken to be prior to the physical apparatus of sight. At the same time, there is the hierarchy of spirit, inner light, and eye. The first two terms define man's essential being and his essential oneness with the being and activity of the heavenly father (hence the male "generic" term here).

This chain of metaphors so fundamental to modern epistemology has been criticized in recent years from various perspectives, including feminism.[36] In the *innermost* chapter of *Speculum of the Other Woman*, ". . . And If, Taking the Eye of a Man Recently Dead, . . .", Luce Irigaray (1985a) pursues the matter of Descartes' (dis)embodiment. Of the many critiques of Descartes offered by feminist thinkers, Irigaray's is important here specifically because it is carried out in a framework that is quite similar to Derrida's. For both there is a deep, historical, coextensive relation between the metaphysics of presence and phallogocentrism (a conflation of the terms "phallocentrism" and "logocentrism," used by both Irigaray and Derrida). More than Derrida, Irigaray is interested in showing how Cartesian epistemology is trapped within phallogocentrism. But, like Derrida, Irigaray does not think that there is any simple "outside" to this phallogocentrism, any more than there is a simple outside of metaphysics.[37] Thus, Irigaray's strategy is also one of deconstruction—the critical occupation of Descartes' text as a form of resistance.

It is in light of this strategy that I turn to a deconstruction of

Descartes carried out more or less in his own period, a critical occupation that has much to teach us about questions of autonomy, subjectivity, and positionality. This deconstruction, significantly (we will discuss
this significance further), is in the form of a poem, "Reply to the Shadow
of Descartes," by Anne de La Vigne, the text of which now follows.

Reply to the Shadow of Descartes

Lo! you appear, illustrious and learned Shadow;
How sweet and astonishing the sight of you!
What joy and happiness I feel this day
To be the reason for your glad return!
My soul is used to apparitions,
And though surprised to see you, is not alarmed;
But already your flattering speeches
With pleasure have interrupted my surprise.
If I but dared, great genius, to believe you,
If your promises were not in vain, Shadow,
What hope would fill my mind and heart,
What learning and honor would I gain!
I'd see by my efforts old errors destroyed,
School and court most happily enlightened.
And all the world excited by my voice,
In your learned texts finally seek the truth.
In vain you flatter me with such a promise.
Badly would I fulfill it: my weakness I know;
Of an old doctor, I haven't the style or airs,
And I don't think it right, lessons to give others.
To great truths I submit with ease,
But am not vain enough to pronounce them;
My mind can be subdued by their weight
Without resolving to defend them.
Courage would fail me in this undertaking.
I leave their artful exposition to our foremost sages,
For I only learn, so as never to speak my learning.
The best and strongest eloquence, I know,
Is often not as worthy as a modest silence.
For us women, custom makes it almost duty
To speak but rarely and to have no knowledge.
And if a lady adopts some other maxims,
She'd better hide them as one hides a crime.
Whether this custom is rightfully established,

Or merely the law of the mightiest,
For her it's surely both safer and wiser
Just to bow before this unpleasant custom.
Yet there are exceptions, in whom heaven so just
Has happily joined all its precious gifts,
Whose mind or rank, greater than the ordinary,
Is dispensed from the laws observed by the common man.
Our bounteous century produces everywhere
Learned beauties who have not these cares:
Wise Elizabeth, whom the universe admires,
The honor of our sex and of the realm,
Did she submit to these laws so strange?
Had she submitted, would she have earned your praise?
Her name, already famous by illustrious birth,
From her rare knowledge drew another luster;
And your rare knowledge, Shadow, extending her renown,
Drew great brilliance from her august name.
'Tis to her name only we can join yours;
We would offend you, in joining it to another.
I myself agree, for I cannot without blushing
See such a fine man's name joined to mine.
That would be a liberty granted in vain:
Even love for a dead man I'm not allowed.
Pure as a woman might be, they'll blame her all the same
In the end, there's always some shame in loving,
And even the least unreasonable of passions,
Far from condoned, are not to be excused.
I see your merit, and without bias,
Wisely I'm content you to admire.
To bear your name to the temple of Mnemosyne,
I leave to your friends the pleasure and the glory.
I know a few of them worthy of this task,
Who consider it an honor and make it their law.
Through them, the court, the bar, and the Sorbonne
Will believe your doctrine best, the only one.
Through them, your texts, your learned treatises
Will be read far and wide, no more contested.
Through them, a thousand triumphs whose great good fortune
Will surpass your hopes, your wishes too,
And render celebrated among us all
Your learning profound, and their love for you.
And so, without great noise and fanfare for myself,

I'll sing your illustrious conquest e'er so softly,
And with a zeal as great as it's discreet,
To your noble triumph I'll give applause in secret.[38]

I should preface my remarks on this poem with the note that I can only
scratch the surface of this very rich piece of writing—which is to say
that I will read the poem as a philosopher rather than as a literary critic
(in the latter capacity I must admit in all honesty that I am not equal to
the task).[39] In its depth of irony, humor, and bitterness, the poem
certainly speaks for itself. Keep in mind, however, Hölderlin's expression, "Without pain we are." What could this mean?

One suspects that a shadow does not feel pain. La Vigne does not
shadow-box with the evil genius, but instead with Descartes himself, or
at least that which he gives expression to but cannot control, his
remainder, his *ombre*—this dissemination that does not return to the
father. To this shadow La Vigne adds her own: "applause in secret," a
singing ever so softly, a zeal as discreet as it is great.

The philosophy that locks out the body is created in a cultural
context that locks out women's bodies. La Vigne can only speak to
Descartes' shadow, and then only softly or in silence. This, for the poet,
is *unthinkable*, in terms of a thinking of the passions, which, however,
"far from condoned, are not to be excused," even the "least unreasonable" of them. Even the passions that are, that is, closest to reason, must
be locked out from philosophy. The poet, therefore, being unable to
think with the philosopher, *sings* with the shadow. The implication is
that singing is a lesser form of expression than "thought," just as the
poet is less than the philosopher. That is an old story (from Plato to
Habermas, we might say). It is also a story of ironic subversion and
excess. While the stifled philosopher in La Vigne extols the virtues of
Queen Elizabeth ("whom the universe admires") and others who, like
Elizabeth, pay no attention to gender in their pursuit of learning (the
poet's reference to these women as "beauties" is a wily move!), the poet
La Vigne evokes the rhythms which confound the eye. The shadow is
pure form, but it is not form; it is the barest imitation; but it follows form
wherever form may go; it is the dance of form—rhythm, poetry, song.
But then the shadow is the embarrassment of form, the remainder of
form. This double gesture, toward the dance and the remainder, demonstrates the necessary complexity as well as the necessary practicality of
feminist self-assertion. The Elizabethan *cogito* pure and simple does not
escape the trap set by modern sovereignty: as Irigaray (1985a, 133) puts
it, "any theory of the subject has always been appropriated by the

'masculine'." The upshot of what I was arguing earlier is that the masculine is what has always already set up all previous theories of the subject.

The poet's song cannot be singular in the way that masculinity aspires to be. Instead, song *only* exists to be disseminated. The genius of La Vigne's "Reply" (her act of responsibility) is its self-conscious parasitism: the parasitism of song on shadow, the parasitism of shadow on substance. Whatever has a shadow, whatever sings, has a body—*is* a body. To banish song is to banish body is to banish mind.

Some salient points in this demonstration can be drawn out for the particular purpose of distinguishing among different kinds of critiques of the self. It is crucial that such distinctions be made. The perils of positionality are simply one aspect of the deeper perils of anti-foundationalism. It is often forgotten or misunderstood by both critics and defenders of anti-foundationalism that not all anti-foundationalisms are the same. The same goes for positionality; therefore, it is imperative within the paradigm of caring that we go some distance in specifying what kind of replacement for self-assertion is politically tenable. There is a basic philosophical question here, concerning foundationalism and its critique, but there is a political question here as well: what sorts of self-deconstructions go no further than self-assertions in providing an alternative to the unified, male self? Politically speaking, not all deconstructions are equal. Radical social theory aims to understand philosophical and political questions together (indeed, it maintains that such questions cannot ultimately be understood apart from one another); fortunately, this mutual understanding is well within reach in the present case.

Let us return to the analysis presented by Diana Fuss in *Essentially Speaking*. Part of her argument is that not only do we often find hidden remnants of essentialism in anti-essentialist constructions (e.g., in the construction of positionalities); it is, moreover, very difficult to see how we could do without "some risk of essence." The way that Fuss explores this point regarding Derrida's work is especially significant for our concerns:

My interest in exploring what Derrida calls "fringes of irreducibility" as they operate in deconstruction itself is motivated not by a desire to demonstrate that Derrida is a *failed* constructionist (this would be a pointless exercise, given the terms of my argument) but by an interest in uncovering the ways in which deconstruction deploys essentialism against itself, leans heavily on essence in its determination to displace essence. (1989, 13; Derrida citation is 1981b, 67)

Elsewhere, Fuss connects this project with "an interest in uncovering the *political* effects of deconstruction's displacement of essence."[40]

Fuss goes on to raise some of the questions that I earlier echoed from Gayatri Spivak. She also makes the further move toward Stephen Heath's provocative suggestion that "the risk of essence may have to be taken" (Fuss 1989, 18–21). Finally, however, in a repetition with a difference, Fuss comes "full circle" to the position that the risk of essence can itself operate as a deconstructive strategy.

How are we to read this "risk of essence" if we are committed to the replacement of notions of subjectivity and self-assertion with a concept of positionality? I think that the best way forward is to augment this "risk," as Fuss conceptualizes it as a deconstructive strategy, with two additional notions. First, in taking this risk we are establishing a set of "border conditions"—this is what "Reply to the Shadow of Descartes" does in a way that will be specified in a moment. That is, we are locating a position that can be staked out, defended, and used as a basis for further political movement (one thinks again of Houston Baker's analysis of minstrelsy). Second, the essence that is risked is always conditional, even if it may constitute a position that remains stable for a particular period—this stability, in any case, is always of a more strategic than ontological character. Again, the conditional self-assertion of La Vigne contributes to this idea. (These augmentations are also, I think, faithful to the strategy set out by Fuss.)

Let us enumerate, then, some relevant features of the meeting between Rene Descartes and Anne de La Vigne. First, there is the emphasis on the body, which must always, in seeming contrast to the pretensions of mind, have a position. Second, there is the genre distinction, between philosophy and poetry, that has traditionally also been a gender distinction. Third, unlike Descartes, who may be said to be interested in intellectual models, La Vigne is interested in role models— out of necessity, to be sure, but also as another instance of the embodiment of thought (or, rather, the inability of thought to not be embodied). Fourth, unlike Descartes, La Vigne must raise the issue of being shut out of a particular set of institutions (in fairness, this is an issue that also concerns Descartes, where church doctrine, as opposed to gender, is concerned; La Vigne, however, raises this institutional factor as one that bears on the intellectual endeavor). Fifth, there is the dissimulating effect that ontologically elusive forms such as song, story, and shadow have on the notion of sovereignty and the autonomy of thoughts (one is reminded of Derrida's discussion of the ontology of smell in *Glas*). Sixth, there is the subversion of sight by hearing, in part a problematization of

Cartesian self-presence in recognition of questions concerning especially the possibility of a private language. Finally, there is the dissimulation of singularity and individualism by poetry, which must be spoken out loud to really breathe (a fact which finds an ironic reference at several places in La Vigne's poem). As Rogers and Hammerstein have it, "A song is not a song until you sing it."

These are very contemporary themes, and La Vigne is a very contemporary writer and *thinker*. In her poem we see the emergence of a theme that runs at least through the work of Virginia Woolf, namely that women's experience plus modernism (or in encounter with modernism) often results in a kind of politically-charged postmodernism, the model of which is set out accurately by Fuss. Furthermore, these seven themes contribute to an argument for positionality. This is perhaps quite clear in a negative sense, specifically in the case of the themes that tend to undermine notions of the singular, sovereign self (points five through seven). Positively (constructively, we might say), the themes concerning the body, role models, genre distinctions (keep in mind that the word, "genre," in French can be translated as either "genre" or "gender"), and institutions are part and parcel of the question of a subject position that is other-asserted. Perhaps the question of the body is the most problematic here—people often want to say that there is a certain plain (I'm tempted to say "bare") *fact* there. Judith Butler (see 1990, 151n9) has argued that even in the case of "biology" (in scare quotes because we are questioning the idea of value-free science) there is no ontological certainty that can be separated from ideology. (Quine *could* say the same thing, although no one expects him to.) Even if there were such a fact, however, the simple "presence" of the body would not determine how that *something* would enter into cultural discourse. (It was, of course, Simone de Beauvoir's contribution to the critique of essentialism that compels us to forever question any strict correspondence between biology and destiny.) By now, everyone with outward eyes with which to see knows this. The point for present purposes is that it is a typical move of classical self-assertion to deny any presence or significance at all to the body, *because* that simple admission opens up these questions of signification. (In other words, we have here a prime example of what Derrida would call an onto-political question.)

The seven themes drawn out from the La Vigne/Descartes encounter constitute a proto-agenda for a politically-situated positionality. This would be a positionality that certainly must continue to question itself in its own terms. Positionality is itself positional, but that does not mean that positionality cannot have a more or less clear sense of why and where and for what purpose a particular position is generated. In other words, this is not "relativism." The positionality that I have argued for is the recognition of the interweaving of subject positions, and it is an attempt to sort out the political possibilities of that matrix.

Let us move, then, toward the reconnection of these themes with what has already been said about the possibility of responsibility. It is sometimes thought that the argument for positionality somehow negates responsibility (i.e., responsible agency). It seems to me, however, that positionality provides a basis for getting away from the individualistic notion of self-responsibility, which to my mind amounts to very little (especially in the recent political atmosphere of truly insipid individualism), and for moving toward a notion of collective responsibility. Notions of self-responsibility have mainly to do with figuring out "who's to blame" in any particular instance, as though this is typically an individual question.[41] Positional responsibility is more akin to a form of collective responsibility, because it is a question of how we respond in a social matrix that is always positioning others and through which we are always being positioned by others. One reason that the philosophical canon resists feminist readings and the inclusion of works by women is that feminism stresses sisterhood. The canon-guards are afraid that, "if you let one in, they'll all want to come in." ("The whole rabble of scribbling women," as Hawthorne put it.)

The notion of positionality allows us to think about sisterhood without having to bring in the philosophically troublesome notion of a "collective subject." This particular notion of positionality was at least implicit, and often explicit, in actual, living sisterhood from the start (i.e., from the beginnings of the marginalization of women). The all-important question for this study is whether this "sisterly" positional form of collectivity can be extended to a rethought brotherhood. This is a very important prospect, for we would then have to say that this brotherhood could not be conceived or practiced apart from sisterhood—quite the opposite of what fraternity has traditionally meant.[42]

In the sense of the word, "responsibility," that Derrida argues for—the ability to respond to the other—positionality implies more, not less, responsibility. But this form of responsibility is somewhat (not entirely) distant from those discourses of "morality" that emphasize blaming, guilt, shame, etc. (all of which may have their place and usefulness, but only when they are displaced from the center of ethico-political concerns), and more toward the question of advocating a feminist or, if you will, "sisterly" political agenda that mainly concerns changing ourselves and the world.

Diversity before community (from autonomy to diversity)

In the preceding analysis, I have positioned a certain women's movement, that part of the women's movement that strains against classical autonomy and toward positionality, as an exemplar of a new politics: a new language of politics inextricably bound up with a new politics of language. In terms of the question of naming, with specific reference to "the name of woman," both Derrida and Irigaray have stressed a productive double-bind or aporia: on the one hand, the sense of "woman" as unnameable; on the other hand, the sense that to give[43] a name to "woman," *finally*, would be to give in to counter-possibility. Counter-finality is that movement which resists this outcome, this final (un)naming.

The strategies of counter-possibility are many and cunning (this is indeed the cunning of history in its search for an outcome). One of these strategies would lure us by attributing a singularity to the unnameability of any particular subject-position, be it woman, Black, Jew, gay, etc. This strategy of singularity recreates a kind of subjectivity by default—a "new," privileged subject.

Politically, coming to grips with this cunning subversion of diversity does not imply that people who have previously been on the underside of privilege should just stay where they are in order to avoid the danger of a resurgent subjectivity. Calls to this effect are commonly heard under the reactionary rubric of "reverse discrimination" and the like. On the contrary, it is necessary to risk "subjectivity" and even "essence," and it is certainly the case that sometimes people have absolutely no choice but to take this risk in an absolutist way. People are sometimes backed into corners. Well-known examples here would be lesbian and Black separatism. Instead of ascribing some pathology to these separatisms, which is an easy and uncourageous act to perform, since it simply rides the tide of identity, the question should be asked, "What specific form of the logic of the Same was able to assimilate the potential space of the other?" This is simply a more theoretical way of answering certain typical questions, e.g., "Why do these women hate men so much?" with another question, e.g., "What is it about men (or better, masculinity) that is so hateful?" But it is also a way of moving the scene of questioning away from subjects only, away from an *ineffective* politics of blaming, toward letting the other speak.[44] The politics of blaming, after all, keeps the focus right where identity-logic wants it, on the Same.

The emphasis thus far has been on the undesirability of community without diversity. In the next chapter I will describe in more detail
what a diverse community might look like and what some of the
problems involved in materializing this conception are. In preparation
for these tasks it is important that more be said about the meaning of
diversity.

A post-secular community, which will in its earlier stages have the
character of post-secular socialism, must be preceded by the flowering
of diversity. To put it in a formula: diversity before community. Any
other sort of community would negate what humanity has learned
through the experience of secular society. (Marxism seems to share with
liberalism the idea that pretty much everything worthwhile humanity
has learned has come from secular society, which is obviously not
something that I accept.) The problem is that, in some important sense,
diversity needs to flower in the midst of our present society *and* at the
same time, again in some important sense, diversity already exists in
present-day Western society. The problem is to distinguish diversity
from pluralism and eclecticism (i.e., the "postmodern pastiche" described by Fredric Jameson).

There are no absolute, hard-and-fast rules for making this
discrimination. One need only turn to Marxist arguments in aesthetics,
from the Benjamin, Brecht, Adorno, and Lukacs debates of the thirties
(see Lunn 1982), to recent controversies concerning, for example, punk
rock (some on the left called it "fascist," some "revolutionary"; see
Marcus 1989), to see that there is no ready-made interpretation that is
attached to diverse social phenomena. Another formula we might well
need here, then, is: "Let a hundred flowers bloom!"

Again, some attention can be focused on this word, "let." There
are some practical signposts here: liberation theology and the Latin
American Christian Base Communities are a flower I would like to let
bloom, while the U.S. Government and most Latin American governments would like to snuff this flower out. But this example, in itself,
does not go far enough. The answer more in line with what we have
discussed thus far is that diversity encourages an active respect for and
appreciation of the other, while pluralism is more akin to mere "tolerance." Again, a practical guideline: in order to let the other speak, *I* have
to do something—I have responsibilities here. Pluralism and eclecticism, on the other hand, do not confer obligations. An example: from the
standpoint of pluralism, there are certain feminist positions regarding
certain "women's problems." From the standpoint of diversity, it
would be essentializing of the other to use the expression "women's

problems"—and this essentializing subjectivizes the other by flattening the dynamic interaction that is possible between I and Thou.[45] There are no "women's problems"—there are issues concerning the situations and the positionalities of "women" and "men," which are received and not immutable categories, issues that call for response to the other who leaves her trace in me. My reference here is to something quite specific: the inability of the Same to acknowledge the mother (this is one case where a semiotic conflation, "(m)other," is entirely appropriate). In an important investigation of the work of Luce Irigaray, Elizabeth Grosz makes this point in terms that are extremely far-reaching, and yet are no exaggeration:

> . . . the son is unable to accept the debt of life, body, nourishment and social existence he owes the mother. An entire history of Western thought is intent on substituting for this debt an image of the self-made, self-created man. One could go even further and suggest that the idea of God itself is nothing but an elaborate if unconscious strategy for alleviating man's consciousness of and guilt about this debt. As man's self-reflecting Other, God usurps women's creativity and their place as the source of the terrestrial. God (and through Him, man) becomes the creator or mother of the mother. (Grosz 1989, 120–21)

Exactly: our "autonomy" is bought at the expense of the most essential and intimate of affective ties. The price that is paid by the other is that it is forced into the straitjacket of pluralism—the material of diversity must hide, must go somewhere else. Irigaray and other feminists of difference are interested in tapping into this energy from a different place (and a different temporality).

Even in societies that are mostly pluralistic there is some diversity, but this diversity is often drained of its energy, an energy of the letter, the semiotic materiality of a cultural history that pluralism tends to flatten into a horizontal train of "interest groups."

A necessary digression: does the question of diversity arise in non-pluralistic societies? A great deal hangs on this question, for the answer will necessarily say something decisive about the historical development of world civilizations. That is, if the answer is that diversity cannot arise in non-pluralistic societies, then at least two major consequences follow. First, non-pluralistic societies, in some sense, do therefore await further *development* in secular society. If that is true, then history does seem to have at least some sort of telos.[46] Second, if we cannot have diversity without pluralism, then don't we have to say, "vive la pluralism"? And, how can we say this if pluralism also undermines diversity? It should not be taken as patently obvious, however, that the initial question, whether diversity can exist in non-pluralistic societies, must necessarily be answered positively simply because there are seeming contradictions and troubling consequences associated with answering in the negative.

This form of dichotomizing is itself exactly what needs to be deconstructed. To pursue examples already raised, the question of the situation of women did not emerge only with the advent of secular society. What happened was that one form of rhetorically addressing this question (a form which, in its negativity—its need to negate women—was perhaps the forerunner of modern subjectivity) was supplemented and largely supplanted by another rhetoric, that of rights and subjects. And, since the earliest periods of Western civilization, there has always been a "Jewish question." Indeed, this latter question, and its persistence through successive discursive regimes, is the most useful for thinking about the historicity of margins, for two reasons: 1) the fact of this persistence; 2) the fact that this question was *never not* a question of difference and undecideability. Derrida even goes so far: "Jew" is the very name of undecideability—therefore for paradox, for the displacement of naming. In the name of the Same, a Holocaust was brought down upon this displacement (see Wyshograd 1985).

What *is* "new" in secular society is a different textual weave of the letter. The subject was spun from the cloth of sovereignty. The question of the undecideable Jew is the question whether all reweaving must be an attempt to clothe undecideability in presence. (This question will concern us further in the next chapter.)

Be that as it may, a rewoven social matrix does standardize certain "new" semantic resources and close off other such resources. The only critique of "newness" and originality intended here, therefore, has it that the letter was always already infinitely unfoldable.

And yet, the matrix of possible semantic positions does seem pretty well filled-out, bringing humanity to a kind of conjuncture. On the one hand, the tensions among *Gesellschaft* and *Gemeinschaft*, secular and traditional societies, diversity and pluralism, diversity/pluralism and the seemingly (but perhaps deceptively so) monological direction of pre-secular societies, lead to a kind of exhaustion. In this exhausted state, all that has been experienced by humanity seems no more than a series of unrelated equations, which are, furthermore, not felt as an enclosing history or home by humanity, more as the endless repetition of the Same, but now in a way typical of consumer society. History does become "bunk" or "just one damn thing after another." The *unheimlich* no longer acts as spur, as in the scenarios of Marx or Freud and their followers. On the other hand, this matrix, if only its diachronic dimension were to be recreated (and "restored" in that sense), presents tremendous possibilities.

And the basis for these possibilities is the fact that it is only humanity, in its present, *dominant* positionalities, that is exhausted, *not* the letter, which is the inexhaustible material, the impossible material, that represents the possibility (or, one should always say, *possibilities*) of a history that continues without beginning or end.

This exhaustion—of humanity—is the quintessence of the postmodern moment. But this matrix of possibilities, this inexhaustibility—of the letter—is also quintessentially postmodern. The quintessential question, therefore, is: who or what will step into this breach?

Marx searched for an answer to a *somewhat* similar question—a different breach, of course (in a way, I'm looking for a breach in Marx's breach, which is quite a case of split breaches!), perhaps even the "wrong" breach, in terms of the perspective outlined here. Marx looked for an answer to what he percieved as a historical conjuncture, an answer that had the ring of necessity and inevitability about it. Who or what will step into the breach?—this is the question Marx looked for the *necessary* answer to.

It hardly needs repeating that Marx found his necessity by pursuing the logic of economic production and class. What does need explanation is the relation of this logic and this necessity to a social theory that reserves a central place for the discourse of margins and the new social movements. For it seems to me that logic and necessity are still needed in these matters. Or, to put it in quite other terms: what about the proletariat? Concerning these questions, this chapter concludes with a set of theses that attempt to remain faithful to the logic of both Marx and postmodern society.

Margin and proletariat

1. Michel Foucault observed that, through the course of the eighteenth century, there evolved a conceptual construct known as "the whole of humanity." Attendant upon this conception, and through the course of the nineteenth century, it came to pass that "the whole of humanity" in fact included almost no one—the conception excluded and marginalized practically everyone.[47]

2. Marx and Engels wrote of a class that has "nothing to lose but its chains" and "a world to win." In their day they located this class mainly in the industrial centers of Europe; since that time, because of the

development of the trade unions, qualitative developments in capitalism, and the emergence of socialist experiments that have indeed transformed the world and given rise to a new set of questions, the location of the proletariat seems to have shifted. (Notice that "location" is a key term here, which deemphasizes the importance of identifying a "subject" in the classical sense.)

3. On the basis of this shift some theorists, for example Habermas and Gorz (1982), argue that the proletariat has "disappeared from the stage of world history." Others, for example Marcuse (see Kellner 1984, 284–90), have argued that the proletariat is no longer the revolutionary subject. While such theses cannot be simply dismissed out of hand (working through their claims can be theoretically valuable), fundamentally there is a failure of certain social theories (especially those that pay little attention to political economy) to take account of class formation as an ongoing and fluid phenomenon.[48]

4. All the same, the rise of national liberation movements, the women's liberation movements, the youth and student movements and others which now go under the rubric of the "new social movements," and the separation of political and cultural avant-gardes (see Burger 1984), have made many wonder, *What happened to the proletariat?* and, *Does it matter?*

5. Marx placed two basic conditions on the definition of the proletariat: dispossession ("nothing to lose") and the situation of having to sell labor power for wages (i.e., the complete commodification of labor). Capital, however, has been a bit more flexible than Marx thought it could or would be, such that the wage system operates at the macro level even though many loci of human work and activity are not directly bound by this condition. For instance, the world peasantry (though not a single class in the conventional sense) is the largest single class group. On the micro level peasants create what can be considered use values, though these values are commodified at a higher and later stage of the economic system. Another pertinent example would be the work for which women are not paid, which is entirely necessary to the present order but which is not directly commodified in the conventional sense.[49] *So much the worse for the conventional sense.*

Pursuing this last point, there are very few women who are not marginalized, economically, politically, and spiritually, from "the whole of humanity." This "whole" in fact *never* included women. The question is *not* how women may integrate themselves into a whole that never existed, nor is it aim for a whole in the future (yes, pun intended; a hole in the present is what we are in need of). Such conceptions can now only inspire wariness: they are constructs built around the suppression of difference, sometimes a supression that is complete and total and—it scarcely needs saying—murderous.

Lenin (see 1979) recognized two great streams of world revolution: proletarian revolution and national liberation (for the imperialized countries). Why is the struggle for women's emancipation not recognized as a stream? It seems to me that there are two reasons. First, national liberation, at least on Lenin's model, is a part of class struggle— it is the passage from feudalism to bourgeois society that sets the stage for socialism. Second, patriarchy and its overcoming do not fit into the theoretical model by which Lenin understands a "stream of revolution," in large part because patriarchy is not as rooted in the state as is class rule. (In fairness, one should not therefore think that Lenin did not stress women's emancipation; the question is more whether Lenin's model of Marxism can really do justice to this fundamental question; see Lenin 1972.) These reasons do not finally hold up. The problems with Lenin's view are important in our quest for understanding the relation between classical and postmodern models of radical social transformation. First, if the network of patriarchy is even more insidious than that of class rule, then perhaps we have to expand rather than contract our model. Furthermore, perhaps we see from trying to understand the workings of patriarchy that Marxism has been beholden to a certain "fetishism of the state" (Foucault). Second, Lenin's conception of national liberation struggles does not finally attend to questions of culture. I say "finally," because Lenin was indeed aware of the degrading effects of one culture imposing its hegemony over another, especially in requiring people to speak foreign tongues and in the suppression, in education, of a people's literature and culture more broadly. In the final analysis, however, Lenin viewed the importance of national liberation as bringing a new set of production relations, and it is no longer a point of controversy that bourgeois relations of production tend to destroy local cultures. Third, there is the question of exactly what is going on when we rank different forms of struggle. In other words, what sort of judgment are we making if we say that the proletarian revolution is of the most central importance, and that other struggles, insomuch as they are legitimate, must follow in the wake of the proletarian revolution? Is this simply a "strategic" issue, as some Marxists would claim? Even if this claim could be maintained (not that I think that it can), the strategic centrality of proletarian revolution has not been proved in practice, at least not where women's emancipation and even a conditional cultural autonomy are concerned.

In *Feminist Theory: From Margin to Center*, bell hooks (1984) offers a compelling model of related struggles in which there is a basic overlap

between the oppressions of gender, race, and class, but there is specificity as well. Early in this text I argued that this basic area of overlapping
concerns can be defined as the condition of marginalization. If we take
this to be the basic condition of the proletariat, then we might reconstitute
something like the Marxist model. In practice, partial reconstitutions
have occurred, especially in the alliances proposed by Mao. But Marxist
theory (or Marxist theorists, at any rate) has not been able to bring this
"Marxism of difference" to the theoretical surface in the way that
feminism has.

The secret to formulating radical social theories of difference is to
find an area of overlap that does not reimpose a logic of the Same. My
proposal is that only the notion of the margin, representative of the
incursion of alterity into identity-logic, could provide such an area.

6. And yet it is the case that only a few people in the world are
qualitatively distant from the wage system and the general process of
the commodification of labor. Marx certainly conceived of this
commodification precisely as marginalization—of the basic human
essence, freedom. The present text has severed ties with the language of
essence, insomuch as this can be done. The difficulty, though a necessary one, is in conceiving freedom and essence in terms of human
possibilities. In fact, there are two difficulties here, which form a double-
bind in which their solution will be found. On the one hand, without
essence, freedom is defined in particular social matrices. We are quite
aware, based on scenarios of the *Brave New World* type, that freedom can
be defined in such a way that we would think it to be unfreedom. On the
other hand, but by the same token, if freedom does not have an essence,
how will we know when we have it? I am simply proposing the pursuit
of this very double-bind as the key to working through these difficulties. On the one hand, then, there is a basis for developing, theoretically
and practically, another logic that defies the logic of commodification.
This was, of course, Marx's goal. On the other hand, however, it is the
non-essentiality of the meaning of freedom that keeps alive, ironically,
the possibility of freedom, through logics of alterity that challenge
essence and foundationalisms. Whether this was also Marx's goal is
open to question. Michael Ryan (1982) argues that Marx did have this
deconstructive side. If this is indeed the case, then that is the side that I
propose building on.

7. The specters of ecological disaster and nuclear war, whether
they are fundamentally related to the process of commodification or not
(I do not think that they are unrelated), are marginalizing on a global
scale. (It is difficult to figure the question of nuclear marginalization in
this period of transition—the late 1980s and the early 1990s. Global

alignments are certainly shifting, but it is not at all clear that the systemic factors that have given rise to the nuclear threat have been ameliorated. At the same time, the threat of ecological disaster has moved even more into the foreground.)

8. The various processes by which our human possibilities are obscured and crushed have the effect, ultimately, of marginalizing practically everyone. It is a question of degrees, but with qualitative distinctions. These would include not only the specificities enumerated thus far (e.g., gender, etc.), but also a distinction between "material" and "spiritual" alienation. By this I mean that there are different forms of not having a stake in the logic of the Same. Marx, in the final analysis, only recognized material dispossession (that is, having no property) as authentic. On his view, disaffected intellectuals, for example, could always turn their skills into capital. The question of "tenured radicals"[50] aside, I do not see that this is always the case. (On the other hand, the 1989 massacre in Beijing, in which the Chinese Government attacked the workers far more viciously than it did the student activists, is indicative of where reactionary governments see the real threat coming from.)[51]

An index of marginalization would serve the strategic purpose of mapping those positionalities where the logic of the Same can best be broken through.

Even if, in a certain sense, the proletariat can be reconceived, under the paradigm of an historical materialism of the letter, as the *margin*, not all of the pertinent questions have been answered. Two questions in particular must concern us. Answering the first creates the basis for answering the second.

The first question concerns the relation between the margin and the existing social structure. Marx argues that the proletariat, owing to its relation to the means of production, must necessarily disrupt and transform existing property relations and from that point of entry disrupt and transform social relations generally (Marx's "four alls"). The interesting thing is that all major Marxists after Marx (and indeed a large part of Marx's work itself), devoted the bulk of their analyses to the larger sphere of social relations rather than to political economy. In this study I have focused on the postmodern juncture, in which the logic of the Same is confronted with diverse, heterogenous positionalities. I leave it to other textual spaces and places to develop further the question whether this postmodern juncture always already exists in other cultural contexts.[52] I would press the point, however, that the collision/collusion of the forces of a flattening identity-logic, called "pluralism" in its late modern and postmodern guise, is especially acute in our time. Equally acute are the disruptions of this one-dimensional pluralism by the marginal positionalities that can be read as the diverse other of this pluralism. This sharpening of the conflict is indeed driven by the logic of a transcendental signifier that stands poised to instantiate its name.

The economic sphere, even in the most ordinary sense, cannot be underestimated. Within the logic of that ordinary economy, however, there must still be the basis for a leap to the larger sense of an "economy" (to Marx's credit, he was never so far from this larger sense). Humanity must deal with the household—but notice that I did not allow the expression "its household" (i.e., humanity's household) to inscribe itself so easily in this text. We inhabit this household as guests, and that fact has consequences for how we might rearrange the house of Being—this house where the other is always knocking at the door, where the other has already left its trace within. I intend here a chain of references, from Kirkpatrick Sale's sense of deep ecology, to Wendell Berry's sense of "home economics," to the Biblical knock at the door of the heart, to Heidegger, Levinas, and Derrida.[53] This chain is directed toward a complication of political economy—a productive displacement of Marx's analyses.

The second question is: Who, or What can answer this knock? Here again I depart from Marx and insist not only on Derrida, but especially on the Nietzschean side of his work. There is not, as Marx supposed, a single answer to that question—a single answer with a single name. Whoever can answer the call of alterity, that is whoever can answer. There is no predetermined subject position here, nor should there be— *of necessity.* We may call this answer to the other by the name "proletariat," or, in another guise, in another positionality, "Jew" or "woman," etc. We may call it a certain "ecology."

At the same time, and this is the Nietzschean-Derridean turn, we must insist on particularity. In rendering the Jew or the proletarian (the connections here could stand examination) "emblematic" we not only place a burden on each that is unjust. I mean this in the sense that Judaism is a material, *not* a metaphysical connection to the possibility of history. To metaphysicalize the Jew or proletarian is both to rob individuals of their feelings and positionalities, and to freeze a positionality into subjectivity. It is therefore, finally, to destroy the form of particularity that is also universal: diverse abilities, of numerous positionalities, to responsibly answer the call of the other.

I have described, then, a minimal basis for unity, coupled with diverse justifications for diversity. There is a further justification that I have not yet mentioned, though it will not surprise the reader in the least bit. I should not fail to mention this justification, however, for it is also a justification for the minimal principle of unity.[54]

Until the beginning of the nineteenth century, it was plausible that some thinkers could claim to know more-or-less all there was to know. These sorts of thinkers, "encyclopedists," could not exist now, for two reasons. First, and obviously, there are just too many subject areas to master, and each of these is too deep. Second, and more significantly, there is a need now for a vigilant skepticism about what it means "to know." When polymaths from Aristotle to Diderot were able to "know everything," what sorts of others were excluded from this "universal" category? (Did they know how to be mothers, for instance?) What was the procedure of thought by which they were able to "master subjects"? The politics of this "knowledge" is readily apparent (see Fox-Keller 1984, Harding 1986). The replacement for *this* knowledge must necessarily be a knowledge that lets the other speak. Hyper-specialization is not a substitute for this impossible knowledge, this open knowledge, even when (*even though*) this specialization presents itself as speaking for the other, having knowledge of the other. Hyper-specialization, perhaps necessary in some contexts, is, as a dominant paradigm, simply the analogue in the pursuit of knowledge to pluralism in politics.

Neither knowing "everything" nor knowing a great deal about a particular subject is a substitute for letting the other speak. (There is an ethics of knowledge here.) The latter must displace (even while, in some respects, encompassing) the former, even when the risk is that of displacing "knowledge" itself.

Encyclopediac and hyper-specialized knowledges must be displaced by diverse knowledge practices (see Fuller 1988) that recognize the limits of their knowledge in the responsibility to the other. This is the place where knowledge will also be extended.

This unnameable community

As we approach sharing let us ask: "What belongs to me?"
Balance sheet of a life ratified by death.
Whatever exists has no existence unless shared.
Possessions under seal are lost possessions.
At first sight, giving, offering yourself in order to receive an equivalent
gift in return, would seem to be ideal sharing.
But can All be divided?
Can a feeling, a book, a life be shared entirely?
On the other hand, if we cannot share all, what remains and will always
remain outside sharing? What has never, at the heart of our posses-
sions, been ours?
And what if all we can share is the vital desire to share, our only means of
escape from solitude, from nothingness?

—Edmond Jabes, *The Book of Shares*

Contamination, 1: some questions about theory and practice

In *of Grammatology*, Derrida sets out a program for contamination;
in *Glas*[1] he enacts this program.

What would it be like to read Marx the way that Derrida reads
Hegel in *Glas*? Who would be Marx's Genet?

What is this *Glas* recently heard "in" philosophy? It is not truly an
end, though it is the sound (what sound?—the sound of opening the
book, *Glas*, or of turning its pages?) of an end, a sound that tells us of an
end.

We are fortunate to hear this sound. You know what they say
about lightning—"As long as you can see it, you're safe." Philosophy
has always been about ends, The End, finality, death, the last word.

What will forestall the last word? Another word.

Life is not worth living at all costs, nor is philosophy worth
preserving at all costs. There can always be another word, until this
sound, this *Glas*, cannot be heard. Two things are meant here. Either the
last word is spoken, the name of names, and meaning is no more—its
riddle is finally solved; or philosophy becomes deaf through repetition
without difference and meaning is no more—its riddle is finally
flattened out of existence. I would like to believe that the latter cannot
happen, that repetition cannot help but propagate difference. But what
is repetition? If I speak the sound, "glub," over and over again, is that
repetition? If I say the words, "Coca-Cola" over and over again, is *that*
repetition? One is reminded of a scene from Don DeLillo's novel, *White
Noise*, in which the narrator and his family find themselves in a shelter in
the midst of an "airborne toxic event":

> A feeling of desperate piety swept over me. It was cosmic in
> nature, full of yearnings and reachings. It spoke of vast distances,
> awesome but subtle forces. These sleeping children were like
> figures in an ad for the Rosicrucians, drawing a powerful beam of
> light from somewhere off the page. Steffie turned slightly, then
> muttered something in her sleep. It seemed important that I know
> what it was. In my current state, bearing the death impression of
> the Nyodene cloud, I was ready to search anywhere for signs and
> hints, intimations of odd comfort. I pulled my chair up closer. Her
> face in pouchy sleep might have been a structure designed solely
> to protect the eyes, those great, large and apprehensive things,
> prone to color phases and a darting alertness, to a perception of
> distress in others. I sat there watching her. Moments later she
> spoke again. Distinct syllables this time, not some dreamy mur-
> mur—but a language not quite of this world. I struggled to
> understand. I was convinced she was saying something, fitting
> together units of stable meaning. I watched her face, waited. Ten
> minutes passed. She uttered two clearly audible words, familiar
> and elusive at the same time, words that seemed to have a ritual
> meaning, part of a verbal spell or ecstatic chant. *Toyota Celica*.
> (1985, 154–55)

If we could be sure that repetition will always give rise to difference—a difference that reaches toward and in respect of the other, not
the repetition of "Coca-Cola," etc.—then we would possess the key to
forestalling the last word. But how can we be sure of a differential
repetition?

There is always the possibility of contamination (in a moment I will practically equate contamination with possibility), as long as there is something to contaminate. Derrida wants to contaminate Hegel with Genet, therefore there is still a need for Hegel (this is perhaps entirely obvious to most readers of Derrida, but it does not hurt to say it). I want to contaminate Marx, *with Derrida*, which is likewise to say that there is still a need for Marx. (But perhaps Marx can sit in the background for a bit—*sit*, because I do not *always* want him looking over my shoulder.) The contamination of philosophy means still needing philosophy.[2]

Perhaps the postmodern political problem is that the room for contamination is being sequestered off. A postmodern cartography needs to show how this might be the case in geographical (one hears of the "reemergence of space"), semiotic, and temporal terms.[3]

For there is a quite active, geographical sense in which "contamination" is sequestered, a sense which resonates with the derogatory name given to proletarians down through history, "the great unwashed." And there is a conceptual apparatus that similarly plays the role of keeping the unwashed "outside," namely the logic of the Same, "the compulsive terror which, above all, forbids contact" (Derrida 1985c, 292). Derrida wants to dispel the notion that it is imperative that we figure out "what came first," this identity-logic in the theoretical sense (and as especially perfected by Kant and Hegel) or the practice of sequestering persons and social groups deemed "impure." This search for "first philosophy," regardless of whether it arrives at a materialist or an idealist starting point, is itself a part of the problem. In the essay on apartheid (written for an exhibition of anti-apartheid artworks), Derrida mentions the "just silence" that must not be consumed by a "discourse [that] would once again compel us to reckon with the present state of force and law [of South Africa].[4] It would draw up contracts, dialecticize itself, let itself be reappropriated again" (1985c, 299). When Derrida says that it is necessary instead to "appeal unconditionally to the future of another law and another force lying beyond the totality of this present" (ibid.; 298), he is simultaneously thinking of the alterity of both philosophy and practice.

Secular society is a hyper-active mode of sequestration, of the drive toward purity, "white mythology." Community is not possible without breaking down the barriers that purportedly keep everything in its own little box with its own name.

Perhaps one kind of box might even be what Marxists call "stages of history." We are presently in the capitalist, bourgeois stage. But part of how Marxism preserves purity is by acting as if these were the only *proper* names of our present Western societies—as opposed to patriarchal, industrial, white supremacist, Christian, etc. This is one way that

Marxism is complicit in the logic of secularism. The problem is that it seems there can be no alternative to the logic of the Same that is free of complicities—for this "freedom" would itself constitute an attempt for purity. Insomuch as socialism and proletarian society represent another self-contained stage, this logic is still operative.

What is needed, instead, is an openness to all of history's possibilities, represented by the still-available, but certainly endangered, semantic resources of history. The price of this openness is the risk of contamination.

Contamination, 2: from grammatology to Glas

One very good example of a contaminated text that is open to the semantic richness of historical possibility is *Midrash*, the practice of rabbinic interpretation. It is a contamination that should be claimed for community, against the efforts of the purifiers, whether their line is a secular insistence on pre-secular community, as in fascism, and its anti-Semitic claims about "mongrelization," or a secular insistence on post-bourgeois society, as with Marx, and his talk about "practice . . . in its dirty-judaical manifestation."[5] The mistake here, in either case, is to think in terms of *manifestation*, as though there were some pre-existing spirit that sullies itself in coming (in)to being.[6] A reclamation of "manifestation" oriented toward its letter would show that it is never not a question of complicity, of dirty hands. (Why a good Marxist should fear a little dirt I do not know.)

Another good example of a contaminated text is Derrida's *Glas*. In both examples of contaminated texts it is important that the source of the contamination be understood—the source and its "science." *Glas* is an encounter between philosophy and its others, but it would be not nearly as significant a work if it were only an exercise in comparative literature. One way to sum up *Glas*: Hegel cannot contain himself.[7] For it is only because the trace of the other informs and forms (pre-forms/performs) the Same that response and responsibility are possible.

Writing is a contaminated activity and process. This basic perspective is what connects Derrida's apparently more "systematic" earlier work, in *of Grammatology* and *Speech and Phenomena*, with his later work. In *of Grammatology* on a straightforward reading, Derrida establishes the priority of the category of arche-writing over speech, and also, a point of at least equal significance, over the duality of nature and culture. Richard Rorty has written that Derrida has, in recent years (and with Rorty's approval) abandoned his search for a "science of writing," turning instead to the more poetic and playful orientations of *Glas* and *The Postcard*:

> . . . Derrida is torn between the negative theologian's urge to find a new pantheon—"trace," "*differance*," and the rest of what Gasche calls "infrastructures"—and the comic writer's urge to make something once held sacred look funny. In his later work, it seems to me, he is less torn. He is content simply to have fun rather than to feel haunted. (1989b, 212)

Rorty goes on to characterize Derrida's earlier work as falling into a negative theology, while the later work is supposedly more "self-referential and esoteric" (see ibid.; 214–15).

Glas is admittedly a very funny work in places, whatever "funny," as opposed to "serious" means (Lenny Bruce and Richard Pryor are funny, too), but whether the work is so self-referential is another question. What sort of "self" can this book refer to?[8]

First and foremost, it is the self who signs this book "Jacques Derrida," which signature also appears on the cover of *of Grammatology*. The textuality that unravels itself in another systematic exposition, "Signature Event Context" (in Derrida, 1982, and its sequel, "Limited Inc"), also unravels that signature—which is another way of saying that grammatology was from the beginning taken as a paradoxical "science." The special purpose of its "pantheon" was to undermine itself, but not in just any old way, rather, in a way such that margins are brought to center, the other speaks.

Again, on a straightforward reading, *of Grammatology* pursues the category of writing through four basic movements. First, there is the critique of the ethnocentrism embodied in Levi-Strauss's notion of "peoples without writing." This might also be called, in shorthand, a critique of "culture." Second, there is the critique of the hypostasized notion of "nature" found in Rousseau. Third, there is the pursuit of the ontology of writing that permits this deconstruction of the nature/culture binary. In other words, Derrida articulates the systematic aspects of writing that seem to make it such a privileged and/or despised category. Fourth and finally, however, Derrida turns this category on itself; he writes writing (undermining its name by a verb), and finds that grammatology, when *pursued most rigorously*, deconstructs itself. Which means, of course, that grammatology both "works" and doesn't work.[9] Which further means that there is a meeting point of "play" and "rigor" (but then, Derrida has stressed this at least since "Structure, Sign, and Play in the Discourse of the Human Sciences").

All of this has its funny side, to be sure (Hegel cannot contain himself), but I don't think that is the complete picture, either in *Grammatology* or in *Glas*. The latter work has a structure that is more complex, but not fundamentally different, I think, from *of Grammatology*. Where the two main critiques contained in *Grammatology*, of nature and culture, are carried out somewhat separately, there is a complete integration in *Glas*. Hegel gets no relief, he is contaminated from the start. Hegel is never not spilling over into Genet, and also, among others, into the Jew whom Hegel would write out of history.

In an unspoken way, the Jew is at the center of *Grammatology*.[10] On the one hand, Derrida commends Levi-Strauss's desire to contextualize French and other Western societies—they are simply cultures among other cultures. But, on the other hand, Derrida is suspicious of the "journey to the East" (or to the Amazon, etc.). The anthropologist enters upon this journey with her or his bags already packed. The "East" itself, along with "Eastern religion," "Eastern philosophy," "Chinese writing," etc., are largely creations of the West, and certainly this is true in the case of the use of these notions by Western philosophers (or "ex-philosophers"), e.g., Plato, Leibniz, Hegel, Levi-Strauss, etc. I would argue that perhaps we should at least keep open the purely analytic possibility of the *not-West* (which is not captured, after all, by the politico-geographical designation, "East"), though here again a certain primacy of the West is obviously asserted. Be that as it may, societies based on "absence" rather than presence are essentially always already spoiled as sources of rejuvenation for the West—one should not put new wine in old bottles (or should it be the other way around?)—and this is becoming increasingly the case for the "East" *qua* East as well. That is, this is the case, or would be, *if* there were no bridges or openings to the "East."

If there were no such openings, however, then the project of letting the other speak would certainly be doomed. There must be *an opening within*, an opening at the margins, for there to be any meaningful sense in which West can meet "East" in any other way than through acts of imperialism. Even in this opening which is the result of an internal rupture (or fracture) there is the danger of a broad, theoretic imperialism. (But there is no unambiguous, safe place to stand.)

The idea of a fracture in the West has as its correlative possibility the dissolution of the myth of the East, a myth of absence that cannot be felt as anything other than as a presence. This dissolution would then have the further consequence of unraveling the West, and not only its myth. The name for this unraveling, in the historical margins of the West since antiquity, is Judaism. And yet, to make this journey to the Middle East of impossibility, of the undecideable and therefore open figure of the possible, it is undeniable and even admirable that the West recognize its limit, even if what it takes to be outside must essentially be the potential fragmentation of its own rhetoric. The West must attempt the journey outward. *Must*, by its nature as a conglomeration, a mostly-unhappy confluence, or better *conflation*, of differences brought under the totalizing logic of *Gesellschaft*.

The names of this outgoingness driven by an unsettled society are double(d): imperialism, on the one hand, and community on the other.

Or, the unsettled society, rather than transforming itself into a new kind of community, a community that builds on the resources of difference and diversity that begin to emerge with pluralism, sets out to annihilate the communities that do exist. The Spirit of *Gesellschaft* is a jealous god. The West invents the East for this purpose, as it also invents other others whom it must both refuse to recognize and seek to dominate.

How, then, to activate the other possibility—indeed, the only field of possibilities (as opposed to the counter-possibility just described)?

Contemporary Western society (and especially the United States, perhaps the nation most concerned to negate history) is not only jaded but also *jealous*—everyone must conform to its law. Contaminants must be destroyed. The contrary trend to this jaded jealousy would involve the *revelation* of the margins, the contaminants, of Western society, paying attention to this society's *Glas* (its undoing and its death-knell), and then two further steps, already presented. First, then, recognition, but recognition in light of the very essence of humanity's possibility. Second, the *institutionalization* of this recognition, through the praxis of renaming. Third, the displacement of even this praxis (i.e., the deconstruction of the name), though in a way that does not ignore questions of strategy.

The first two steps here are inseparable. My primary example of this inseparability has been the way that new social movements come to recognize the possibilities of renaming in necessarily undertaking its praxis. In the formulation of this thesis just presented, however, something new, another dimension, has appeared, which is marked by the term "institutionalization." An argument heard more and more concerning the possible politics of Derrida's philosophy (we only accept this separation of philosophy and politics in a purely analytic sense, of course), asks how such a politics would critique existing social institutions and propose new, counter-institutions. Such criticisms, proposed by Nancy Fraser, Thomas McCarthy, etc., have their point: what is the institutional form of deconstruction, grammatology, and the recognitions of alterity, marginality, possibility, and *Glas*?[11]

In other words, the question is *not* what the "final form" of community is. The question is rather, what institutional structures will allow people to both reinvent community and to continually postpone the question of community's "final form." I have associated the latter praxis with the possibility of a reinvented, diverse community. I call it a praxis to emphasize the fact that human practice remains essential— there is no question of institutions alone instituting community. That Habermas and McCarthy (and Seyla Benhabib 1986, etc.) are *so* inclined toward a purely procedural framework indicates their secular difference from the directions I am pursuing.

I do not accept that institutions can "commune" (I doubt, of course, that Habermas would claim otherwise), and I have argued throughout that only a reinvented community can save humanity from the flattening, narrowing drive of hyper-secularism. Finally, I use the expression "continually postpone" rather than "permanently postpone" for the following, closely related, set of reasons. First, "permanence" itself, and its destruction of openness to possibility is what must be postponed. Second, to attempt to create social institutions that would "permanently postpone" the outcome of history would, through this attempt to institute permanence, bring about a kind of historical outcome. Third, these sorts of institutions would necessarily undermine interpretive activity—the grammatological praxis that, in light of *Glas*, must be open to contamination and reweaving.

None of these reasons, however, excuses us from thinking about institutions, a task to which I now turn.

Breaking with apartheid

In terms of the criticisms of proceduralism just outlined, it is clear that there can be no complete "blueprint" for the future. But the theory set out in this study must be capable of generating models and these models must be susceptible of empirical disconfirmation. In other words, as Habermas (1984) has rightly stressed, we need a *fallible* social theory. A fallible theory, however, need not necessarily be purged of every utopian, alterian impulse. As Davidson has demonstrated especially well, an anti-naturalistic philosophy and social theory need not be separated from an empirical basis.[12]

Though the notion of renaming as a political strategy was thematized in the fourth chapter, in terms of what is already motivating the new social movements, we did not discuss specific examples. In order to answer the criticisms raised by Habermas and other critical theorists, however, we must turn to the critique of particular institutions. I will propose two examples in what follows immediately, with others to follow in the next (and final) three sections.

First, consider a thought experiment that brings out the elements of renaming. Suppose that a certain university were to erect a building, naming it perhaps the "Robert Dole Human Development Center." As the reader undoubtedly knows, Robert Dole is a U.S. Senator known in recent years for his support for a constitutional amendment outlawing the "desecration" (interesting word, that) of the U.S. flag, for the defunding of art that is deemed "obscene," and, of course, for various adventures of U.S. imperialism (e.g., the 1989 invasion of Panama, the *contras*, etc.). A building, having something to do with "human development," could conceivably be named after this man who, to all outward appearances, has little to do with such development—analogous to the U.S. Navy's proposal to name a nuclear submarine "the body of Christ" (i.e., the "Corpus Christi"). Suppose that a strategy counter to this naming were to be conceived. Perhaps the building in question could be renamed, for example, as the "Robert Mapplethorpe AIDS Research Center." There are various ways that this could be accomplished, the most obvious of which is graffiti. This, of course, is not enough, but it is already a challenge to the system of legality that alone claims to have the right to name. (And, frankly, it is a better start than many liberal-procedural schemes.) However, to really change the name of this imaginary building, relations of power must be addressed.

The point is to make a reinterpretation of the world that *does* change it. In this quasi-Nietzschean appropriation of Marx's Eleventh Thesis it must be clear that the word "interpretation" is already a category of praxis—it essentially *is* praxis and the essence of praxis. Rewriting the social structures that give low priority to finding a cure for AIDS and related diseases[13] and that are only willing to vilify people identified (in an especially cruel turn of identity-logic) with AIDS—gay men, "AIDS kids," IV drug users, prostitutes, etc.—means more than changing the name of a building. But the struggle to rename is central to this general rewriting. This struggle is the initial opening of the letter, and I mean this in the sense that renaming and rewriting are not "mere metaphors" in the narrow sense. Another significant example will demonstrate further this line I am drawing out of the matrix. Such a demonstration must necessarily be "topical" (can there be politics without topos?), but it must also reveal a political model that is adaptable to other cases.

We know, certainly, that it is possible to institutionalize apartheid—to inaugurate and perpetuate apartheid by a set of social institutions. The reference here is both to what is typically referred to by "apartheid," namely the system that oppresses the Black African majority (the Azanian people) in South Africa, and to other forms of institutionalized racial oppression that exist around the world, and certainly in the United States.

The way to proceed here, according to the model already developed, is to generate the pertinent questions concerning the name, to reflect on the possibility of the other, its warrant to speak its own name, and to devise strategies for displacing names that are enforced by identity-logic—not forgetting that this logic has its police, its army, and other instruments of subjugation (instruments for designating people as certain kinds of subjects, based on a set typology).

In the case of South Africa, we are dealing with a white minority that has perpetuated a name of the region colonized by white Europeans, "South Africa," and at the same time perpetuated the tribal names of the Black African majority. This triple reversal—what is originally Black is called by its white name, what is derivatively white, the peoples living within the imposition of the European nation-state in the southern part of Africa, is called by its purportedly original (Black) name—serves to show that my aim is certainly *not* to restore some "original" name—on the contrary (though it does not hurt to show the bitter irony of the white citizens of South Africa calling themselves "South Africans" and the Black residents by tribal names). The question is one of who and what controls the discourse of names—are names being used here to create an openness to the other's possibility, or are they being used to close off that possibility?

This system of naming has its institutions. I do not see any way of breaking with this system that does not have its own institutions, though the distinction between instituting possibility over against the institution of counter-possibility must be carefully preserved—which is to say, preserved in an analytic sense, for the very reason that the historical relationship of impossibility, possibility, and counter-possibility (the relationship is written here in a linear portrayal of the actual tensions) is necessarily not such a neat and tidy affair.

Institutions institute, first of all, a mode of discourse. Simply "destroying the state machinery," as recommended by Marx in the period of the Paris Commune and by Lenin in the period from *State and Revolution* forward, may indeed do little to challenge prevailing and entrenched discursive formations. Sometimes just the opposite is achieved.

An old problem is being addressed here. Traditionally the problem has been understood as the question of a "beginning" in political struggle—a beginning with either consciousness or with institutions, or, as I prefer to put it, with subjects or structures. In either formulation, it is fairly obvious that I stress the latter of the pair. But the "structure" that I want to emphasize first of all is language. That is, writing is the key to addressing the subject/structure configuration, which is always an *underwritten* matrix, no less than writing underwrites our binarizations of nature and culture. Remembering the arguments from previous chapters, it should be clear that the immediate institution of a new writing is out of the question. On the other hand, the ground can be prepared for the *revelation* of this writing, through the exercise of writerly politics.[14]

How does this allow people to liberate themselves from the state of apartheid? In "deconstructive politics" thus far there has been a kind of deeply academic evasion of such questions. Let it be said: there is no way out of apartheid, or any other form of institutionalized counter-possibility, without struggle. In South Africa this means, almost certainly, civil war. Personally, I feel more than a little self-conscious about the discourse of "violence and metaphysics"[15] when this talk seems utterly distinct from institutionalized, brutal violence. There is no better place to begin in the elaboration of a deconstructive politics than with the question of strategy, the *orientation* of struggle.

Language reveals our human possibilities. The strategy of counter-possibility is always to bring these diverse possibilities under a single logic. In this century the name given to this logic is "reason," and accordingly, all who resist this logic are running "counter to reason." (This is the sort of logic, by the way, that continues to justify U.S. investment in South Africa.) "If only everyone would listen to the voice of reason!" This voice takes it as a virtue that it can stifle all other voices. And yet again the point is that these other voices would indeed have no hope of being raised and heard if there was not a fracture in reason itself. Reason based in real, social institutions occasionally chokes on its own words—and can sometimes be made to choke; especially at these times, opportunities for name-displacement come into play.

However, what has just been described is an almost classical case of capitalism in crisis, in which supposedly "universal" interests are, in a very short period, revealed as class-bound. The situation in South Africa can be considered an almost permanent form of such a crisis, so permanent that this very fact makes struggle difficult. Here the South African case is exemplary. The problem is not one of seeing that the ruling class does not rule in the name of universal interest—there is little pretense to that. The problem is in forming a coherent sense of the margin that must displace those who claim a name only for themselves. "Forming a coherent sense," however, has its military and strategic side as well. The permanence of this crisis makes struggle difficult, but so does the fact that, to be sure, South Africa exists in an international order, supported by other powers for economic as well as military-strategic reasons. In practical terms, the only claim to universality that can be asserted by the ruling party (as of this writing) is in comparison to openly fascist elements that make no such pretense—and in comparison to the system of tribal names that the white rulers have violently imposed upon the Black masses.

In the U.S., identity-logic functions much more smoothly and subtly. Public rhetoric is managed in such a way that there are very few chokes, very few openings for something other. But, by its very nature, as a flattening form of counter-possibility that must necessarily deal in the media of rhetoric and sign-systems, this "management" must indeed contain fissures and fractures.

What justifies this sudden leap from the theoretical and practical dimensions of breaking with apartheid in South Africa to commentary on the corporate media of the U.S.? It has everything to do with the orientation of the struggle.

Fascism has never been easy to define.[16] Sometimes fascism is defined as the open, terroristic dictatorship of the bourgeoisie (see Wolff 1983). In this respect, South Africa is a fascist country (more so than Nazi Germany, in this particular sense, because Hitler and the ruling caste were not exactly the bourgeoisie). But what is "open," in this formulation? In South Africa there is the open rule of counter-possibility. The state proclaims openly: we have no need or use or desire for your diversity, we will do what we can to destroy it. In the U.S. this is not openly proclaimed, or at least not very often (not as a "policy" anyway). On the contrary, diversity is brought under the category of pluralism. It is also the case that the question of the "state" is somewhat different in the U.S. But then, South Africa does very much have need of the labor of those it will otherwise prevent from naming themselves. In South Africa there is a tight intertwining of super-exploitation and racial oppression.

Where there is an intertwining, however, there is also a separation: in other words, the logic of racial oppression cannot simply be brought under the production paradigm.

In the U.S. there has been in recent years a mounting and ever more deadly war on Black people, which is being called "the war on drugs." It is easy enough to see how the media has built consensus on this question, with its racist imagery of "street crime" (also a by-word in the 1988 Presidential campaign of George Bush) and "gang activity," etc. Who could be against this war on drugs?[17]

If apartheid is going to be deinstitutionalized, then the institution of racist discourse has to be dealt with at both its points of "origin" and points of dissemination. More and more, the media has to be seen as the key institution, for the media has the power to confer names. This is especially true in countries like the U.S.—but *because* it is true for the U.S., Japan, West Germany, England, France, etc., i.e., centers of media monopoly, it is also true for South Africa.

We will return to this point.

Media

We are living in the age of semiotic capitalism. In flattening the sign, capital has indeed achieved a kind of victory. Like all its other "victories," this victory will also undermine its own basis in capital. Unlike other capitalist victories, however, this semiotic victory of capitalism in the (not coincidentally) nuclear age, does not leave the same sorts of possibilities for victories by the other.[18] Two parallel, flattening logics are at work here. There is a military logic predicated on the use of weapons that will ensure that capital will "win" only if it, and everyone on this planet, loses. (I do not believe that this fact alone will prevent capital from pursuing such a "victory.") And there is the impoverishment of semantic resources, which has the effect of *originating* consciousness as always already pacified and complacent. This strategy subverts what revolutionaries have always taken as a basic and dependable law—the idea that "where there is oppression there is resistance." This "law" still holds to some, not insignificant, degree. Not everyone has been turned into a smiley-face button (i.e., J. Danforth Quayle) yet. But originating consciousness as already euphorically cynical *is* one of the key strategies of post-60s capitalism.

The strategic question I want to raise is whether, in concentrating on a thoroughly televisual and telemetric form of bread-and-circuses spectacle, capitalism is not picking up a rock that it might be made to drop on its own foot.

For the spirit of the letter is to work through mediations, mediations that cannot be so easily commanded to "start" and stop and remain in their proper containers.

Counter-institutions must confront those institutions that are central to the imposition of counter-possibility. I have argued that counter-possibility is institionalized, in the contemporary world, through a semiotic capitalism that relies first of all on the power to name. There is

no single "source" of this power, but the role played by "the media" is
crucial to the functioning of semiotic capitalism. In recent years, a
debate has emerged concerning the media, and television in particular,
that largely replicates the argument between Adorno and Benjamin
concerning popular art. I would like to make a few comments on that
argument as a prelude to turning to the question of media.

The details of this dispute are well known and can be found
elsewhere.[20] Adorno, it might be said, never accepted that there could be
such a thing as "popular art." For him, there is no distinction between
popular art and "mass art," the latter being explicitly designated as a
product of the "culture industry."[21] In his famous essay, "The Work of
Art in the Age of Mechanical Reproduction," Benjamin (1969, 217–51)
argues that the "loss of aura" that accompanies the technical reproducibility of works of art, by means of photography, sound recording, film,
etc., has the liberating effect of bringing art closer to the masses. People
do not feel so threatened by the artwork; indeed, they feel a sense of
participation that Benjamin associates with a potential flowering of
radically democratic tendencies. As Derrida puts it,

Benjamin insists on this: as soon as the technique of reproduction
reaches the stage of photography, a break line and also a new front
traverses the whole space of art. The presumed uniqueness of a
production, the being-only-once of the exemplar, the value of
authenticity is practically deconstructed. Religion, cult, ritual, the
aura, stop hiding, in art, the political as such. As soon as one can
reproduce, not only works of art which lent themselves, or so one
thought, to the distinction production/reproduction, but also
others in which reproduction breaches the original structure . . . ,
"the function of art is no longer grounded in a ritual but on another
praxis: it has its foundation in politics." (1987b, 175–76)

Benjamin's prediction, however, that reproducability would ensure the production of a radical left praxis, did not come to fruition. For
Adorno, the world order that took shape with the end of the Second
World War gave the lie to any attempt to create "popular art." Such
art—Adorno would not even allow that "popular art" is art, of course—
can only play an "affirmative" role.[22]

Adorno, in search of "negation," can only settle with the avant-
garde. To his way of thinking, the only hope lies in an art that speaks a
language that is virtually incomprehensible (thus Adorno is especially
interested in avant-garde music, whereas Benjamin is more inclined
toward literature, theatre, and film). Anything less than the artistic

experiment at the limits of comprehensibility is liable to be quickly recuperated. Furthermore, Adorno sees the cultural arena as the only real stage for political struggle in the post-war period; more "direct" political engagements (which Adorno always refused) were just as liable to be coopted by identity-logic.

Nothing could be easier than to agree with Adorno. The reproductive image turned out, in the longer run, to be just as useful to fascism and capitalism as it could be to radical programs. And yet there is a side to Adorno's argument that is not simply elitist, but, more to the point, radically impractical. Adorno's program for culture seems, in its more extreme form, to take up a position not simply at the limits of comprehensibility, but rather in a whole other world. Not a world that is "incomprehensible"—insomuch as Adorno wants to test limits and draw out the critical mind I am with him. Instead, Adorno seems to want to take up a position that is simply beyond the sway of identity-logic. There are two problems with this: such a position is not obtainable and, more significantly, such a position is basically ineffectual. The real problem is to find the fracture within identity-logic.

There is a further problem, of course, with Adorno's position: the avant-garde simply does not exist anymore, even if it pretends to.[23]

I have outlined the Adorno/Benjamin dispute (which Adorno had the luxury of thinking about for thirty more years after Benjamin's death) mainly in order to put forward a position that I hope will not simply be taken as a sign of an impasse or equivocation (although it is the postmodern impasse that gives rise to this position). That is, I do not think that it is either possible or desirable to "decide" between Adorno and Benjamin on the question of mass art and high art. I doubt that we can afford the luxury of deciding. It is quite true that attempts at radical expression in popular art are often recuperated, sometimes at a blinding speed. (For instance, break dancing, a popular dance form created by inner-city Black youths, was featured in a Selective Service television commercial within a matter of weeks of its initial appearance on the streets.) At the same time, however, I do not think that it can be said that such expressions have no effect whatsoever—they simply do not have the effect that Adorno was hoping for. Perhaps Adorno placed too much hope in the cultural sphere. (In a moment we will turn to the question of the role that the media of reproducibility plays in recuperation.) Furthermore, one would be hard put to measure the actual radical effect, if any, of the avant-garde in the second half of the twentieth century. (Popular art does at least seem to play a radicalizing role every now and then.) And yet, Adorno has his point as well: the strategy of straining comprehensibility, in order to make the familiar strange, and in order to create discomfort with complacency, is both viable and necessary. But this cannot be the only strategy, and, even where this is the strategy, the Adorno approach must remain anchored in the very logic that it seeks to subvert. That is, this strategy must be deconstructive.

This debate, as I mentioned earlier, has resurfaced around the question of the media, especially electronic media. With the emphasis so shifted, however, there is less room for a double strategy. The media tend to blend everything into the same mush, whether it is "high," "popular," or what have you (some would say that the media cannot help but to make everything "low"). Furthermore, it seems that this media is by nature *not* "popular."[24] And yet, if there is anything in the advanced capitalist countries that plays the role of what Althusser called "Ideological State Apparatuses," it is the media. This is the case even where, as in the United States, the media are not state owned or controlled. To put it crudely: the state could not do what it does without the deep complicity of the media and, with that complicity, the political system has far-reaching powers. My question, to put it simply, is whether the media can be deconstructed and, in what would this deconstruction consist?

There is a kind of euphoric postmodernism that intends an emptying out of the modern self into the electronic media. This euphoria was foreshadowed, most famously, by Marshall McLuhan's pathbreaking study, *Understanding Media: The Extensions of Man*. This is still very much a current book, essential for thinking about the writings of Lyotard (*The Postmodern Condition*, that is), Baudrillard, and other "televisual" thinkers. Readers of McLuhan will realize, better than those who take a quasi-Adornoian stance on this quesion, that to pose the question as one of "for or against TV" is to miss certain crucial aspects of the new technologies. Mark Crispin Miller (1988), a media critic who is influenced by Adorno, argues that "Big Brother is you, watching." It does not seem that this formulation appies only to those who "watch TV." We live, after all, in a televisual society—like it or not, we are all plugged in; like it or not, we are already watching TV.

Television and other forms of telecommunication constantly bombard us with "information," through an ever-broadening, ever-deepening net that is more and more global (see Bagdikian 1983). McLuhan may be credited with two basic insights into the development of this net. First, he argued that the new media "affect the entire field of the senses" (1964, 45). Indeed, the new media get involved at a deeper level than our senses because, "it extends, not our eyes, but our central nervous systems as a planetary vesture" (ibid.; 147) We are, however, not well prepared for this epistemological shift, because, in a literate society, "it is how [media] are used that counts" (ibid.; 18). This was McLuhan's claim in 1964. It is a claim against which the further insinuation of media into all areas of life, into our "epistemology," as McLuhan would have it, should be measured. For McLuhan's second insight was that the new media would make possible the "global village."

McLuhan is right on both counts, I think. As soon as the epistemology of the new media takes hold, we *are* in a global, post-literate village. There is, however, one very big problem, a problem that is pointed out in superb fashion in two recent books, *Fast Capitalism* by Ben Agger, and *The Telephone Book* by Avital Ronell. That is, the "global village" is a world-level recreation of the pre-secular community. Agger points out that the "post-literate" society is one in which not only the book has been destroyed, but significance along with it. Indeed:

> Fast capitalism whittles down and otherwise so reduces opposition that it is difficult even to pose the problem of the degradation of signification. The stronger the center, the more it marginalizes dissent; and the more dissent is coopted, the stronger the center becomes. The fateful circuitry exists through which it is so difficult to think another society without borrowing so much from its fast texts that they reduce the dissenting writing merely to terms of a given discourse.
>
> ... In fast capitalism textuality is swallowed in its own objectifications and thus is so quickly received that it cannot be remembered. Such instantaneity utterly overwhelms the capacity to remember, let alone rewrite, what one has read. (1989b, 59, 45)

Such an agenda is not foreign to McLuhan. As Baudrillard put it, summarizing McLuhan, "The media make—indeed they are—the revolution, independently of their content..." (1981, 177). In other words, a revolution without people, or at least without people for whom autonomy could be a value. What McLuhan never thematized, for reasons that seem transparently political and indeed a bit ominous, was that life for the post-literate person in the global village is little different from life in the homogenous, pre-secular community.

One might say that Derrida's problematics of "the end of the book and the beginning of writing" presuppose the book and all that goes along with literate culture—it is not a problematics "before the book." (Following Derrida, we might question whether there could be a "before the book," any more than there are "peoples without writing.")

In *The Telephone Book*, Ronell (1989) argues that to answer the telephone is to say "yes" to fascism, because of the opening that one allows to the global net that technologizes beings, deepening even further the rift between beings and Being.

My question is: suppose that everyone mentioned in this discussion of media thus far, McLuhan, Miller, Agger, and Ronell, is right—then what? For it seems to me that society is already plugged into the global media network and, despite Agger to the contrary, it is not going to be possible to launch critique by struggling to slow the pace of fast capitalism. One is certainly welcome to try, and there may be no harm in trying, up to a point—up to the point, that is, where "figuring out how to write books again" diverts attention from the circuitry that must be disentangled from the inside.[25]

The self-contained "environment" that I alluded to in Chapter 2 is a fully-mediated "world" in one sense, namely that there is no specific point at which this world must insist on some essential contact with some other "reality." This world carries with it all that, from within this world, can be taken as "reality," and, for that matter, all that can be understood as "good." Thus it becomes difficult to ask questions of the sort, "If the new media have brought broad and deep changes in their wake—more appropriately, through their "circuits"—is this necessarily all to the good?" For it would be difficult to define "good" apart from this "world." One endpoint of this sort of thinking is the conscious decision—but what is "consciousness," at this stage of things?—to voluntarily become the "brain in a vat": "the evil genius is me." But there may be another sense of the fully-mediated world that is not captured by the enveloping homogeneity of televisual society. The telecommunicative environment is fully-mediated in the sense specified above, but it is not fully-mediated in the sense of participating in all the possible mediations, all the possible possibilities. Thus its modality tends toward the counter-possible, and its politics tends toward the limiting of human possibilities, toward the screening of the other only within the channels of the Same.

And yet, if this screening is our metaphysics in this postmodern period, as celebrated by Baudrillard, then there is no other strategy than the occupation of this space in a deconstructive way. Turning the TV off, in conventional terms, may be a good strategy for self-purification, if one thinks that such purification is really possible. It is undoubtedly a good way to gain some time to think. But there must be more creative ways to act against the televisual, ways that operate the possibilities of television. Certainly, one of these ways may be to explode television, at the margins of legality.[26] Other subversions of telecommunications will involve computer hacking and alternative networks. And still other subversions will involve the mediation of mediation: a rethematization of other areas of the general text.

Brutality and the sign (and more thoughts on breaking with apartheid)

The sign can either be oriented toward impossibility, toward "all" (an unknowable and impossible quantity) of its possibilities, or toward counter-possibility. There is nothing essential about the sign other than its iterability. It may be that repetition necessarily underwrites the possibility of difference and diversity, but the future of our planet cannot depend on this any more than this future can depend on the good will of politicians. In this Pepsi generation, diversity has to contend with Coca-Cola repetition. The sign oriented toward counter-possibility is the sign of brutality.

In a key section in *of Grammatology*, "The Battle of Proper Names" (1976, 107–18), Derrida makes a seemingly paradoxical argument about the relationship between names and the practice of writing:

If writing is no longer understood in the narrow sense of linear and phonetic notation, it should be possible to say that all societies capable of producing, that is to say of obliterating, their proper names, and of bringing classificatory difference into play, practice writing in general. (1976, 109)

The seeming paradox is in essentially relating the production and obliteration of proper names. The name, however, as a sign among signs, must, no less than any other sign, remain unstable. The name, after all, especially the name that we call the "proper" name, is, on the one hand, that place in writing where the sign is most oriented toward absolute proximity (or, as Derrida puts it, "consciousness"), but on the other hand, and for the very reason of that orientation, where the sign is most unstable and most subject to the violence of origins. By this violence is meant the turbulence generated between these two poles, which have already been named as the impossible—that which draws us away from the seeming presence (let us also call it a certain dream of autonomy) of absolute proximity—and the counter-possible, an obsti- nate holding to the proper. This turbulence is perhaps not transcendable: there will perhaps always be some "risk of essence" that has to be taken. We have distinguished, however, between a strategic risk as opposed to a metaphysical commitment. This distinction, to be sure, is "merely analytic"—"in the final analysis." This proviso, however, is of the very nature of strategy, of strategic thinking and action.

Keeping this in mind—that our best strategy is to fend off "the final analysis," I propose a concluding variation on the political modalities (impossible/counter-possible) that have framed the analysis here. We may provisionally consider the "unnamed" and the "unnameable" as different categories. The unnameable participates in the responsibility of the impossible (toward the other), while the unnamed is a category of counter-possibility. It is the erasure of possibility through the erasure of an emergent name. The person (or movement) who is unnamed can be subjugated or destroyed without notice (this is another way of saying, "We represent the universal discourse—too bad if you don't fit in"). Without notice—but not necessarily without remainder.[27] The margins must create a new machinery of naming, and yet this machinery must also engage with, and subvert, the counter-possible machinery of unnameing.

There is no "inside" to the sign—only an infinite outside, only context. The closest that one can come to an inside is to the mechanisms of the symbolic order. This is the political topos that must necessarily be emphasized.[28]

The only element that needs to be added, in conventional terms, is sacrifice. To liberate territory by the displacement of the name that unnames takes sacrifice: the risk of being unnamed. But who demands this sacrifice? Of whom is this sacrifice demanded?

This sacrifice is demanded by those who are already making it, those whose lives are impossible, those who risk being unnamed, those who are in the margins—those who "are" not, those who are unnameable. Those, and *that which.*

This sacrifice is demanded of those who are, in whatever "present," open to the fracture that will always haunt the logic of the Same.

This sacrifice is no more than responsibility—and no less.

Taken together, the impossible and those who could hear the call of the other, of impossibility, are humanity—are all who can make a claim on the name, "human."

That is almost everyone.

After the age of originality: this unnameable community

The secular age is peculiar for its sense of originality. The sign must have its origin, a community must have its origin, etc. "As it was in the beginning, is now, and ever shall be" is a secular theme. Anything that has a beginning has an end. Therefore, a sign with no end must have no beginning. And community with no end must have no beginning. (But it has yet to be determined whether community has no end—which is the essence of "not having an end" that I am trying to evoke here.)

The movements that will reinvent the community have names and must have names. They must have beginnings and ends.

Community is here, it is the matrix of possibilities called by the impossible. Responsibility and recognition, letting the other speak: these are community's "beginnings."

The matrix that must be inhabited in order to displace the machinery of unnameing is a global information net that will, in the last decade of the twentieth century, only reach further into every aspect of people's lives. The effect of this net (not entirely planned, but increasingly recognized and capitalized upon) is to create formations in information—to form in informing. The net does not simply reach into different areas of people's lives—it increasingly defines those areas in so reaching. As Mark Crispin Miller (1988) has argued, this net does not at all "bring us all closer together" (also see Ryan 1989, 89–90). On the contrary, it merely ensures the dominance and cynical repetition of the deadening (deafening) logic of the Same. Unlike Miller, I propose inhabiting this net differently, though the dangers of recuperation so well documented by Miller and others cannot be ignored (but it is those very dangers that are intimately bound up with the fact that fissures may be exploited as sites of possibility). And I propose a kind of graffiti politics aimed at disrupting the sameness of the net and at creating alternative nets (punk rock, rap, xerography, portable video, alternative women's health care, computer hacking and networking, postering, and other forms that have yet to be invented).

The kind of question that the emerging, diverse community will face is, for example, whether this global information net, which is capable of enforcing the most brutal unnameings, can be displaced by a global communications net, where there is as much emphasis on commune in communication, as there is on formation in information. In other words, an *interactive* global net.

Such a net, however, is as far as post-secular community should go toward globalism. The hyper-secular insistence on mobility has been achieved (for a few, basically, at least if we mean voluntary mobility) at the cost of the destruction of the capacity for affective bonds between people and between people and the earth. We need to know the other, and that means to *live with* the other, and truly be a possibility for the other and let the other be a possibility for us. I know of no good way to say this "in theory," if by theory we mean a kind of panoramic view, for the point is to revalorize the sense of locality and local participation. Without such participation, diversity is groundless (pluralism might even be defined as "groundless diversity"). I find much to admire on this score in the essays of Wendell Berry (esp. 1987), which argue and demonstrate the virtues of the "Great Economy," as rooted in local, non-corporate, subsistance farming, without descending into mere sentimentality or nostalgia.[29] There is also much "local knowledge" in the future vision of Marge Piercy's *Woman on the Edge of Time,* in which different cultures are not taken to be either essential or permanent (insomuch as one must remain a member of such a culture), and yet are at the same time held to be centrally important in the formation of human life as possibility.[30]

Simply seeing the other on television cannot allow us to commune with our fellows—on the contrary. Right now the problem is that the other can be put on the screen as this or that abomination, and just as easily be taken off the screen or never put on to start with—i.e., unnamed. Community without origin or outcome requires the possibility of the proximity of the impossible. The problem is not that media transmissions are "too mediated." Derrida does not turn away from media for this reason, and neither do I. The problem is that the *fullness* of mediation—meaning not its presence, but its possibility, its opening, all the possibilities that we now know but would lose—is not captureable by foreseeable modes of electronic information. All that you are, and all that I am, in all our possibilities and mediations, cannot at present be perpetuated, postponed indefinitely, without beginning or end, by existing modes of telecommunication, even if new possibilities are emerging with these modes. Perhaps this will not always be the case, but that is all the more reason that a diverse community, open to its impossibility and aware of the threat of the counter-possible which unnames, must maintain the memory and open-endedness of human possibility by diverse means.

Afterword: Postmodern social theory at loose ends (points for further research and discussion)

The foregoing text was conceived from the start as an initial exploration, albeit in somewhat large scale, into the possibilities of Derridean social theory. As much as any text, this one remains open-ended, but purposely so. Work on this book began, at least in a very preliminary way, in the summer of 1987, with a long conversation with Professor Derrida at the School of Criticism and Theory at Dartmouth College. At the School and in the three and a half years following that truly wonderful experience (for which I thank not only Professor Derrida, but also especially the School's Director for that year, Professor Geoffrey Hartman, and Professor Houston Baker, with whom I had many hours of fruitful study and warm friendship—I think that I already indicated somewhere in this book that I'm a bit sentimental), I had the opportunity for extremely valuable discussion concerning the work-in-progress. A paper, "Elements of a Derridean social theory," generated from the original proposal for the project, which then was transmogrified into section three of the first chapter, was presented at various forums, including the Society for Phenomenology and Existential Philosophy annual meeting at Duquesne University and the Society for Social and Political Philosophy annual meeting at Iowa State University. From these presentations I received many valuable comments, criticisms, and questions that are represented, in one form or another, in the final product.

There will always remain more questions than answers, however. On the whole this is a very good thing, not only for those who are occupied by philosophy and social theory (I hope that this phrase is sufficiently ambiguous), but also for those who seek those possibilities of society and community that are open-ended. I thought that it might be useful to give an account of what I think still remains to be done, especially in terms of issues that are either raised directly by this text, or concerning issues that must necessarily be part of an ongoing investigation of this sort. This account is presented in the form of a series of questions and answers, a kind of informal self-interview, sometimes with words, and certainly with questions and comments, given to me by others. I wish in advance to thank them all, but I would especially like to thank Gary Shapiro, Steve Fuller, Diana Fuss, Roger Gottlieb, and Svetozar Stojanovic, all of whom raised important questions concerning the final formulation of the book.

Q: It seems that, on the one hand, there has been a resistance to "the social" by some thinkers who have been called "postmodern" while, on the other hand, there has been a resistance to deconstruction on the part of philosophers. We might add that, in the former case, there seems to be an analogy (and the question is whether there is also a complicity) between a postmodern resistance to politics and neo-conservative market ideology (an ideology which is, at the same time, a claim for the "end of ideology"). What are the sources of these resistances?

A: In the first place, the question depends on two conflations that are typical and that should be resisted. This is not to rule out what is important in the question, but still, we should be careful. First, and perhaps this is not such a deep point to make but it should be made all the same, I am quite concerned to *not* conflate all thinkers who happen to write in the French language into a single paradigm. (I often joke that my two favorite "French" philosophers, Derrida and Levinas, are not exactly French—although, as important practitioners of the French language, perhaps they are more French than many who are native-born; this is not an insignificant question of identity politics.) Unfortunately, it still has to be pointed out that Derrida is not Lyotard is not Foucault is not Cixous, etc. I realize that this makes life a little more difficult for those who depend on such groupings, either positively or negatively. Second, and more importantly, an important aspect of the argument in Chapter 3, concerning "poetry" and "communication," was to make clear the dangers of taking "the social" as a category apart. At the same time, perhaps I did not show sufficiently how political responsibility does not thereby devolve/disappear into a general, "everything is political," mush. (Dick Howard has some interesting things to say about this question in his *Defining the Political.*)

There are, however, more interesting dimensions to this question of resistance. I wonder if the two resistances are not two sides of the same coin. Part of the issue has to do with the institutional setting in which Derrida's work was first received in the U.S. (In the last few years Derrida has said, in various interviews, that "something called deconstruction," as he puts it, is essentially a product of the academy in the U.S. The further interesting thing that Derrida has said is that, not only is deconstruction "American," but "America is deconstruction."

One can only hope!) That institutional framework itself should be subjected to a great deal of critical scrutiny in dealing with the question of resistances. That our subject matters are determined somewhat by intellectual "turf" conflicts is something that deconstruction (and for that matter, structuralism and semiotics before it) is especially interested to address. This is not to say that deconstruction ignores the developments and special methodologies of particular disciplines, but certainly where there is both institutional hierarchy and a core of positivistic assumptions that not only guide individual disciplines, but also compartmentalize them in a way that seems to close off more possibilities than are opened up, then there is some work for deconstruction to do. This is a big chore, part of which involves pedagogy, part of which involves the university as an institution and its relation to other social and economic structures, and part of which involves addressing positivism in theoretical and practical terms. Derrida's extensive work in the latter project is brought to bear on the question of the university (and education more generally) in a number of essays, including "The Principle of Reason: The University in the Eyes of Its Pupils." Gregory Ulmer is taking this pedagogical project in interesting directions with his *Applied Grammatology* and other writings. Perhaps all of this work is building toward an engagement between the texts of Derrida and Paulo Freire, which to me would be a welcome development.

After setting out this larger project, the following observations will undoubtedly seem a bit facile. But then, Rome wasn't deconstructed in a day!

On the one hand, much of the deconstructive establishment in the U.S. has not wanted to get very close to political questions thematized as such. Perhaps it is important to note that, in no small measure, this "establishment" consists in students (either first or second generation) of the "Yale School" and especially of Paul de Man. The reaction of many of these students to the question (blown out of all proportion by opportunists both inside and outside of the academy) of Paul de Man's politics as a young man has been, unfortunately, to battle for the turf that they had gained in literary studies during the seventies and eighties. That is, they worried about their reputations, careers, and fortunes—not a pretty sight in a group that was already plenty fortunate. The more significant point is that the "de Man affair" presented the opportunity for a larger political engagement that the establishment in literary deconstruction was resistant to. This was an opportunity to say, "You want to talk about fascism and complicity with the machinations of authoritarian governments? Good—let's really open this question up." I believe that it is not too late for this debate to take such a direction, but obviously there is a resistance that has to be dealt with—indeed, deconstructed. I would like to make just one small remark about the more practical dimensions of this deconstruction: although Derrida can be read in the French context as attempting to avoid the political metaphysics and the metaphysical politics of that person who indeed dominated the intellectual scene when Derrida was a young man, Jean-Paul Sartre, I don't think that Derrida, in problematizing Sartre's model of the engaged intellectual, ever attempts or intends to mark some absolute distance from the possibility and indeed the necessity of engagement. In this respect, perhaps one most sees the resistance to the social in a certain standard, but entirely one-sided, reading of the end of Derrida's "The Ends of Man."

On the other hand, where "literary deconstructionists" *have* been more politically engaged (for example, Gayatri Spivak, Michael Ryan, and Gregory S. Jay—the first chapter of his recent *America the Scrivener*, "Values and Deconstructions," is a major contribution to the project of deconstructive politics), the social theorists have been a bit snooty and unreceptive. Perhaps the larger point, the one that shapes this social theory/literary criticism bifurcation, and certainly the point that I want to stress (from my privileged position seemingly apart from the institutional turf war, you might say—fair enough), is that Derrida provides the basis for a new language of politics. This is quite a different project than what we are used to in social theory. One sees its emergence in the work of Tracy Strong, William Corlett, William Connolly, Michael Shapiro, Mark Warren, and others. (Interestingly enough, these theorists, some of whom are in political science departments—possibly the worst place to try to carry out this project, given that most such departments are bulwarks of both "Americanism" and positivism, a natural combination—find that they must, of necessity, mainly work with colleagues in other departments.) In relation to their work, I have tried to do two things: 1) to not only call for a different language of politics and a different politics of language, but, at least some of the time, to engage in the very interpretive praxis that I thematize; 2) to insist on a stronger connection between, on the one hand, Nietzschean-Heideggerian themes (which are primary in the aforementioned thinkers) and the concerns of Marxism.

Perhaps it is crucial to point out that, as a social theorist, I feel that I can only "engage in the very interpretive praxis that I thematize" part of the time. The rest of the time I am trying to address issues in something like the standard languages of philosophy and social theory. Given that the development of a new language of politics must necessarily be gradual—one cannot simply leap to a new language without some principle of translation, which is why Derrida never claims to "think beyond the concept," but rather at its limit—perhaps one can expect the breakdown of certain resistances to be somewhat gradual also. I suppose that I do, however, hope to see a leap in terms of the desire to deconstruct the resistance to the social and the resistance to deconstruction.

I cannot help noting, at the conclusion of these remarks, that the term, "deconstruction," is probably used more times here than in the entire preceding text. Recently it seems that, after a period of resistance to this, Derrida is using the term more often, although sometimes couched in the expression (as noted above), "something called deconstruction"—as though he is no longer responsible for the term, which is indeed the case. I think that I would prefer at least *some* resistance to the term, insomuch as "deconstruction" gets in the way of a broader and deeper analysis of Derrida's work.

Q: Why the confessional, almost apologetic tone of the self-identification in the vignette on difference in the first section of Chapter 2? More problematically than the tone, this self-identification—"I, a white male theorist...," homogenizes your identity when the force of the argument is to work against such essentializing tendencies in theories of identity. It does not strike me, in any case, as a particularly exhaustive description (as if such a thing were possible) and so could be easily dropped.

A: I too have worried about the confessional tone—am I oversensitive here? Am I just trying to cover myself? I'm trying to deal, in part, with the "men in feminism" question here. I don't think that anyone quite knows what to do with this yet. I thought that it might mark a new direction here to take a kind of "oath," to make a "profession of good faith." This can have the effect of simply reifying the very form of subjectivity that I hope to disrupt. And yet the other side of this issue is the sort of "critical cross-dressing" that feminist critics have quite rightly lambasted. It is important to walk a certain tightrope here, not simply homogenizing my own subject position, and yet not relieving myself of a fundamental responsibility either. At the same time, what am "I" doing in this? The idea is that the theorist is not disembodied. Working out the possibilities here will probably be a matter of ongoing strategies and negotiations in a situation that itself is continually changing. There is even a certain embarrassment in the words I've used, marking a position that is not fully "mine," and yet which I cannot mark an absolute difference from—meaning that, the words of this oath do become somewhat disembodied, or at least separated from my particular body, and then they haunt me with responsibility. This is one way that responsibility can work, however—in "myself" I have nothing to respond to.

The formulation of the oath also cannot be taken as something entirely separate from other formulations of self-assertion and positionality generated in the text. The oath is a moment that, while not entirely disrupted, is part of a larger sequence. Still, in this particular cultural moment, I would like to retain the oath as perhaps something that needs to be risked (for "now," realizing that there really is no such thing).

Q: A question concerning this text which still awaits an answer is, What is a social theory? While the text articulates, for example, an argument for Derrida's superiority to Habermas on the issue on normative grounding, the attempt to move from such points to a fully-developed social theory leaves out many of the familiar concerns that social theorists address: What are the essential social structures? How do they condition other structures and historical change? What historically immanent grounds are there for believing that emancipation is possible? Who or what is to be the agent of emancipation? While the text provides normative support from a deconstructed, "different" social agent(s) perspective, it does not really deal with these other questions. The text is thus open to a traditional Marxist critique: e.g., that the issue of naming is superstructural, not essential; or that the politics of this text are idealist (renaming the building in Chapter 5 instead of re-owning it).

A: In some sense, it was part of my purpose to be "open" to a traditional Marxist critique, though hopefully in a way that requires Marxism to be open as well. I have taken it for granted that Marxism does a good job of dealing with some of the questions just raised, and that there is no need to "go beyond" Marxism on these questions. Of course, that is also to take for granted that "Marxism" is not a monolithic text—something that these questions do not seem to recognize—and that there are forms of Marxism, for example of Adorno or Benjamin, that are not so distant from some of the central concerns of Derrida. The expression, "traditional Marxist critique," too, is funny—given that Marxism purports to be a critique of all tradition. Perhaps that phrase, as much as any, locates this text: it is a text of the period when Marxism has become a tradition. On the other hand, I certainly could have done a better job of saying what parts of Marxism are taken for granted (or what parts of whatever Marxisms). I didn't get deeply involved in that project in part because it was not my primary intention to stage another encounter between Marxism and Derrida, but rather to see what in Derrida's text might be of use in social theory.

When I say, in Chapter 1, that all of the elements are there in

Derrida's text for the sort of social theory that I then try to articulate, it may seem that an overly-extravagant claim is being put forward. But I have a special sense of "in Derrida's text" in mind, or perhaps two special senses. First, I'm thinking of Derrida's sense of supplementarity (especially as set out in of Grammatology) and the sense in which Derrida (quite intentionally, it seems to me) supplements Marx. These points of supplementarity need to be better marked in future research. Second, Derrida writes further of the "dangerous supplement," that which seems to only add on, but which in reality transforms the thing supplemented. Derrida's dangerous supplement to Marxism is, to my mind, his approach to language and meaning. But again, I did not want to primarily make the text a staging of Derrida's dangerous supplement to Marx, though undoubtedly this is a project to which future research should turn.

There has been a longstanding debate over the question of language in terms of the base/superstructure distinction (then again, there has also been an important debate over how to make this distinction and, in particular, how to get beyond some of Marx's and especially Engels' cruder formulations of it). My line on this question has been much influenced by Althusser. (Some of the research I am presently engaged in has to do with how to really take stock of structuralist Marxism while not succumbing to what still might be called "theoretical Stalinism." The first chapter of Fredric Jameson's The Political Unconscious is very useful here.) At any rate, if language is not basic, I don't know what is—therefore, I reject the criticism, raised by some, of "linguistic idealism." (And, as noted more than once in the text, I am agreeing with Habermas in a pretty significant way on this point.) What remains to be shown, however, is how "linguistic materialism," or what I call "intertextual materialism," can be articulated as a (it's embarrassing to say this, but forgive me this momentary lapse) "full-blooded ontology."

If intertextual materialism were to be boiled down to a more practical orientation, I think that it would consist in two principles. First, always support the oppressed, the downtrodden, and the marginalized. Second, be open to learning from many sources. The second of these principles seems easily connected to materialism, but I want to argue that it has to be subordinate to the first principle. That prioritization also seems materialist (theory follows practice), but why say then that the guiding principle is "materialist"—why isn't it a purely "ethical" standpoint? These questions get us into the discussion between Derrida and Levinas, which I invoked in my second chapter. The problem is to show that this very undecideability is itself "materialist." This question has to be addressed in terms of the problematics of alterity and signification. I tried to make a start in this direction in the first chapter, but a great deal more remains to be done. (The work would involve writing a longer text of the sort that I am not used to writing, one that is not very overtly "political." Still, this problem, of a more-articulated intertextual materialism, needs to be taken up as a somewhat separate issue.)

I realize that little of what I have just said sounds much like Marxist materialism (at least of the more orthodox sort), and yet the references to Lenin (on the inexhaustibility of matter) are not gratuitous—they are meant to show that there is an opening, a possibility of supplementation, even in the midst of a fairly orthodox materialism.

Q: The emphasis on difference misses (avoids?) some hard questions. While we all want a space for women and men, blacks and whites, etc., it is not clear that "we" all want a space for, say, fundamentalist religion or pedophilia. How will the marginalized lesbian feminist deal with the marginalized orthodox Jew (whose religion is patriarchal, to say the least)? They may coexist in a conversation, and thus if everything is language or constituted by language they can simply be different signifiers. But social space is not infinite (any more than a library or the page of a book is) and therefore some choices, and some conflict, will arise. Just supporting difference is inadequate here. Which laws will be in place? Which schools will get government funding?, etc. Concerning the development of the idea of positionality, building on feminist theory, in Chapter 4: Doesn't the emphasis on difference leave out the ultimate conflict we have with those who are just too different, for example the Nazis?

A: This is the question that has perhaps come up the most in discussions of the book and in presentations of the "Elements" paper and, of course, in discussions of the possibility of a social theory of difference more generally. The strategic (one might say "metaphysical," except that it is meant to be anti-absolutist) distinction that I rely on is that between the logic of the Same (or, "identity logic") and the disruptive, counter-logic of *differance*. There is, and should be, the practical question of what is to be done about certain practices (and I think it helps to raise the question in terms of practices rather than subjects), e.g., pedophilia. (Everyone seems interested in this one— what's the fixation/fascination?!) It is furthermore important that the distinction I theorize does not give *a priori* answers to these hard questions—and it seems that it is this aspect of the distinction, that it does not issue in a calculus or science of values, that many people find troubling. I, in turn, find it troubling that it is such a calculus that people seem to want, the point being that this would not only be a cure worse than the disease(s), it *is* the disease.

To come down to cases, I am not willing to say that, for instance, pedophilia (since this is everyone's favorite example, along with "the Nazis") is absolutely wrong, if by that one means "wrong because of some foundationalist criteria." On the other hand, if by "absolute" is meant, "in terms of the social weave that we find ourselves in and are responsible for, this thing is absolutely wrong," then that sort of judgment is possible, correct, and even necessary, for it places the emphasis on our responsibility for our ongoing social project. (I still would be wary of an absolute judgment concerning pedophilia—more on this point in a moment.)

In my view, there is very little danger, under a hard look, to thinking that Nazis are "too different." In my argot, Nazism and other versions of violent fascism are the most vicious forms of the logic of the Same. Most forms of sheer intolerance would come under this designation. The real question is in the "live and let live" types of practices—the pedophile is not necessarily proposing that his/her practice be the norm. Of course, such practices are generally not "proposed" period, and therefore there is no participatory responsibility concerning such practices. Again, there is no formula or calculus for generating an answer in the case of any particular practice. In a sense the question was one of present social structures, which is a way of asking which reforms might be supported. That is not an invalid question, for it may in fact be decisive at key points for changing social structures; the question of abortion rights is an important example here. But the larger question is one of whether we are capable of creating social structures in which there is real participation in determining what is Same and what is different. What practices, regardless of whether I participate in them myself, open humanity to new possibilities? Fecundity becomes a key criteria here. Forms of fascism are of course "new possibilities" in the slightest sense (though perhaps not anymore, they've been tried—but there is always some "new" form of cruelty on the horizon), but they close off many other forms of possibility even in the very short run. I think that we have to be able to trust people to see these things, in an environment of participation in which the social structures are always open (at least in principle) to restructuration in order to encourage the greatest degree of participation and responsibility. (This would obviously be a social environment quite different than, say, the present environment for a question like flag-burning, where yokels and professional right-wing ideologues dominate the "debate" because there is always freedom of expression, in this society, for such people. Of course,

Afterword

in the fall and winter of 1990–91, the U.S. Government found a solution to the flag-burning issue: war with Iraq and even more compulsory patriotism.) In such a context, not every practice has to be tried, although every new idea can be given a hearing. There will have to be debate, then, about what is a "new" idea. For instance, the idea of "creationism" is not a new idea—it has little or no currency in the world of evolutionary biology, and there is no scientific reason why our society had to be submitted to this debate. It was a "debate" created artificially in the media by powerful people in support of the Reagan/neo-conservative agenda. (Which was in support of a President who not only did not attend church, but who also seemed truly ignorant of religious practices or traditions, as evidenced by a humorous episode in which Ron and Nancy attended an Episcopal service with George Bush. During communion, Nancy accidentally dropped her wafer into the cup of grape juice. Thinking this was the tradition, rather than an accident, Ron dunked his wafer too. Of course, this happened after Reagan left office, so now we're just supposed to be cynical about Reagan's cynicism—which is of course the main ideological strategy of this system in this period.) However, that is not to say that some of the spiritual/religious impulses that made the media debate popular with some sections of the general population are not themselves valid subjects of debate. They are. I would even go so far as to say that it cannot be ruled out *a priori* that something like creationism could be the subject for a real participatory debate. (I take it, by the way, that "creationism" has nothing to do with creation myths in Genesis or other ancient texts, which do not purport to be "scientific theories," i.e., open to the criteria of falsification.)

But then, by the same token, it seems very clear that we need an open, participatory, and responsible debate about sexuality. I do not see any reason why the question of pedophilia would not be a part of this debate. However, as the original question makes clear, there is still the difficult problem of what to do with those practices that participatory debate deems to not contribute to the opening of human possibility. This, too, would have to be a matter of discussion, but it seems clear that some things would be forbidden, and that there would have to be mechanisms for ensuring that certain social codes are not abridged.

As to the "finitude" of social spaces and libraries and pages of books: I take it that there is a sense in which such texts are open and infinite, although perhaps not for "me" (whoever "me" happens to be at any particular point in the matrix).

Q: For a book that seeks to be rooted in the profound problem of community, there is little attention given to the fact that contemporary

America (and other parts of the world) is (are) experiencing a dramatic increase in spirituality as a way to deal with life and to form communities. And this is the case not just intellectually, but in terms of how "ordinary" people conceive of their lives. The breakdown of positivism which gave rise to deconstruction also gave rise to forms of thought and practice and social duty based on identification with transcendent experiences and forms of consciousness. The "postsecular socialism" proposed in this book looks quite secular from the point of view of, say, a 12-step program, a Buddhist meditation center, the Catholic Sanctuary movement, etc. For such people the world is not "thoroughly secular." The world may be thoroughly secular in the social circles the author is in, but then he has to restrict his grand claims about what his subject matter is, and recognize that he simply is not addressing the vital concerns of a whole host of people from David Griffin to Joanna Macy to Kubler-Ross, to Ram Dass to Charles Curran or Carter Heyward, etc. This issue goes along with the author's critique of Habermas. Suppose, for instance, we were to say that humanity aims at love rather than logos?

A: I agree with much of the spirit of this criticism. A similar, and to my mind even more important, criticism might be raised about the lack of discussion of the historical experience of community. In terms of my current work, I find myself returning to these questions again and again. Therefore, I'm partly inclined to say that I should leave these historical/empirical questions for future research.

However, I do have some problems with the examples offered. I imagine that people have entered such diverse groups as the sanctuary movement, Buddhist meditation, etc., primarily because they also see the world as overwhelmingly secular and therefore spiritually barren. Their analyses of the meaning of secularism and the possible alternatives is, I'm sure, different than mine, and, at least in some cases, I'm sure that I could learn many things from their analyses. Still, much of what goes under the name of the "new spirituality" seems almost straightforwardly to be a new age salve on the conscience of the greedy West. And, to me there is a world of difference between the sanctuary movement and liberation theology, on the one hand, and the "wisdom" of Shirley MacLaine and other crystal-rubbers. I realize that that is a pretty tendentious way to put it, but I remain sceptical of the almost entirely white, middle-class "new age movement." The "spirituality" there doesn't seem to go very deep. The aim of this movement seems to be transcendence without difference. Of the people mentioned in the question, I would have to put David Ray Griffin's "postmodern theology," which is basically warmed-over process theology, in this category as well. That isn't to say that we shouldn't study Whitehead; rather it is simply to wonder what happens when process theology reaches California.

Sarcasm aside, it does seem necessary that "intertextual materialism" deal with its, shall we say, "religious overtones." It does seem to me that there is something like a "religious sensibility," which consists in a basic wonderment at, as Wittgenstein put it, not "how things are," but "that they are." The question is one of finding a principle within this wonderment itself that is oriented toward the call of the other, as opposed to quietism. (Incidentally, for a brilliant look at what a structurally-oriented Marxism coupled with a kind of Buddhist spirituality might look like, see the wonderful novel by E. P. Thompson, *The Sykaos Papers*. I am still waiting for discussion of this novel to open up.)

The idea that humanity is aiming or could be aiming for love rather than logos is quite interesting. Is it so different from the possibility that humanity could aim for a fundamental regard for the other rather than for an "ethics" of calculation and personal advantage-seeking? "Love" is not a term that I know how to use in this context at this point. I'm certainly not opposed, in principle, to the idea. Indeed, understanding love seems crucial to addressing the concerns of, as the original question puts it, the "ordinary people." I'm not sure, however, that we know at this point how to have it both ways, i.e., a structural (Marxist or otherwise) analysis of society coupled with an appreciation of love. A "structural analysis of love," as useful as it may be in some respects, seems to crucially miss the point.

Q: Isn't the deconstruction of pure thought precisely what feminism has aimed for from the start, but not from the guise of an absent play, like Derrida, but rather from the vantage point of self-consciously situated persons? Why do we need Derrida at all, when we have this much more comprehensible feminist literature doing the same thing?

A: First let me say that I received questions of the "why do we need Derrida at all, when we have *X*?" sort from various quarters, where *X* equals not only feminism and Marxism, but also, for example, John Dewey, Foucault, Lacan, Hegel, etc. Besides the fact that one motivation of these questions seems to be inattentiveness to what Derrida is doing (because it is "incomprehensible," etc.), it seems that, when one takes all of the queries and their *X*'s together, then one would see the need for an open text that could reach out to these various possibilities. That is what I find most of all in Derrida.

On the specific point, perhaps Derrida's work could be seen as a feminism rendered in terms of quasi-transcendental arguments, taking feminism's concern with difference to a more general plane—and then, unfortunately, so this story would run, not bringing that analysis back down to earth again. Derrida's concerns seem broader, but perhaps Derrida's theoretical model of difference is not unlike that of at least some feminist theories. I think that the question might be more appropriately focused on feminist practice, but then there is the same general question as concerns the possibility of going from Derrida to social theory.

Q: The suggestion that reality is like a book remains opaque. The model of a book presupposes readers who are subjects—with ideas to be sure, but also with bodies and emotions. It also presupposes the physical book which is produced under certain economic relations— and at once both the subject and the Marxist materialist dimensions return.

A: Of course, I never suggest that reality is like a book—Descartes is the one who said that we need to learn to read the book of the world. Derrida has said more than once that no one would or should give deconstruction five minutes of their time if its central claim was that the world is a book. This has been discussed at such length by Derrida and others that I wonder why certain critics of Derrida are so fastened on the idea. In fairness, I do think that there is a relation between intertextuality and Kantian intersubjectivity that makes this "book" question keep coming back, especially in contrast to Marxist materialism. It is a question of the relation of meaning to matter. As a matter of fact, I do think that the intertextual model has something to contribute to what could be, and what has sometimes been, a very "cold" practice of materialism in Marxism, in which bodies and emotions can have no real standing. Furthermore, it is a little disingenuous to talk about the "subject coming back in" or "returning." From a purely structural materialist standpoint, Marxism might have a hard time distinguishing the bodies and emotions of people from the mere blips of "carbon-based units" (an expression used by a computer intelligence in one of the *Star Trek* movies, which made the point quite well). Why should we attach any meaning or significance to these blips? I don't think that we can, without a theory of meaning and a theory of corporeality.

Of course, it does not hurt, in the quest for such theories, to consider the problem of how there can be meaning in books.

Q: If human identity is constituted by language, what of those— for instance the senile, the severely retarded—who cannot speak?

A: A distinction should be drawn between those who literally cannot speak and those who cannot use language. The latter group would include people who cannot engage in symbol manipulation, period. There is a very big difference. Those who cannot use language at all of course have a very difficult time taking their place in human society. However, and this is really by far the more important point, to focus primarily on who can and who cannot speak in this sense is to look at people from the standpoint of subjectivity rather than positionality. "Not being able to speak" is the standard condition of most people in an anti-participatory society. Furthermore, in my model (which is Kantian in important ways), one's humanity is always in relation to others, and this goes no less for the senile, severely retarded, etc. I should hope to be able to say that, on my model, the sense of responsibility is even much greater toward such people.

I have the feeling that the same general problematics extends to the question of listening elsewhere to those entities that do not, in the now conventional sense, have a voice: rivers, forests, ecosystems in general. All of this remains to be worked out.

Q: Is being in the margins of intellectual discourse the same as being in the margins of social power and mass culture?

A: Not necessarily. There are real material differences. Sometimes there is more sheer frustration in being in the margins of intellectual discourse (or in being an intellectual in a society in which intellectual discourse is marginalized), as most readers of this text well know. But it seems likely that the more, shall we say, directly "material" forms of marginalization are more difficult to live with—when it is a matter of holding body and soul together. I hesitate to simply say, however, that we intellectuals can simply "live with" our marginalization. This is the sort of thing that Marxist activists often say with regard to intellectuals, supposedly coming from the basis of some "class analysis" that auto-matically tells one that intellectuals are "middle class" and therefore "comfortable." As an intellectual who tries to live up to my responsibili-ties as such, I have a difficult time "living with it," and I think that that has to be true of other engaged intellectuals. It is true that, generally speaking, we are not starving, imprisoned, etc., but it is also true that we have to operate within confines, mostly manifest in terms of countless acts of self-censorship, that can be restrictive and that can certainly make one sick in the heart. It is also the case that there still are various, sometimes subtle and sometimes not-so-subtle forms of blacklisting and repression at work in the only space in U.S. society allocated for intellectual work, namely, the academy. One wonders what effect the dissolution of the Eastern Bloc will have on all of this, when the U.S. no longer has to contrast its record on human rights with the other side. These are purely personal musings, hopefully a little more alarmist than is strictly speaking necessary.

I would still not compare the marginalization of the intellectual with, say, the marginalization of the homeless person. But then, the point is not to have to get into the business of "comparative marginalizations," except as an accounting of what strategic resources are most important for building a movement of the marginal that will transform society. Here I will simply reiterate the argument given at the end of Chapter 4: we need to rethink the idea of the proletariat in terms of marginalization.

Q: Isn't human finitude a form of ultimate counter-possibility? Don't we "freeze ourselves" by our actions, by making choices? Don't we give ourselves a final identity not by claiming an ultimate metaphysics of presence but rather by *being* a presence through living one form of life rather than another?

A: These are interesting points, all of which need to be taken account of by my scheme of possibility/impossibility/counter-possibility. These are good Sartrean questions. I would begin to respond by deconstructing the individualist thrust of these questions. The human finitude that I discuss is collective; in that respect, the counter-possibility represented by human finitude as a whole—the whole "human project"—indeed is a form of ultimate tragedy. It is a "useless passion." (Incidentally, in deconstruction, one sees this Sartrean current especially in the work of Paul de Man.) That makes it all the more sublime, in my view, and it makes the human project all the more urgent.

Who is the "we" who "gives ourselves a final identity"? "I" don't ever have such an identity, except perhaps in the destruction of our species, in which case, of course, I really don't have an identity (no one does).

On a quite different level, I would respond to the question in what I think is good Sartrean fashion by saying that, if anything (and I do mean, "if anything") makes us free, it is our choices, and if anything imprisons or freezes us in an identity, it is the avoidance of choices. There is no better example here than that of the person who chooses the supposed "freedom" of promiscuity over "getting stuck" in the "frozen identity" of a relationship.

Q: Suppose—as in nuclear war or the poisoning of the environment—that nature dies. Does the letter also die?

A: Yes, unless there is someone else out there to read it!

Q: If we are really in doubt about who the self of *Glas* is, can't we just see who picks up the royalty check? Whatever the pretensions of deconstructionist theorists, aren't they as wedded to their egos as anyone else? And isn't that the reductio of their position? Don't we find Derrideans proclaiming the death of the subject by reading individually authored papers at the front of rooms at conferences, then waiting for questions and defending "their" position? If I offered Derrida $3000 to give a lecture and then gave him $3, wouldn't he know who the subject was, what the text *really* said, and which interpretation was critical?

A: Well, a similar thing might be said about Marxism and the critique of private property—are Marxists simply hypocrites for accepting lecture fees or book royalties, or owning their own cars, etc.? At least some Marxists are using these things as part of the critique of private property. This critique is at the heart of the question regarding the self, and I try to extend that critique in this text. Marxists who do try to use private property against itself have to walk a very fine line, as do those who critique the discourse of subjectivity from the inside. Do I need to add that, in either case (private property, subjectivity), there is not at this time some pure outside from which to launch the critique? It does seem to me that many "deconstructionists" are not walking this line too well, which means that they are not taking Derrida's ideas very much to heart. What can I say? I try to. (I feel another "oath" coming on!)

By the way, when I give a paper, I at least try to not get into the "defending one's position" thing, as though a colloquium is some sort of military struggle between presenter and audience. On the other hand, "I," by "myself," do not define contexts. However, that should not be used as a cop-out, but rather as a spur to question the institutional contexts of intellectual production.

Q: The use of the Jews as Hegel's other is troubling. While I appreciate Fackenheim's argument, the Levinas-Derrida version of what Jewishness is would hardly square with the fundamentalist strain which combines open-ended discourse on the Torah and Talmud with an untouchable faith that they are God-given and that the mitzvahs must be performed. The Jewish tradition cannot be so simply represented as proto-deconstructionist while keeping faith with the religious experience of that tradition.

A: In response to this question I would add the following pair of codas to the section entitled "The Jews who bother Hegel." I realize that the actual working out of the positions in these questions is a much more complicated task.

First, when I take a certain "Jewishness" (to put it in the term offered by the question) and consider the possibility of "translating into a more general rubric," of deconstruction or whatever, is this not the Hegelian strategy *par excellence*? What is the meaning and what is the cost of my statement, "These questions," of Jewish internal self-mediations that occur in response to Hegel's external mediations of Jewish history, "can be translated into the rubric thus far established," namely the rubric of alterity and the logic of the Same? A number of questions surface here; these must be considered as a cluster: 1) the question of some "other history," apart from "Hegel's"; 2) the question of translation and its relation to particularity, specifically to the particularity of the name; 3) the question of the ontology of the same/other relation, and the question of the relation of that ontology to the ethico-political.

In *this* encounter with Hegel, is the Jew lost in translation (or never found, which amounts to the same thing)? I think that the danger is certainly there. Perhaps more than any other Jewish philosopher, Fackenheim has risked this loss in the encounters that he arranges between Judaism and modern philosophy. It seems to me that there is no avoiding this risk and its attendant dangers. (You may ask, however, Who are *you* to stage this risk? My answer is that I am nobody to do this.) What does finally resist this translation? Derrida reminds us that it is the name that is not translateable, the name resists translation. But that is to say that the name is not finally captureable in the other parts of our common tongues. It is a well-established theme in Judaism (and here Derrida is certainly "thinking Jewishly," as Stephen Schwarzschild liked to say) that this radical alterity of the name touches (marks) every aspect of language (and therefore life). And yet we must work from inside the languages that we have. There *is no* history "other" than Hegel's, not one that we can in any case name. There *is no* "rubric" other than "the more general rubric." But these things, paradoxically, do not begin to address the deeper responsibility that is called forth by the unnameable. In one very real, deadly serious sense, to accept this responsibility, to live in the shadow of it, is what it means to be "Jewish." I think that this definition would be accepted by many Jewish philosophers—it is certainly accepted by thinkers as diverse as Fackenheim and Levinas, on the one side, and Hermann Cohen and Stephen Schwarzschild on the other (in my next coda I will explain the reason for this dichotomizing). But is this the definition of "*the* Jew"? To say that the Jew is undefineable is surely on one level a cop-out. The language of "both circumscribed and circumscriber," employed by Derrida in "Shibboleth," is a more general rubric: "Anyone or no one may be 'Jewish'"—or a poet, for that matter. Is there a call, from within either Judaism or language, for the "particular" Jew or the "particular" poet? Or is there a specific bind that is generated by liberal-secular society, in which one has to "come up with" some particular, namely an "individual"? It is this bind that forms the background for a certain fundamentalist response to the question, one that certainly would not take the responsibility defined above as the definition of "Jewishness." Of course I have sympathy for the bind and its difficulties (we're all in it), but I do not take the fundamentalist response (and here we might say, "Jewish or otherwise," because there are certain commonalities to fundamentalist responses in general, even if there is a real particularity to Jewish fundamentalism—or Jewish anything else, for that matter—because of the Holocaust) to be the only legitimate response. Indeed, the fundamentalist response seems self-defeating and historically one-sided. It may be the case that Judaism is not "evangelical," but there has always been an openness, at least in principle, to the idea of conversion in Judaism, an openness which goes hand-in-hand with being "a light unto the nations."

Second, there has been another form of questioning of the leap to a more general rubric, as expressed in the challenge to Fackenheim's internal self-mediation of Hegel by Judaism. For thinkers and practicioners of "Kantian" Judaism such as Stephen Schwarzschild, Fackenheim's sense of "God's presence in history" is simply a fall toward pure immanence. I have to admit that, until I read Schwarzschild (specifically the collection of his *Jewish Writings* issued by SUNY Press in 1990) it had never occurred to me that any Jew (or anyone else) would essentially affirm Spinoza's expulsion from the Synagogue. (Many large cities, as the reader no doubt knows, have Spinoza Societies, which are largely made up of Jews. I should add, too, that even Fackenheim, as much as he rails against Spinoza, in *To Mend the World* and elsewhere, never comes out in favor of the expulsion, at least to my knowledge.) Spinoza, for both Schwarzschild and Fackenheim, is the opening to the "adventure of immanence" (as Yovel puts it) which culminates with Hegel (or perhaps Marx). Schwarzschild resists the overall drift toward historicism; for him, the pursuit of the unnameable is the pursuit of transcendence. This argument between immanence and transcendence (which Schwarzschild frames as not only an argument between Kant and Hegel, but also between Plato and Aristotle) is precisely where Derrida's project begins.

Perhaps it is also a good place for this potentially infinite text to end.

Notes

Chapter One: Modalities, politics

1. Derrida (1984b, 113).

2. This classical ideal type schema comes from Tönnies (1988); see also O'Hagen (1988).

3. On Derrida's relation to the term and institution, "philosophy," see Derrida (1984b, passim); also Norris (1987, 18–27).

4. Two essential references here are Husserl (1970) and de Man (1983, 3–19).

5. On "traditionalism," see Derrida (1985d, 7–8).

6. It would be unfair not to mention the notion that secular society actually begins in writing: alphabetization in McLuhan's and Ong's sense, "the coming of the book," the proliferation of legal codes, constitutions, etc. Whether this writing is actually "writerly" (Barthes) or textual (Barthes, Derrida) is, however, another question. I do not want to close off any avenues: one could certainly imagine a textual approach to constitutions that unfolded these documents in a democratic way. On the other hand, the prevailing sense of constitutions in most constitutional societies, of a magical document that regulates signifiers rather than being regulated by signifiers, is very much resistant to intertextual politics. (Of course, part of the point is that Derrida has a special sense of "writing.")

7. Heidegger recognized this, I think, even though he did not admit his own complicities, in his essays on technology. See Heidegger (1977). The term "techno-capitalist" is taken from Kellner (1989b).

8. See Gross (1980). Although I agree with Gross that there are elements of fascism in the recent U.S. administrations (i.e., those of Reagan and Bush— Gross's book was written before the full story unfolded, of course, but it seems that, if anything, things came out even worse than Gross expected), for example, the racist "war on drugs," attacks on women's reproductive rights, art censorship, movements toward mandatory flag-worship, etc., on the whole I think that the present U.S. social formation is not best-described by the term "fascism." But that is not to say that this formation is not, in its own insidious ways, as bad as fascism (and the U.S. could indeed become an outright fascist country—the machinery is there; until recently, Lt. Colonel Oliver North was in

charge of that machinery, and there was certainly no move to even discuss this machinery, much less dismantle it, around the "Iran-Contra" scandal).

9. See Deutscher, "Marxism and Primitive Magic" (1971). Although he is not specifically thinking in terms of secularism and its alternatives, Isaac Deutscher gives a penetrating account of the contours of Stalinist socialism that fits in quite well with the analysis pursued here.

10. There are many conflations of fascism and Stalinism in the literature on these questions; I will simply cite one recent example that forthrightly depends on the secular (and, in this case, "postmodern" as well, which is why the example is significant) logic that I am criticizing here: Rorty (1989, 174).

11. This privileging also still charges an historical debt to the post-Leninist Marxisms of Trotsky and Mao.

12. Is tradition, in other words, only a "chain"? We might play on the meanings of this term. Here I also want to mark an encounter that has begun to take place in the same staging ground I map here, but which I will not pursue in this study: that between Derrida and Gadamer. See Michelfelder and Palmer (1989).

13. Fortunately, there are now some comprehensive, systematic studies of Derrida's work that begin to make such caricatures less feasible. Two studies in particular should be mentioned: Gasche (1986) and Harvey (1986). Some (e.g., Rorty 1989, 123–25) have criticized these two books for being "too serious." My feeling is that the "seriousness" of these books is fully justified by some of the "playfulness" of some Derrideans, but even more so on independent grounds; that is, Derrida is a serious philosopher. Of course, for those analytic philosophers and others who do not feel that Derrida must be read in order to be condemned, there is little that even the work of Harvey and Gasche can do. My proposal is simply that, whenever people of this bent say something negative about "Derrida" (i.e., something or someone they think of as Derrida), they should always be challenged to cite their source (and not just let such people off the hook with some protestation that, "I've *tried* to read Derrida—it's just not possible"). It's time to get serious with these people who are helping to destroy philosophy through promoting a proud illiteracy—there are enough forces outside of the academy promoting this; we don't need our colleagues adding to the anti-intellectual climate. (I apologize for the sudden manifesto, but enough is enough!)

14. On the other hand, it is most certainly true that Derrida does not provide the basis for any form of dialectical materialism (perhaps even on the contrary).

15. One of the most satisfying treatments of the question of Derrida and Marx is found in "Values and Deconstructions," the first chapter of Gregory S. Jay (1989).

16. It may be added that, for Derrida, for a word to differ from another word, a word must also in some sense be "associated" with that other word. Here Derrida is foreshadowed by Freud, but also, interestingly enough, by Hume.

17. A useful book that works through the interconnections of language and subjectivity is Smith (1988). (Incidentally, the book develops a Marxist-feminist position fundamentally at odds with Derrida.) An important work that puts forward a position somewhat similar to the one that I will develop in the third chapter is Schrag (1986). Finally, a book in the analytic tradition which also outlines the language/subjectivity relation is Hattiangadi (1987).

18. For example, see "The agency of the letter in the unconscious, or Reason since Freud," in Lacan (1977), and "To Speculate—On 'Freud'," in Derrida (1987a). Heidegger is of course essential here, as we shall see in Chapter 3.

19. In the new "Afterword" to the book version of *Limited Inc*, Derrida distinguishes what he means by "undecideability" from what is typically meant by "indeterminacy" in the analytic tradition. The former includes, but goes beyond, the latter. See Derrida (1988a, 114–31).

20. On the question of social theory in the pragmatic mode, see Rochberg-Halton (1986, esp. 273–77). Derrida's notion of "pragrammatology" is developed in Ulmer (1985).

21. For useful introductions to the traditions of this problematic, see Taylor (1987) and Dallery and Scott (1989).

22. A very helpful discussion on this point is found in Rorty (1989, 3–43). Davidson got the ball rolling on this question with "On the Very Idea of a Conceptual Scheme," in Davidson (1985).

23. For Derrida, difference itself is different, hence the grouping of all the possible effects of the economy of difference under the general heading *différance*. The principle may be explained simply as follows: rather than, "In the beginning was Identity" (substitute whatever name for Identity that you like), it is instead that, "In the beginning there was difference—which really means that in the beginning there was no beginning, and before that there was no beginning either, etc." This is in a sense simply an arche-ontological application of the context principle.

24. This position on the coextensive possibility and impossibility of language is perhaps not so different from a certain reading of Wittgenstein's *Tractatus*. See, for example, Nieli (1987). Perhaps Nieli goes a little overboard on some of the mystical aspects of the problems that Wittgenstein was raising concerning language (while at the same time undoubtedly being fair to what seems to have been Wittgenstein's own mystical leanings). Nieli would have

been well-served by a better sense of the problematics of language and otherness in Heidegger, Levinas, and Derrida.

25. Derrida raised this point in his first presentation to a U.S. audience, in "Structure, Sign and Play in the Discourse of the Human Sciences" (1978, 278–93).

26. This question is raised with explicit reference to Wittgenstein in Derrida (1989c).

27. I find it curious that this question is not taken up in Stanton (1984). Thus far it seems that comparisons of Derrida and Wittgenstein have remained on the level of linguistic analysis.

28. Comprehensiveness is part of what distinguishes, for me, a "social theory" from a "political philosophy." The other main point of distinction, not unrelated to comprehensiveness, is that a social theory aims toward an understanding of the broader culture that the theory hopes to address. One might compare, in this light, Habermas's *Theory of Communicative Action* with Rawls's *A Theory of Justice*. I do not find the latter especially culture-specific in any very deep sense (and, even though Rawls claims in his later work that his theory is more or less specific to "Western" societies, one does not get from him a very interesting sense of what "Western" means).

29. It should be added that the term "repeatability" does not cover the range of possibilities that Derrida signifies with the term "iterability." On this point, see Derrida (1988a, 127–28) and Gasche (1986, 212–17).

30. Lately I have begun to wonder, however, whether an opening to the other is possible within the terms and thematics of Davidson's philosophy—I tend to think that this is a real possibility.

31. Among the many important references here would be Levinas, Buber, and Fackenheim. See especially "The Shibboleth of Revelation: From Spinoza Beyond Hegel," Chapter Three of Fackenheim (1982). Also see Richard L. Rubenstein, "Civic Altruism and the Resacralization of the Political Order" and Manfred H. Vogel, "The Social Dimension of the Faith of Judaism: Phenomenological and Historic Aspects," both in Bryant (1985).

32. I have already set up this notion, "the time after postmodernity," to generate a paradox, if it is indeed true that postmodernity is also post-periodization (Gary Shapiro's term). The impasse of postmodernity keeps itself alive by cancelling the notion of "after." I must, therefore, think that things are not so dire as all that—there must be something significant in postmodernity that does not submit to its flattening tendencies. Although I do deal with this paradox at some length in the second and fourth chapters, I cannot say that I have entirely overcome it. This will have to be an area for more research.

33. See, e.g., Fodor (1987), Schiffer (1987), and Dretske (1981).

34. I should distinguish even at this point (the theme is developed further in Chapter 3) between Chomsky, who is not first of all concerned with semantics (but rather syntax), and Chomsky-inspired theories, which are concerned with a general theory of meaning.

35. See, e.g., the first chapter of Dews (1987).

36. See Kim (1989) and Rorty (1979, 70–127). Davidson responds to Kim in "The Measure of the Mental" (forthcoming).

37. These are the "nice" terms, so to speak. There are also terms for the abject: dirt, refuse, shit, etc. On this point, see Taylor (1987, 115–48).

38. See Ryan (1982, Chapter Two), on Marx, Derrida, and materialism.

39. Lenin (1972).

40. This characterization may be more accurate of certain contemporary Hobbesians, e.g., David Gauthier and Jean Hampton. Another side of Hobbes is presented in Shapiro (1980).

41. The point is, however, that the paradox need not therefore be avoided, in the manner of the Vienna positivists (who disparaged Heidegger's reflections on "Being" and "nothing." Thinking about infinity may not be entirely "scientific," but it can be philosophically productive (especially if one is not overly logico-mathematical about doing philosophy). Levinas is perhaps the most important reference here (see Taylor 1987, 185–216).

42. See Mao (1977, 1–22, 23–78) and Avakian (1979, 154–58).

43. See Derrida (1976, 6–26) and (1982, 207–71).

44. On these figures in relation to materialism, see Martin (1989c).

45. An argument could be constructed, I think, that the part of my claim that *is* in Marx comes from a reading of some of the same sources that Derrida reweaves: Judaism (and even the tradition of Kaballah, as Habermas, 1985, 63–80, argues), Rousseau, Hegel, utopian thought, etc.

46. I did not want to point a finger in the text proper, but Scholes (1985) is a good example of all of these problems. Undoubtedly it will also be argued, however, that the present work is also a part of this same problem, of "intertextual politics" that are not "concrete" enough (I try to get plenty "concrete" in places), and the point is certainly not to get into some sort of "lefter-than-thou" contest.

47. This question is taken up in an analysis of the Nazis' use of Nietzsche in Derrida (1985a, 27–33).

48. I am responding to certain formulations of Rorty's (1989, 44–69).

49. In another context, of course, the context problem would not be called

a "problem," because there is no way to abolish contextuality—indeed, attempts to do so result in real disaster.

50. On one level, however, we might ask, What choice is there? The point is that the opening to possibility, as a diverse and plural movement, really is more socially-advantageous than a foundational declaration of a single possibility which must be realized through a single movement (apart from which all deviations must be squashed).

51. I deal with the possible nostalgia of this position, which Derrida has of course criticized in his reading of Rousseau (1976), in the second and fourth chapters.

Chapter Two: History past its end

1. Two important distinctions are bracketed here: 1) that between subject and object, which I take up in Chapter 3; 2) that between a "dialectic of nature" and a "dialectic of thought," as thematized in much Marxist literature, perhaps reaching its most acute formulation in Sartre's *Critique of Dialectical Reason*.

2. On Marx's continued debt to Hegel, even in the later work, see Allen Wood (1981, 207–18).

3. This is Gary Shapiro's expression.

4. Cited in Warren (1988, 162).

5. Cited in Warren (1988, 161).

6. For opposing views on the thesis that multinational corporations have outgrown the bourgeois nation state, see Lotta (1984) and Mandel (1978).

7. I am playing off of the conceptions in Jameson (1988).

8. Lecture delivered at the International Association for Philosophy and Literature conference on "Postmodernism: Texts, Politics, Instruction," at the University of Kansas, April 1987.

9. These two points are: 1) the idea of a historical break that did not already inhabit the semiological structure of *anthropos*; 2) those subjects who have yet to be—whom Foucault is, however, recognizing in some sense.

10. See Foucault (1977, 139–64). By "genealogy," Foucault means reading history "backwards," to points of difference, rather than "forwards," in terms of a story of overall development and progress.

11. See Lyotard (1984, 38–39).

12. See, e.g., Abrams (1973) and Hyppolite (1974).

13. See also Fuss (1989), esp. Chapter Six.

14. See Fuss (1989, 86–93) on the work of Houston Baker in this connection, and see Baker (1984, 64–112). We will return to these texts in Chapter Four.

15. On the passing of existentialism as a social trend, see Hollier (1986).

16. See also Eagleton (1986, 149–65) and Martin (1989b).

17. See Gibson (1984, 1986, 1988).

18. The literature on this question is now quite vast, but I would be remiss in not noting Barthes, "The Death of the Author" (1977).

19. On this particular point, one would have to cite the entire book, *Glas* (Derrida 1986). I here cite it against Rorty's reading, which is discussed in some detail in Chapter 5.

20. On historicizing historicism, see Dean (1988); the book contains discussions of Rorty, Derrida, and Mark Taylor.

21. See Derrida (1988a, 116–18) on the "logic of the concept." The relation between dialectic and difference is discussed.

22. See Gasche (1986, 98–99).

23. On deconstruction and political economy, see Spivak (1987, 154–75).

24. This is a reference to the Hebrew alphabet, in which letters also stand for numbers.

25. See the essays by Rubinstein and Vogel in Bryant and Mataragnon (1985).

26. We have just questioned whether the latter (existentialism), and indeed we will have to question whether the former (Marxism), lives on as anything more than an area of specialized study in academic philosophy.

27. Cited in Nadel (1989, 89).

Chapter Three: What is at the heart of language?

1. Shapiro (1985, 187). For further discussion of the idea of nomad thought, in relation to Nietzsche, Marx, Deleuze, and Shapiro, see Martin (1986).

2. For example, see Ferry and Renaut (1990).

3. See Voloshinov (1973), Stalin (1972), and Coward and Ellis (1987).

4. See Althusser (1971, 107–25; 1979, 119–44), Benton (1984, 55–58), and Elliot (1989, 115–86).

5. See "Excursus on the Obsolescence of the Production Paradigm" in Habermas (1987b).

6. See, e.g., Bloor (1983), Carnap (1959), Jacobs and Otto (1990), Michael Root, "Davidson and Social Science," in LePore (1986, 272–304), Putnam (1987), Margolis (1986, 1987, 1988). I am leaving aside analytical Marxism, which has not on the whole done much with the question of language thus far.

7. Marx's only explicit statement on the question of language is the early formulation, "language is practical consciousness," which does not get us very far in terms of language itself.

8. Holderlin (1984, 117). I would be remiss if I did not cite Paul de Man's influential readings of this poem, in the second and third essays of *The Rhetoric of Romanticism* (1984).

9. Derrida's "answer," of course, is in a form that Habermas and many others do not recognize—a form which I hope to have the audacity to tease out without expecting the "answer" to necessarily be something that Derrida would recognize either.

10. A very useful discussion of these issues, as they relate to both analytic and continental philosophy, is Rorty (1989, 3–22).

11. The literature on this question is now very extensive, but see, e.g., Eco (1986), Handelman (1982), Bloom (1984), and Idel (1988).

12. This story is told very well in Corlett (1989, 164–81).

13. See, e.g., Margolis (1986, 1987, 1988), Cavell (1984), and Bernstein (1983).

14. See Quine, "Two Dogmas of Empiricism," in (1953). Also see Koppelberg (1987).

15. See Davidson, "The Myth of the Subjective" (1989) and "What is Present to the Mind?" (1989).

16. See Davidson (1985, 3–15) and Hattiangadi (1987, 18–20).

17. Cited in Roderick (1986, 79).

18. On strategic action and communicative action, see Roderick (1986, 108–09).

19. See Rawls (1982) and Pogge (1989, 125–34, 161).

20. See Habermas (1984, 70–71; 1987a, Part iv).

21. On the concept of "home" as it relates to Habermas, see Trey (1989).

22. Helmut Peukert (1984) bases his Habermas-inspired theology on just this point. See also my review of Peukert, Martin (1987).

23. Two points need to be raised here. First, Habermas's conflation of the views of language in the work of Michael Dummett and Donald Davidson

indicate that there is a bit of confusion and perhaps carelessness in Habermas's investigation of theories of communication; see Habermas (1984, 276, 316–18). Dummett discusses his differences with Davidson in "What is a theory of meaning?" (1975). Second, there is the problem that speech act theories tend to be both foundationalistic and relativistic: foundational in their positing of a self-present subject who knows and speaks, relativistic in what Dagfinn Follesdal and others have tagged a "Humpty-Dumpty theory of meaning" ("a word means just what I say it means").

24. See the chapter titled "Meaning as Soliloquy," in Derrida (1967, 32–47).

25. See the essay on Habermas and communicative competance in Culler (1988). Also see Ingram (1987, 212–13, n. 51).

26. On the conceptual schemes argument, see Ramberg (1989, 114–37) and the essays in Part IV ("Language and Reality") of LePore (1986, 307–429).

27. See Marcia Cavell, "Metaphor, Dreamwork and Irrationality," in LePore (1986, 495–507). Also see Davidson's "Deception and Division," in LePore and McLaughlin (1985, 138–48).

28. On the "question of literature," see Derrida (1983b). Also see Norris (1987, 18–27) and Johnson (1982).

29. Quoted in Ingram (1987, 90–91).

30. An extremely interesting analysis of this question is Parker (1986).

31. Again, see Habermas (1985), as well as (1989).

32. Habermas calls Heidegger a "mandarin" in *Political-Philosophical Profiles* (1985, 55–62).

33. Cited in Zimmerman (1990, 43).

34. Zimmerman (1990, 43). My only qualm with this analysis concerns the idea that the Germans were the only perpetrators—a problem that I also have with the left-wing arguments in the *Historikerstreit*. Of course, it is admirable that people like Habermas take responsibility for the German people. It is something else, however, when non-Germans take comfort in this (this seems somewhat a defect of Maier's book).

35. See Dummett (1981, 521–23). I do not mean to say that the way that Frege came by his Platonism was in any way simple-minded, only that Frege's ontology, as far as he was concerned, simpy falls out of his logic. See also Quine, "On What There Is" and "Logic and the Reification of Universals" (in 1953).

36. See Dummett, "The Context Principle" (1981, 360–427).

37. On Davidson and naturalism, see Martin (1989). I disagree with Rorty (1989, 15) and many other "Davidsonians" on this question.

38. In asking if this is perhaps Jewish, I am following Derrida's lead; see (1989b).

Chapter Four: Radical diversity/radical confluence

1. Derrida (1989a, 60).

2. Perhaps *Glas* would be the most outstanding example of Derrida's practice with regard to different genres of philosophy. The further point may be made that, even when Derrida is especially concerned to discuss a particular poet or "writer," he does not thereby become a "philosopher of literature" (contrary to the claims of Boyne 1990, 1), any more than he is ordinarily a "philosopher of language."

3. On "ruins," see Derrida (1986a, 33b).

4. In "The Myth of the Subjective," Davidson (1989a) argues that the empirical fact of ostensive definition (and the role that it plays in language learning) does not in itself earn a central place for naming.

5. See Quine, "Two Dogmas of Empiricism" (in 1953) and "Ontological Relativity" (in 1969); also see Davidson (1985, 215–41); for Derrida on reference, see (1988a, afterword).

6. My reference is not so much to deviant logics as to Davidson's idea that logic is just what we make of it. A good demonstration of this point is found in Davidson (1982b).

7. William Corlett goes so far as to argue that authoritarian logics also have their diachronic dimension in the notion of linear time. See Corlett (1989, 65–140). "Reassurance" is Corlett's term.

8. Habermas (1987b) criticizes Derrida for trying to get outside of the "concept." Derrida responds in (1988a, afterword).

9. See Spivak (1980).

10. See Derrida (1976, 74–93). Also see Han-Liang Chang (1988).

11. In *The Media Lab: Inventing the Future at MIT*, Steward Brand (1988, 224–25) discusses the attitute toward William Gibson's *Neuromancer* at a major computer research facility. The technocratically-minded researchers are enthusiastic about the world that Gibson portrays, one suspects, because in such a world these technocrats would be in charge.

12. See the discussion of "civic friendship" in Gauthier (1990) and the failure to link capitalism and liberalism in Dworkin (1990).

13. Neurath, incidentally, was a Marxist. He was interested in substituting logical positivism for dialectical materialism as the philosophical ground of socialism. See Jacobs and Otto (1990).

14. Before the Bolshevik Revolution, people were more willing to accept that idea that socialism would find its own course and could have no "blueprint." After Stalin, people do not so readily accept this idea. The comparison, however is between a leap into the dark (socialism) and a leap in the dark (capitalism), not much of a choice. The Cultural Revolution in China (contary to recent anti-Mao chic orthodoxy) did represent some alternatives, to my mind. Radical change is never made under conditions of choice and planning. To call for blueprints for the radical alternative, as Rorty (1989) does, is to have little sense of the material conditions in which the question of social relations is decided. Rorty's vision of change, depending as it does on the need for blueprints, is essentially technocratic (following Dewey and the whole idea of social engineering). We do need plans and manifestos for a future society, but it is not the lack of such plans that is holding back radical change.

15. The structure that makes such variations possible, however, must in some sense be encompassed by grammatology—that is, the structure of ahistoricity that permeates and motivates so much liberal political theory and postmodern discourse needs to be understood systematically. Otherwise, it is difficult to resist, in a deconstructive way, this sort of language.

16. Malcolm Bradbury spoofs the idea of overnight, massive language reform in *Rates of Exchange* (1985).

17. On Burke, concerning this question, see Corlett (1989, 116–40) and Blakemore (1988).

18. For a series of useful studies on Derrida and the canon, see Silverman (1989).

19. See MacGregor (1984) and the discussion of MacGregor in Duquette (1990).

20. See the chapter on Marx and Mill in Cohen (1978).

21. On the "Proletcult" ("Proletarian Culture") debate, see Trotsky (1960, 1970); on Marxism, aesthetics, and tradition, see Eagleton (1990).

22. See Firestone (1971) and Sayers, et al. (1987).

23. See the special issue of *Signs: Journal of Women and Culture* on women in medieval society. Kathleen League made me more aware on this question.

24. On the possibility of "communitarian liberalism," see Buchanan (1989). Also see Eisenstein (1981); she is not a "liberal feminist," but she demonstrates this point quite well.

25. As in the well-known scenario in Robert Heilbronner's *An Inquiry Into The Human Prospect*, in which ecological disaster brings about an international authoritarian social order.

26. See Sartre (1976b) and Aronson (1987).

27. See Corlett (1989, 179–83) on "silence."

28. See Derrida (1976, 101–40; the quotation from Levi-Strauss is from p. 130). A useful summary and explanation of "the writing lesson" is in Norris (1987, 127–41).

29. Derrida analyzes "is" and the conditions of its use in "*Differance*" and especially in "The Supplement of Copula"; see (1982, 1–27; 175–205).

30. Which speaks more in the voice of Hobbes than Locke; see Dolan (1988) and Portis (1988). Also see David Ingram (1988).

31. I am quoting Barbara Johnson quoting Gayatri Spivak, from the seminar on "The Politics of Poetry," School of Criticism and Theory, Dartmouth College, Summer 1987.

32. Perhaps the expression, "male theorist," is itself redundant. Is *theory* itself "male," in that it aims for the total scene, the "view from everywhere" (Susan Bordo's expression)? This does seem to follow from the arguments of Irigaray and Derrida on phallogocentrism.

33. These remarks were occasioned by the presentation of a different version of this section as a paper at the Society for Phenomenology and Existential Philosophy meeting in October 1988. I here take the liberty of presenting further remarks I made at that session concerning my placement on a panel titled "Re-reading as a Woman": "I stand before you as I have been positioned by others, as someone who will re-read as a woman. I do not know all the machinations, either the more simple, straightforward ones that pertain entirely to this conference and this session, or the highly-complex ones that pertain to gender-positioning in general that have positioned me thus. In the fomer case I know that it has to do with the process of blind review, which was initiated in SPEP in part as a way of eliminating the possibility of sexism in paper selection. I leave the examination of the insight in this blindness to further discussion.

"It does seem, though, that there is a clear upshot in terms of the 'men in feminism' question. I must admit, and this will be (I promise) my last purely personal note, that after several years of trying to be 'in feminism'—and of course, the question is , *as what?*—'a man'?" (but perhaps that shouldn't be the question)—I have had serious doubts in the past year. And these have everything to do with the problem of positionality, or more to the point, the opposite position, which I would call *essentialism*. Under the rubric of positionality it may seem perfectly legitimate that a man might re-read as a woman. But this is conditional upon the acceptance of others. But who *are* these others? It would be very easy to fall from the notion of other-assertion into something like the idea of an "honorary woman" or an "honorary man" (as silly as that sounds once a name is given to it). But that is the very essentialism that we have to overcome. The problem is that the concept of positionality that upsets other-assertion upsets itself as well."

34. See Derrida (1979), and related texts, such as Krell (1986).

35. Fuss (1989, 19). More needs to be said about the political effects of referring to "the undecideability of woman"; the phrase makes one think of the stereotypical phrase, "Women can't make up their minds," or Freud's "What do women want?" We might also think here of Derrida's discussion of the "undecideable Jew," in relation to Edmond Jabes, in Derrida (1978, 295–300).

36. See, e.g., Flax (1983), Keller and Grontkowski (1983), Bordo (1987), and Rorty (1979).

37. On Derrida and Irigaray, see Grosz (1989, 26–38); on Irigaray, see Fuss (1989, 55–72).

38. The translation is by Dorothy Becker, in Stanton (1986). I have substituted the word "shadow" for the word "shade" in the title; I think that, in the context of philosophical discussion, this is a preferable translation of the word "*ombre*." Some dates, for purposes of comparison: Rene Descartes (1596–1650), Anne de La Vigne (1634–1684).

39. I realize, of course, that I spilled much ink in Chapter 4 in order to make such a distinction, between philosophy and literature, untenable. I only mean by this remark that I am not sufficiently skilled in the terminology of poetics to make an analysis of the poem in these terms. Literary critics, of course, cannot help but engage in the philosophical analysis of literary works, while philosophers would do well, to my mind, to attend to the letter of philosophy as well as to its spirit.

40. Diana Fuss, "The Risk of Essence" (earlier version of the first chapter of her 1989), p. 14.

41. An especially acute example of this would be the attempt to portray the Exxon Valdez oil spill as though it were just another individual case of drunk driving.

42. Perhaps in the midst of these transformations, however, the terms "brotherhood" and "fraternity" would have outlived their usefulness (one suspects that this is almost the case already).

43. This term, "give," could itself be interrogated in terms of the question of property that is inseparable from the question of naming.

44. An investigation into the question of lesbian separatism, from a lesbian-feminist point of view, that (I think—I want to be careful in such cases, and non-appropriative) shares some of the general features of the framework developed here, is Phelan (1989).

45. Corlett (1989, passim), following Foucault, traces the relation between subjectivity and subjugation.

46. In terms of the sacred and secular, this argument finds an interesting expression in Cox (1965).

47. Foucault somewhere uses the example of a "world literature" that came into existence around the end of the nineteenth century. This was the literature of a handful of European countries.

48. Although I do not entirely agree with her answers, Ellen Meiksens Wood (1986) has raised the appropriate political-economic questions about the "retreat from class." These questions cannot be dismissed as merely "orthodox." Significantly, Mao and Maoism are often pointed to as prime culprits (by Wood, as well as by Callinicos [1990], Eagleton [1990], and others) in this retreat. I disagree on this point for reasons that are implicit in the present study—I will have to postpone the explicit enunciation of these reasons to another discussion. (See also Lotta 1984, Part Three, on this point.)

49. See Mies (1986). This work was brought to my attention by William Corlett.

50. This is a reference both to the right (and the book that has the title, *Tenured Radicals*—see Kimball 1990, and review by Lambrose 1990), e.g., Alan Bloom, Hilton Kramer, etc., and to the left, e.g., Jacoby (1987).

51. See Munro (1990) on the real story of the Tienamen massacre.

52. See Lyotard, "What is Postmodernism?" (in 1984), where he contends that there has always been a dialectic of modernism and postmodernism, on the model of T. S. Kuhn's analysis of "normal" and "revolutionary" science.

53. See Sale (1985) and Berry (1987).

54. The circuit of this minimalism is now complete. Derrida, like Davidson, places the sign with minimal attributes before the subject, but finds this sign sufficiently motivated to displace the subject. Where Davidson also has a minimal conception of the other, however (a conception that is largely opaque and unthematized in Davidson's philosophy), Derrida continually refolds this material, the sign and its other, to maximum effect—and this is his "realism," for language itself effects this infinite unfolding.

Chapter Five: This unnameable community

1. The word, "*glas*," means roughly, "knell," as in the ringing of a bell, especially a death knell. A good introduction to Derrida's *Glas* is found in Geoffrey Hartman, *Saving the Text* (1981). The book is set out in two columns, with additional inset columns appearing intermittently, not unlike a Rabbinic text. Broadly speaking, the left-hand column concerns Hegel, while the right-hand column is commentary on Jean Genet. The idea is that these two seeming opposites cannot be kept separate.

2. In *of Grammatology*, Derrida raises the question of Levi-Strauss's "turn away from philosophy," the discipline in which he was trained, toward anthropology, as a turn toward the "empirical" and "concrete."

3. On the "reemergence of space," see Soja (1989); on the semiotic dimension, see Kroker and Cook (1986); on the temporal dimension, see Corlett (1989, 65–141) and Wood (1989).

4. In the essay Derrida is careful to trace the international network that allows (to say the least) apartheid to exist.

5. The translations of the "Theses on Feuerbach" are interesting in their attempts to mask Marx's anti-Semitism. For instance, some versions use the term "dirty Judaical." This question has not been squarely faced from within Marxism. See Padover's (1979) "Introduction" to his edition of Marx's letters.

6. Compare this formulation with Derrida's (1989b, Ch. 10) argument about how Heidegger subverts the letter by the letter in order to protect spirit from contamination—a protection with quite direct political implications.

7. Following Mark Taylor's line on Hegel and Kierkegaard (see 1987, Ch. 1 and 10), perhaps Marx's others were Helen Demuth and the child that Marx had with her.

8. It can be added parenthetically that there are many texts by Derrida since 1975 that are *so* serious that one needs a little comic relief.

9. The reference here is also to Nancy (1986).

10. See Handelman (1982, 167–69).

11. See Fraser (1984) and McCarthy (1989-90). I find many arguments that "question" whether deconstruction has "political implications," or whether "deconstruction is at all political," etc., a bit disingenuous. McCarthy's article seems to me another failure by the Habermasians to engage Derrida.

12. Here again I take issue with Rorty's (1989a) and Callinicos's (1985) interpretations of Davidson as a naturalist.

13. I put it this way because "AIDS" itself cannot be separated from the intersection of interpretive practices and epidemiology; it is not even clear at this point that AIDS is necessarily a single disease. In any case, the discourse of AIDS is certainly a clear case of the politics of naming.

14. The very idea of a writerly politics must have the political deployment of irony as its central conception. I pursue this question in (1989b), a radical reading of some of Paul de Man's essays, especially "The Rhetoric of Temporality" (1983, 187–228). My analysis runs, of course, quite contrary to the whole drift of Rorty's (1989b) on the question of irony. For Rorty, irony is essentially a "private" affair, useful for the creation of a personally edifying vocabulary.

15. The explicit reference is to Derrida (1978, 79–153), but I am more concerned with the discourse as it has been used by literary critics.

16. The left has often made strategic mistakes based on superficial definitions of fascism—which is also to indicate that fascism is not so easy to "define," in the sense of "to limit." It is never so easy to know that one is "outside" of fascism. I was especially reminded of this important truth by remarks made by Charles Scott at the conference on Heidegger at Loyola University, September 1989.

17. Perhaps I should provide empirical documentation of the racist dimension of the "war on drugs." Instead, however, I will simply cite one recent example of this most recent form of slander against African-Americans. As part of his campaign for the governorship of Massachusetts, John Silber remarked that he "would not take his campaign to the black neighborhood of Roxbury" because "[T]here is no point in my making a speech on crime control to a group of drug addicts." (This sort of thing plays well in Boston.) That this statement was made by one of our "fellow philosophers" (a "Kantian" no less) hardly lessens its vileness. See "Tarnished Silber," *The Nation* 8 October 1990: 365.

18. One is entitled to hear echoes of Paul Piccone's "artificial negativity" thesis here. In short, Piccone has it that most of what passes as "opposition" or "dissent" is actually created by the dominant social order itself as a way of generating a creativity that it no longer can produce through establishment channels. (One is, furthermore, entitled to hear echoes of Adorno in Piccone.) To my mind, this analysis, although not developed at great length by Piccone, bears more consideration from critical theorists than it has received thus far. See Piccone (1977) and Luke (1978).

19. One crucial aspect of this cynical strategy is the attempted return to the "happy days" of the 1950s, with the deeper purpose of not simply recreating the post-war euphoria that middle class white people experienced at that time (or now think that they experienced), but further of creating a continuity of complacent generations. This continuity is very useful for making anyone from the middle class or upper part of the working class who questions the social order feel isolated. The basic idea is to create an '80s generation that thinks along the same lines as their parents.

20. For accounts of the Adorno/Benjamin dispute, see Buck-Morss (1977, 1989), Eagleton (1981), and Lunn (1982).

21. See Adorno and Horkheimer (1972) and M. Jay (1984, Ch. 4).

22. Also see the essay, "Affirmative Culture," in Marcuse's *Negations* (1968).

23. Adorno had some sense of this; see "The Aging of the New Music" (1988); also see Barbiero (1989) and Hullot-Kentor (1989).

24. Mark Miller (1988) argues that television, especially, is not a part of "popular culture."

25. Agger (1989b, 133, slightly modified). I very much disagree, incidentally, with Agger's analysis of Derrida.

26. Perhaps "illegal art" is the only remaining arena of the avant-garde, e.g., Dread Scott Tyler, Fiona Burns, Robert Mapplethorpe. See the interesting discussion of the work of Fiona Burns in Ryan (1989, 98–110).

27. Why is it that, for now, we have to remember Somoza, for instance, more than those who were "disappeared" under his regime? This is a sickening irony that the movement of the mothers of the disappeared, in Somoza's Nicaragua and elsewhere in Latin America, have tried to address, in the light of their daughters' and sons' possibility: I think that I can say without sentimentality that *they are our community*.

28. In coming close to a Lacanian terminology I should mention the fascinating book by Slavoj Zizek, *The Sublime Object of Ideology* (1989).

29. I do wonder if there isn't something of a patriarchal note in Berry's praise for the family farm. I would warn, however, against oversimplification of this question. I think of Berry as a "real communitarian," someone for whom the value of community is practiced as well as theorized. Perhaps the thing I like most about him is that his writings, especially *Home Economics* (1987), evidence a kind of "radical common sense." He is providing a fundamental critique of our present social system, but in terms that any ordinarily intelligent person would find hard to deny.

30. In her novel Piercy imagines a future society in which the problematics of naming, and their relation to questions of propriety, is thematized in a way very much in line with Derrida and the analysis presented here.

Bibliography

(As mentioned in the "Preface," texts that mark important intersections for this study are noted with an asterisk to the left of the entry.)

Abrams. M. H. 1973. *Natural Supernaturalism: Tradition and Revolution in Romantic Literature*. New York: Norton Books.

Adorno, Theodor W. 1973. *Negative Dialectics*. Translated by E.B. Ashton. New York: Continuum.

————. "The Aging of the New Music." 1988. Translated by Robert Hullot-Kentor and Frederic Will. *Telos* 77 (Fall), 95–116.

Adorno, Theodor W., and Max Horkheimer. 1972. *Dialectic of Enlightenment*. Translated by John Cumming. New York: Continuum.

Agger, Ben. 1989a. *Socio(onto)logy: A Disciplinary Reading*. Urbana: University of Illinois Press.

————. 1989b. *Fast Capitalism: A Critical Theory of Significance*. Urbana: University of Illinois Press.

Althusser, Louis. 1971. *Lenin and Philosophy*. Translated by Ben Brewster. New York: Monthly Review Press.

Anderson, Perry. 1983. *In the Tracks of Historical Materialism*. London: Verso Press.

Aronson, Ronald. 1987. *Sartre's Second Critique*. Chicago: University of Chicago Press.

Arrighi, Giovanni, Terrence K. Hopkins, and Immanuel Wallerstein. 1989. *Antisystemic Movements*. London: Verso Books.

Avakian, Bob. 1979. *Mao Tsetung's Immortal Contributions*. Chicago: RCP Publications.

Bagdikian, Ben H. 1983. *The Media Monopoly*. Boston: Beacon Press.

*Baker, Houston A, Jr. 1984. *Blues, Ideology, and Afro-American Literature: A Vernacular Theory*. Chicago: University of Chicago Press.

————. 1987. *Modernism and the Harlem Renaissance*. Chicago: University of Chicago Press.

Barbiero, Daniel. 1989–90. "After the Aging of the New Music." *Telos* 82 (Winter), 144–50.

Barrett, R., and R. Gibson, eds. 1990. *Perspectives on Quine*. Oxford: Basil Blackwell.

Barthes, Roland. 1977. *Image/Music/Text*. Translated by Stephen Heath. New York: Hill and Wang.

Baudrillard, Jean. 1981. *For a Critique of the Political Economy of the Sign*. Translated by Charles Levin. St. Louis: Telos Press.

———. *America*. 1988. Translated by Chris Turner. London: VersoBooks.

Benhabib, Seyla. 1986. *Critique, Norm, and Utopia: A Study of the Foundations of Critical Theory*. New York: Columbia University Press.

Benjamin, Walter. 1969. "The Work of Art in the Age of Mechanical Reproduction." in *Illuminations*. Translated by Harry Zohn. New York: Schocken Books, 217–51.

Benton, Ted. 1984. *The Rise and Fall of Structuralist Marxism: Althusser and his Influence*. New York: St. Martin's Press.

Bernasconi, Robert. 1985. *The Question of Language in Heidegger's History of Being*. Atlantic Highlands, NJ: Humanities Press.

Bernstein, Richard. 1983. *Beyond Objectivism and Relativism*. Philadelphia: University of Pennsylvania Press.

———. 1989. "Pragmatism, Pluralism and the Healing of Wounds." *Proceedings and Addresses of the American Philosophical Association*, v.63, n.3 (November), 5–18.

*Berry, Wendell. 1987. *Home Economics*. San Francisco: North Point Press.

Blakemore, Steven. 1988. *Burke and the Fall of Language: The French Revolution as Linguistic Event*. Hanover, NH: University Press of New England.

Blanchot, Maurice. 1988. *The Unavowable Community*. Translated by Pierre Joris. Barrytown, NY: Station Hill Press.

Bloch, Ernst. 1988. *The Utopian Function of Art and Literature*. Translated by Jack Zipes and Frank Mecklenburg. Cambridge: MIT Press.

Bloch, Ernst, et al. 1977. *Aesthetics and Politics*. London: New Left Books.

Bloor, David. 1983. *Wittgenstein: A Social Theory of Knowledge*. New York: Columbia University Press.

Bloom, Harold. 1984. *Kabbalah and Criticism*. New York: Continuum.

Bogue, Ronald. 1989. *Deleuze and Guattari*. London: Routledge.

Bordo, Susan. 1987. *The Flight to Objectivity: Essays on Cartesianism and Culture.* Albany, NY: SUNY Press.

Bowles, Samuel, and Herbert Gintis. 1986. *Capitalism and Democracy: Property, Community, and the Contradictions of Modern Social Thought.* New York: Basic Books.

Boyne, Roy. 1990. *Foucault and Derrida: The Other Side of Reason.* London: Unwin Hyman.

Bradbury, Malcolm. 1985. *Rates of Exchange.* London: Penguin Books.

Brand, Stewart. 1988. *The Media Lab: Inventing the Future at M.I.T.* London: Penguin Books.

Bryant, M. Darrol and Rita H. Mataragnon, eds. 1985. *The Many Faces of Religion and Society.* New York: Paragon House.

Buchanan, Allen E. 1989. "Assessing the Communitarian Critique of Liberalism." *Ethics* v.99, n.4 (July), 852–82.

Buck-Morss, Susan. 1977. *The Origin of Negative Dialectics: Theodor W. Adorno, Walter Benjamin and the Frankfurt Institute.* New York: Macmillan Free Press.

———. 1989. *The Dialectics of Seeing: Walter Benjamin and the Arcades Project.* Cambridge: MIT Press.

Burger, Peter. 1984. *Theory of the Avant-Garde.* Translated by Michael Shaw. Minneapolis: University of Minnesota Press.

*Butler, Judith. 1990. *Gender Trouble: Feminism and the Subversion of Identity.* New York: Routledge.

Callinicos, Alex. 1985. *Marxism and Philosophy.* Oxford: Oxford University Press.

———. 1990. *Against Postmodernism: A Marxist Critique.* New York: St. Martin's Press.

Caputo, John D. 1988. "Beyond Aestheticism: Derrida's Responsible Anarchy." *Research in Phenomenology,* v.xviii, 59–73.

———. 1990. "Thinking, Poetry and Pain." *The Southern Journal of Philosophy,* v.xxviii Supplement (Spring), 155–81.

Carnap, Rudolf. 1959. "The Elimination of Metaphysics Through Logical Analysis of Language." in A. J. Ayer, ed., *Logical Positivism.* New York: The Free Press.

Cavell, Stanley. 1984. *Themes Out of School: Effects and Causes.* Chicago: University of Chicago Press.

Chomsky, Noam. 1975. "Quine's Empirical Assumptions." in D. Davidson and

J. Hintikka, eds., *Words and Objections: Essays on the Work of W. V. Quine.* Dordrecht: D. Reidel, 53–67.

Churchland, Patricia. 1986. *Neurophilosophy: Toward a Unified Science of the Mind-Brain.* Cambridge: MIT Press.

Cohen, G. A. 1978. *Karl Marx's Theory of History: A Defense.* Princeton: Princeton University Press.

*Corlett, William. 1989. *Community Without Unity: A Politics of Derridian Extravagance.* Durham: Duke University Press.

Coward, Rosalind, and John Ellis. 1977. *Language and Materialism: Developments in Semiology and the Theory of the Subject.* London: Routledge and Kegan Paul.

Cox, Harvey. 1965 *The Secular City: Urbanization and Secularization in Theological Perspective.* New York: Macmillan.

Culler, Jonathan. 1988. *Framing the Sign: Criticism and Its Institutions.* Norman: Oklahoma University Press.

Dallery, Arleen B., and Charles E. Scott, eds. 1989. *The Question of the Other.* Albany, NY: SUNY Press.

Daubier, Jean. 1974. *A History of the Chinese Cultural Revolution.* Translated by Richard Seaver. New York: Vintage Books.

*Davidson, Donald. 1982a. *Essays on Actions and Events.* Oxford: Oxford University Press.

———. 1982b. "Expressing Evaluations." The Lindley Lecture. University of Kansas.

*———. 1985. *Inquiries into Truth and Interpretation.* Oxford: Oxford University Press.

———. 1986. "Judging Interpersonal Interests." in Jon Elster, ed., *Foundations of Social Choice Theory.* Cambridge: Cambridge University Press.

———. 1989a. "The Myth of the Subjective." in Michael Krausz, ed., *Relativism: Interpretation and Confrontation.* Notre Dame: Notre Dame University Press.

———. 1989b. "What is Present to the Mind?" in J. Brandl and W. Gombocz, eds., *The Mind of Donald Davidson. Grazer Philosophische Studien* 36; pp. 3–18.

———. 1989c. "The Conditions of Thought." *Le Cahier du College International al de Philosophie.* Paris: Editions Osiris, 165–71.

Dean, William. 1988. *History Making History: The New Historicism in American Religious Thought.* Albany, NY: SUNY Press.

Deleuze, Gilles. 1985. "Nomad Thought." Translated by David B. Allison. in David B. Allison, ed., *The New Nietzsche*. Cambridge: MIT Press.

DeLillo, Don. 1985. *White Noise*. New York: Penguin Books.

Delphy, Christine. 1977. *The Main Enemy: A Materialist Analysis of Women's Oppression*. Translated by Lucy Roberts and Diana Leonard Barker. London: Women's Research and Resources Centre Publications.

De Man, Paul. 1983. *Blindness and Insight*. 2nd ed., rev. Minneapolis: University of Minnesota Press.

———. 1984. *The Rhetoric of Romanticism*. New York: Columbia University Press.

*Derrida, Jacques. 1973. *Speech and Phenomena, and Other Essays on Husserl's Theory of Signs*. Translated by David B. Allison. Evanston, IL: Northwestern University Press.

*———. 1976. *of Grammatology*. Translated by Gayatri Chakravorty Spivak. Baltimore: Johns Hopkins University Press.

———. 1978. *Writing and Difference*. Translated by Alan Bass. Chicago: University of Chicago Press.

———. 1979. *Spurs: Nietzsche's Styles*. Translated by Barbara Harlow. Chicago: University of Chicago Press.

———. 1981a. *Dissemination*. Translated by Barbara Johnson. Chicago: University of Chicago Press.

———. 1981b. *Positions*. Translated by Alan Bass. Chicago: University of Chicago Press.

*———. 1982. *Margins of Philosophy*. Translated by Alan Bass. Chicago: University of Chicago Press.

———. 1983a. "The Principle of Reason: The University in the Eyes of Its Pupils." *Diacritics* v.13, n.3 (Fall), 3–20.

———. 1983b "The Time of a Thesis: Punctuations." Translated by Kathleen McLaughlin. in Alan Montefiore, ed., *Philosophy in France Today*. Cambridge: Cambridge University Press, 34–50.

*———. 1984a "No Apocalypse, Not Now (full speed ahead, seven missiles, seven missives)." Translated by Catherine Porter and Philip Lewis. *Diacritics*, v.14, n.2 (Summer), 18–31.

———. 1984b. "Interview with Richard Kearney." in Richard Kearney, ed., *Dialogues with Contemporary Continental Thinkers*. Manchester: Manchester University Press, 83–105.

———. 1985a. *The Ear of the Other: Otobiography, Transference, Translation*.

Edited by Christie V. McDonald. Translated by Peggy Kamuf and Avital Ronell. New York: Schocken Books.

———. 1985b. "Des Tours de Babel." Translated by Joseph F. Graham. in Joseph F. Graham, ed., *Difference in Translation*. Ithaca, NY: Cornell University Press.

———. 1985c. "Racism's Last Word." Translated by Peggy Kamuf. *Critical Inquiry*, v.12, n.1 (Autumn), 290–99.

———. 1985d. "Deconstruction in America: An Interview with Jacques Derrida." Translated by James Creech. With James Creech, Peggy Kamuf, and Jane Todd. *Critical Exchange*, n.17 (Winter), 1–33.

*———. 1986a. *Glas*. Translated by John P. Leavey, Jr., and Richard Rand. Lincoln: University of Nebraska Press.

———. 1986b. *Memoires for Paul de Man*. Translated by Cecile Lindsay, Jonathan Culler, and Eduardo Cadava. New York: Columbia University Press.

———. 1986c. "Shibboleth." Translated by Joshua Wilner. in Geoffrey H. Hartman and Sanford Budick, eds., *Midrash and Literature*. New Haven: Yale University Press.

———. 1987a. *The Post Card: From Socrates to Freud and Beyond*. Translated by Alan Bass. Chicago: University of Chicago Press.

———. 1987b. *The Truth in Paining*. Translated by Geoff Bennington and Ian McLeod. Chicago: University of Chicago Press.

*———. 1988a. *Limited Inc*. Edited by Gerald Graff. Translated by Samuel Weber and Jeffrey Mehlman. Evanston, IL: Northwestern University Press.

———. 1988b. "The Politics of Friendship." *Journal of Philosophy*, v.LXXXV, n.11 (November), 632–44.

*———. 1989a. "Psyche: Inventions of the Other." Translated by Catherine Porter. in Lindsay Waters and Wlad Godzich, eds., *Reading de Man Reading*. Minneapolis: University of Minnesota Press.

———. 1989b. *of Spirit: Heidegger and the Question*. Translated by Geoffrey Bennington and Rachel Bowlby. Chicago: University of Chicago Press.

———. 1989c. "How to Avoid Speaking: Denials." Translated by Ken Frieden. in Sanford Budick and Wolfgang Iser, eds., *Languages of the Unsayable: The Play of Negativity in Literature and Literary Theory*. New York: Columbia University Press.

Deutscher, Isaac. 1971. "Marxism and Primitive Magic." in *Marxism in Our Time*. Edited by Tamara Deutscher. Berkeley: Ramparts Press.

Dews, Peter. 1987. *Logics of Disintegration: Post-Structuralist Thought and the Claims of Critical Theory*. London: Verso Books.

Dolan, Frederick M. 1988. "Hobbes and/or North: The Rhetoric of American National Security." *Canadian Journal of Political and Social Theory*, v.12, n.3 (Fall), 1–19.

Dretske, Fred I. 1981. *Knowledge and the Flow of Information*. Cambridge: MIT Press.

Dreyfus, Hubert L. and Harrison Hall, eds. 1982. *Husserl, Intentionality, and Cognitive Science*. Cambridge: MIT Press.

Dummett, Michael. 1975. "What Is a Theory of Meaning?" in Samuel Guttenplan, ed., *Mind and Language*. Oxford: Oxford University Press.

————. 1978. *Truth and Other Enigmas*. Cambridge: Harvard University Press.

————. 1981. *The Interpretation of Frege's Philosophy*. Cambridge: Harvard University Press.

Duquette, David. 1990. "Civic and Political Freedom in Hegel." *Southwestern Philosophy Review*, v.6, n.1 (January), 37–44.

Dworkin, Ronald. 1986. *Law's Empire*. Cambridge: Harvard University Press.

————. 1990. Lindley Lecture. The University of Kansas.

Eagleton, Terry. 1981. *Walter Benjamin or, Towards a Revolutionary Criticism*. London: Verso Books.

————. 1986. "The Critic as Clown." in *Against the Grain*. London: Verso Books, 149–65.

————. 1990. *The Ideology of the Aesthetic*. Oxford: Basil Blackwell.

Eco, Umberto. 1986. "The Return of the Middle Ages." in *Travels in Hyperreality*. Translated by William Weaver. New York: Harcourt, Brace, Jovanovich, 59–85.

Eisenstein, Zillah R. 1981. *The Radical Future of Liberal Feminism*. New York: Longman Press.

Elliot, Gregory. 1987. *Althusser: The Detour of Theory*. London: Verso Books.

Elster, Jon. 1985. *Making Sense of Marx*. Cambridge: Cambridge University Press.

Erckenbrecht, U. 1973. *Marx's Materialische Sprachtheorie*. Kronberg: Scriptor.

*Fackenheim, Emil L. 1980. *Encounters Between Judaism and Modern Philosophy: A Preface to Future Jewish Thought*. New York: Schocken Books.

———. 1982. *To Mend the World: Foundations of Future Jewish Thought.* New York: Schocken Books.

Ferry, Luc, and Alain Renaut. 1990. *French Philosophy of the Sixties.* Translated by M. S. Cattani. Amherst: University of Massachusetts Press.

Firestone, Shulamith. 1971. *The Dialectic of Sex: The Case for Feminist Revolution.* New York: Bantam Books.

Flax, Jane. 1983. "Political Philosophy and the Patriarchal Unconscious: A Psychoanalytic Perspective on Epistemology and Metaphysics." in Sandra Harding and Merrill B. Hintikka, eds. *Discovering Reality.* Dordrecht: D. Reidel.

Fodor, Jerry. 1987. *Psychosemantics: The Problem of Meaning in the Philosophy of Mind.* Cambridge: MIT Press.

Foucault, Michel. 1973. *The Order of Things: An Archaeology of the Human Sciences.* New York: Vintage Books.

———. 1972. *The Archaeology of Knowledge.* Translated by A.M. Sheridan Smith. New York: Pantheon Books.

*———. 1977. "Nietzsche, Genealogy, History." in Donald F. Bouchard, ed., *Language, Counter-Memory, Practice.* Translated by Donald F. Bouchard and Sherry Simon. Ithaca: Cornell University Press, 139–64.

———. 1980. *Power/Knowledge.* Edited by Colin Gordon. Translated by Colin Gordon, Leo Marshall, John Mepham, and Kate Soper. New York: Pantheon Books.

Fraser, Nancy. 1984. "The French Derrideans: Politicizing Deconstruction or Deconstructing Politics." *New German Critique,* n.33 (Fall), 127–54.

Fuller, Steve. 1988. *Social Epistemology.* Bloomington: University of Indiana Press.

*Fuss, Diana. 1989. *Essentially Speaking: Feminism, Nature and Difference.* London: Routledge.

Gadamer, Hans-Georg. 1981. *Reason in the Age of Science.* Translated by Frederick G. Lawrence. Cambridge: MIT Press.

*Gasche, Rodolphe. 1986. *The Tain of the Mirror: Derrida and the Philosophy of Reflection.* Cambridge: Harvard University Press.

Gauthier, David. 1989. "Constituting Democracy." The Lindley Lecture. The University of Kansas.

Genova, Anthony C. 1983. "The Metaphilosophical Turn in Contemporary Philosophy." *Southwest Philosophical Studies,* v.ix, n.2, 1–22.

———. 1984. "Good Transcendental Arguments." *Kant-Studien*, v.75, n.4, 469–95.

Gibson, William. 1984. *Neuromancer*. New York: Ace Science Fiction.

———. 1986. *Count Zero*. New York: Ace Science Fiction.

———. 1988. *Mona Lisa Overdrive*. New York: Bantam Books.

Gilbert, Sandra M., and Susan Guber. 1979. *The Madwoman in the Attic*. New Haven: Yale University Press.

Gorz, Andre. 1982. *Farewell to the Working Class: An Essay on Post-Industrial Socialism*. Translated by Michael Sonenscher. Boston: South End Press.

Gross, Bertram. 1980. *Friendly Fascism: The New Face of Power in America*. Boston: South End Press.

Grosz, Elizabeth. 1989. *Sexual Subversions: Three French Feminisms*. North Sydney: Allen and Unwin Australia.

Habermas, Jurgen. 1979. *Communication and the Evolution of Society*. Translated by Thomas McCarthy. Boston: Beacon Press.

*———. 1984/1987a. *The Theory of Communicative Action*. 2 Vols. Translated by Thomas McCarthy. Boston: Beacon Press.

———. 1985. *Philosophical-Political Profiles*. Translated by Frederick Lawrence. Cambridge: MIT Press.

*———. 1987b. *The Philosophical Discourse of Modernity: Twelve Lectures*. Translated by Frederick Lawrence. Cambridge: MIT Press.

———. 1989. *The New Conservatism: Cultural Criticism and the Historians' Debate*. Edited and Translated by Shierry Weber Nicholsen. Cambridge: MIT Press.

Han-Liang Chang. 1988. "Hallucinations of the Other: Derridean Fantasies of Chinese Script." Working Paper n.4, Center for Twentieth Century Studies, University of Wisconsin-Milwaukee.

*Handelman, Susan. 1982. *The Slayers of Moses: The Emergence of Rabbinic Interpretation in Modern Literary Theory*. Albany, NY: SUNY Press.

Harding, Sandra. 1986. *The Science Question in Feminism*. Ithaca, NY: Cornell University Press.

Hartman, Geoffrey H. 1981. *Saving the Text: Literature/Derrida/Philosophy*. Baltimore: Johns Hopkins University Press.

Hartsock, Nancy. 1985. *Money, Sex, and Power: Toward a Feminist Historical Materialism*. Boston: Northeastern University Press.

*Harvey, Irene. 1986. *Derrida and the Economy of Differance*. Bloomington: University of Indiana Press.

Hattiangadi, J. N. 1987. *How is Language Possible?*. La Salle, IL: Open Court.

*Hegel, G. W. F. 1975. *Lectures on the Philosophy of World History, Introduction*. Translated by H. B. Nisbet. Cambridge: Cambridge University Press.

————. 1977. *Phenomenology of Mind*. Translated by J. B. Baillie. New York: Humanities Press.

————. 1984. *Lectures on the Philosophy of Religion*. Edited by Peter C. Hodgson. Translated by R. F. Brown, P. C. Hodgson, and J. M. Stewart. Berkeley: University if California Press.

*Heidegger, Martin. 1977. *Basic Writings*. Edited by David Farrell Krell. New York: Harper and Row.

————. 1977. *The Question Concerning Technology and Other Essays*. Translated by William Lovitt. New York: Harper and Row.

Heilbroner, Robert. 1975. *An Inquiry Into The Human Prospect*. New York: Norton.

Hennelly, Alfred T., ed. 1990. *Liberation Theology; A Documentary History*. Maryknoll, NY: Orbis Books.

Hobbes, Thomas. 1968. *Leviathan*. Edited by C. B. Macpherson. London: Penguin Books.

Holderlin, Friedrich. 1984. *Hymns and Fragments*. Translated by Richard Sieburth. Princeton: Princeton University Press.

Hollier, Denis. 1986. *The Politics of Prose: Essay on Sartre*. Translated by Jeffrey Mehlman. Minneapolis: University of Minnesota Press.

Hooks, Bell. 1984. *Feminist Theory: From Margin to Center*. Boston: South End Press.

Huhn, Thomas. 1988. "Jameson and Habermas." *Telos*, n.75 (Spring), 103–23.

Hullot-Kentor, Robert. 1989. "From Uplift to Gadgetry: Barbiero, Eno, and New Age Music." *Telos* 82 (Winter), 151–56.

Husserl, Edmund. 1970. *The Crisis of European Sciences and Transcendental Phenomenology*. Translated by David Carr. Evanston, IL: Northwestern University Press.

Hyppolite, Jean. 1974. *Genesis and Structure of Hegel's Phenomenology of Spirit*. Translated by Samuel Chernick and John Heckman. Evanston, IL: Northwestern University Press.

Idel, Moshe. 1988. *Language, Torah, and Hermeneutics in Abraham Abulafia.* Translated by Menahem Kallus. Albany, NY: SUNY Press.

Ingram, David. 1987. *Habermas and the Dialectic of Reason.* New Haven: Yale University Press.

———. 1988. "The Retreat of the Political in the Modern Age: Jean-Luc Nancy on Totalitarianism and Community." *Research in Phenomenology,* v.xviii, 93–124.

*Irigaray, Luce. 1985a. *Speculum of the Other Woman.* Translated by Gillian C. Gill. Ithaca, NY: Cornell University Press.

———. 1985b. *This Sex Which Is Not One.* Translated by Catherine Porter. Ithaca, NY: Cornell University Press.

Jabes, Edmond. 1989. *The Book of Shares.* Translated by Rosemarie Waldrop. Chicago: University of Chicago Press.

Jacobs, Struan, and Karl-Heinz Otto. 1990. "Otto Neurath: Marxist Member of the Vienna Circle." *Auslegung,* v.16, n.2 (Summer), 175–89.

Jacoby, Russell. 1987. *The Last Intellectuals: American Culture in the Age of Academe.* New York: The Noonday Press.

*Jameson, Fredric. 1984. "Postmodernism, or The Cultural Logic of Late Capitalism." *New Left Review,* n.146 (July/August).

———. 1988. "Cognitive Mapping." in Cary Nelson and Lawrence Grossberg, eds., *Marxism and the Interpretation of Culture.* Urbana: University of Illinois Press, 347–57.

Jay, Gregory S. 1990. *America the Scrivener.* Ithaca, NY: Cornell University Press, 1990.

Jay, Martin. 1984. *Adorno.* Cambridge: Harvard University Press, 1984.

Johnson, Barbara. 1982. "Teaching Ignorance: *L'Ecole des Femmes.*" *Yale French Studies,* n.63, 165–82.

———. 1987. *A World of Difference.* Baltimore: Johns Hopkins University Press.

Keller, Evelyn Fox, and Christine R. Grontkowski. 1983. "The Minds Eye." in Sandra Harding and Merrill B. Hintikka, eds., *Discovering Reality.* Dordrecht: D. Reidel, 207–24.

Kellner, Douglas M. 1984. *Herbert Marcuse and the Crisis of Marxism.* Berkeley: University of California Press.

———. 1989a. *Jean Baudrillard: From Marxism to Postmodernism and Beyond.* Stanford: Stanford University Press.

———. 1989b. *Critical Theory and Modernity*. Baltimore: Johns Hopkins University Press.

Kim, Jaegwon. 1989. "The Myth of Nonreductive Materialism." *Proceedings and Addresses of the American Philosophical Association*, v.63, n.3 (November), 31–47.

Kimball, Roger. 1990. *Tenured Radicals*. New York: Harper and Row.

Kockelmans, Joseph J., ed. 1972. *On Heidegger and Language*. Translations by Joseph J. Kockelmans. Evanston, IL: Northwestern University Press.

Koppelberg, Dirk. 1987. *Aufhebung auf analytische philosophie: Quine als Synthese von Carnap und Neurath*. Frankfurt am Main: Suhrkamp.

Krell, David Farrell. 1986. *Postponements*. Bloomington: University of Indiana Press.

Kroker, Arthur, and David Cook. 1986. *The Postmodern Scene: Excremental Culture and Hyper-Aesthetics*. New York: St. Martin's Press.

Lacan, Jacques. 1977. *Ecrits: A Selection*. Translated by Alan Sheridan. New York: Norton.

Laclau, Ernesto, and Chantal Mouffe. 1985. *Hegemony and Socialist Strategy*. Translated by Winston Moore and Paul Cammack. London: Verso Press.

Lacoue-Labarthe, Philippe. 1987. *La Fiction du politique*. Strasbourg: Association de Publications pres les Universites de Strasbourg.

Lambrose, R. J. 1990. Review of Roger Kimball, *Tenured Radicals*. *The Nation*, v.250, n.22 (June 4), 791–95.

Lenin, V. I. 1967. "The Proletarian Revolution and the Renegade Kautsky." in *Selected Works*, v.3. New York: International Publishers, 39–121.

———. 1972a. *Materialism and Empirio-Criticism*. Peking: Foreign Langauges Press.

———. 1972b. *The Emancipation of Women*. New York: International Publishers.

———. 1979. *Imperialism: The Highest Stage of Capitalism*. New York: International Publishers.

Lentricchia, Frank. 1983. *Criticism and Social Change*. Chicago: University of Chicago Press, 1983.

LePore, Ernest, and Brian McLaughlin, eds. 1985. *Actions and Events: Perspectives on the Philosophy of Donald Davidson*. Oxford: Basil Blackwell.

LePore, Ernest, ed. 1985. *Truth and Interpretation: Perspectives on the Philosophy of Donald Davidson*. Oxford: Basil Blackwell.

Levinas, Emmanuel. 1969. *Totality and Infinity.* Translated by Alphonso Lingis. Pittsburgh: Duquesne University Press.

Lotta, Raymond, with Frank Shannon. 1984. *America in Decline.* Chicago: Banner Press.

Luke, Tim. 1978. "Culture and Politics in the Age of Artificial Negativity." *Telos,* n.35 (Spring), 55–72.

Lunn, Eugene. 1982. *Marxism and Modernism: An Historical Study of Lukacs, Brecht, Benjamin and Adorno.* Berkeley: University of California Press.

*Lyotard, Jean-Francois. 1984. *The Postmodern Condition: A Report on Knowledge.* Translated by Geoff Bennington and Brian Massumi. Minneapolis: University of Minnesota Press.

MacGregor, David. 1984. *The Communist Ideal in Hegel and Marx.* Toronto: University of Toronto Press.

MacIntyre, Alasdair. 1984. *After Virtue.* Second edition. Notre Dame: University of Notre Dame Press.

———. 1988. *Whose Justice? Which Rationality?* Notre Dame: University of Notre Dame Press.

Magliola, Robert. 1984. *Derrida on the Mend.* West Lafayette, IN: Purdue University Press.

Maier, Charles S. 1988. *The Unmasterable Past: History, Holocaust, and German National Identity.* Cambridge: Harvard University Press.

Mandel, Ernest. 1978. *Late Capitalism.* Translated by Joris de Bres. London: Verso Books.

Mao Tsetung. 1977. *Five Essays on Philosophy.* Peking: Foreign Languages Press.

Marcus, Greil. 1989. *Lipstick Traces: A Secret History of the Twentieth Century.* Cambridge: Harvard University Press.

Marcuse, Herbert. 1968. *Negations: Essays in Critical Theory.* Boston: Beacon Press.

Margolis, Joseph. 1986. *Pragmatism without Foundations: Reconciling Realism and Relativism.* Oxford: Basil Blackwell.

———. 1987. *Science without Unity: Reconciling the Human and Natural Sciences.* Oxford: Basil Blackwell.

———. 1988. *Texts without Referents: Reconciling Science and Narrative.* Oxford: Basil Blackwell.

Martin, Bill. 1986. "Nomad and Empire: Nietzsche, Guerilla Theatre, Guerilla War." *Arena,* n.77 (Winter), 88–95.

————. 1987. "Return to the land of weird theologies." *Social Epistemology*, v.1, n.2 (April), 203–209.

————. 1988. "Apocalypse Derrida." *Auslegung*, v.14, n.2 (Summer), 201–210.

————. 1989a. "The Feminist Path to Postmodernity: Virginia Woolf's *To the Lighthouse*." *Philosophy and Literature*, v.13, n.2 (Summer), 307–315.

————. 1989b. "Politics of Irony in Paul de Man." *Canadian Journal of Political and Social Theory*, v.13, n.3 (Fall), 16–30.

————. 1989c. "How Marxism Became Analytic." *The Journal of Philosophy*, v.LXXXVI, n.11 (November), 659–66.

————. 1990a. "The Moral Atmosphere: Language and Value in Davidson." *The Southwest Philosophy Review*, v.6, n.1 (January), 89–97.

————. 1990b. Review of Solomon, *Discourse and Reference in the Nuclear Age*. *Auslegung*, v.16, n.2 (Summer), 209–214.

Martin, Rex. 1985. *Rawls and Rights*. Lawrence: University of Kansas Press.

Marx, Karl. 1964. "Critique of Hegel's Philosophy of Right." in Tom Bottomore, ed., *Karl Marx: Early Writings*. New York: McGraw Hill.

Matthews, Richard K. 1984. *The Radical Politics of Thomas Jefferson*. Lawrence: University of Kansas Press.

Mazlish, Bruce. 1984. *The Meaning of Karl Marx*. Oxford: Oxford University Press.

McCarthy, Thomas. 1984. "Translator's Introduction." in Jurgen Habermas, *The Theory of Communicative Action*, v.1. Boston: Beacon Press, v–xxxvii.

————. 1989. "The Politics of the Ineffable: Derrida's Deconstructionism." *Philosophical Forum*, v.XXI, n.1–2 (Fall/Winter), 146–68.

McLuhan, Marshall. 1964. *Understanding Media: The Extensions of Man*. New York: McGraw-Hill.

Merleau-Ponty, Maurice. 1973. *Consciousness and the Acquisition of Language*. Translated by Hugh J. Silverman. Evanston, IL: Northwestern University Press.

Michelfelder, Diane P., and Richard Palmer, eds. 1989. *Dialogue and Deconstruction: The Gadamer-Derrida Encounter*. Albany, NY: SUNY Press.

Mies, M. 1986. *Patriarchy and Accumulation on a World Scale: Women in the International Division of Labor*. London: Zed Press.

*Miller, Mark Crispin. 1988. *Boxed In: The Culture of TV*. Evanston, IL: Northwestern University Press.

*Miller, Nancy K. 1989. "Changing the Subject." in Elizabeth Weed, ed., *Coming to Terms: Feminism, Theory, Politics*. London: Routledge.

Mohanty, J. N. 1985. *The Possibility of Transcendental Philosophy*. Hingham, MA: Martinus Nijhoff.

Moses, Stephane. 1988. "Franz Rosenzweig in Perspective: Reflections on His Last Diaries." in Paul Mendes Flohr, ed., *The Philosophy of Franz Rosenzweig*. Hanover, NH: University Press of New England, 185–201.

Munro, Robin. 1990. "The Real Story of the Slaughter in Beijing." *The Nation*, v.250, n.23, 811–22.

Nadel, Ira B. 1989. *Joyce and the Jews: Culture and Texts*. Iowa City: University of Iowa Press.

Nancy, Jean-Luc. 1986. *La Communaute desoeuvree*. Paris: Christian Bourgeois.

Nehemas, Alexander. 1985. *Nietzsche: Life as Literature*. Cambridge: Harvard University Press.

Nieli, Russell. 1987. *Wittgenstein: From Mysticism to Ordinary Language*. Albany, NY: SUNY Press.

Norris, Christopher. 1987. *Derrida*. Cambridge: Harvard University Press.

O'Hagen, Timothy. 1988. "Four Images of Community." *Praxis International* 8:2 (July), 183–92.

Oliver, Kelly. 1988. "Nietzsche's Woman: The Poststructuralist Attempt To Do Away With Women." *Radical Philosophy*, Spring, 25–29.

Padover, Saul K., ed. 1979. *The Letters of Karl Marx*. Translated by Saul K. Padover. Englewood Cliffs, NJ: Prentice-Hall.

Parker, Andrew. 1985. "Between Dialectics and Deconstruction: Derrida and the Reading of Marx." in Gregory S. Jay and David L. Miller, eds., *After Strange Texts: The Role of Theory in the Study of Literature*. University: University of Alabama Press.

———. 1986. "Ezra Pound and the 'Economy' of Anti-Semitism." in Jonathan Arac, ed., *Postmodernism and Politics*. Minneapolis: University of Minnesota Press.

Peukert, Helmut. 1984. *Science, Action, and Fundamental Theology: Toward a Theology of Communicative Action*. Translated by James Bohman. Cambridge: MIT Press.

Phelan, Shane. 1989. *Identity Politics: Lesbian Feminism and the Limits of Community*. Philadelphia: Temple University Press.

Piccone, Paul. 1977. "The Changing Function of Critical Theory." *New German Critique*, n.12 (Fall), 29–37.

*Piercy, Marge. 1976. *Woman on the Edge of Time.* New York: Fawcett Crest.

Pogge, Thomas W. 1989. *Realizing Rawls.* Ithaca, NY: Cornell University Press.

Portis, Larry. 1988. "On the Rise and Decline of Totalitarian Liberalism: Schlesinger, Bell, Larouche." *Canadian Journal of Political and Social Theory*, v.12, n.3 (Fall), 20–36.

Poster, Mark. 1984 *Foucault, Marxism and History: Mode of Production versus Mode of Information.* Cambridge: Polity Press.

*Pradhan, S. 1986. "Minimalist Semantics: Davidson and Derrida on Meaning, Use, and Convention." *Diacritics*, v.16, n.1 (Spring), 65–77.

Putnam, Hilary. 1987. *The Many Faces of Realism.* LaSalle, IL: Open Court.

———. 1988. *Representation and Reality.* Cambridge: MIT Press.

Quine, W. V. 1953. *From a Logical Point of View.* Cambridge: Harvard University Press.

———. 1969. *Ontological Relativity and Other Essays.* New York: Columbia University Press.

Ramberg, Bjorn. 1989. *Donald Davidson's Philosophy of Language.* Oxford: Basil Blackwell.

Rawls, John. 1980. "Kantian Constructivism in Moral Theory: The Dewey Lectures 1980." *Journal of Philosophy*, v.LXXVII, n.9 (September), 518–72.

———. 1982. "The Basic Liberties and Their Priority." *The Tanner Lectures on Human Values*, III. Edited by Sterling M. McMurrin. Salt Lake City: University of Utah Press.

Rochberg-Halton, Eugene. 1986. *Meaning and Modernity: Social Theory in the Pragmatic Mode.* Chicago: University of Chicago Press.

Roderick, Rick. 1986. *Habermas and the Foundations of Critical Theory.* New York: St. Martin's Press.

Ronnel, Avital. 1989. *The Telephone Book: Technology, Schizophrenia, Electric Speech.* Lincoln: University of Nebraska Press.

Rorty, Richard. 1979. *Philosophy and the Mirror of Nature.* Princeton: Princeton University Press.

———. 1982. *Consequences of Pragmatism.* Minneapolis: University of Minnesota Press.

*———. 1989a. *Contingency, irony, and solidarity.* Cambridge: Cambridge University Press.

———. 1989b. "Two Meanings of 'Logocentrism': A Reply to Norris." in Reed Way Dasenbrock, ed., *Redrawing the Lines: Analytic Philosophy, Deconstruction, and Literary Theory*. Minneapolis: University of Minnesota Press.

Rosenzweig, Franz. 1985. *The Star of Redemption*. Translated by William H. Hallo. Notre Dame: Notre Dame University Press.

*Ryan, Michael. 1982. *Marxism and Deconstruction: A Critical Articulation*. Baltimore: Johns Hopkins University Press.

———. 1989. *Politics and Culture: Working Hypotheses for a Post-Revolutionary Society*. Baltimore: Johns Hopkins University Press.

Sale, Kirkpatrick. 1985. *Dwellers in the Land: The Bioregional Vision*. San Francisco: Sierra Club Books.

Sartre, Jean-Paul. 1956. "Existentialism is a Humanism." in Walter Kaufmann, ed., *Existentialism from Dostoevsky to Sartre*. Cleveland: Meridian Books, 287–311.

———. 1976a. *Critique of Dialectical Reason*. Translated by Alan Sheridan-Smith. Edited by Jonathan Ree. London: Verso Books.

———. 1976b. "Socialism in One Country." *New Left Review*, n.100 (November), 143–63.

Sayers, Janet, et. al., eds. 1987. *Engels Revisited: New Feminist Essays*. London: Tavistock Publications.

Schiffer, Stephen. 1987. *Remnants of Meaning*. Cambridge: MIT Press.

Scholes, Robert. 1985. *Textual Power: Literary Theory and the Teaching of English*. New Haven: Yale University Press.

Schrag, Calvin O. 1989. *Communicative Praxis and the Space of Subjectivity*. Bloomington: University of Indiana Press.

Searle, John. 1982. "What Is an Intentional State?" in Hubert L. Dreyfus, ed., *Husserl, Intentionality, and Cognitive Science*. Cambridge: MIT Press, 259–76.

Shapiro, Gary. 1980. "Reading and Writing in the Text of Hobbes's *Leviathan*." *Journal of the History of Philosophy*, v.xviii, n.2 (April), 147–57.

*———. 1985. "Nietzschean Aphorism as Art and Act." in J. N. Mohanty, ed., *Phenomenology and the Human Sciences*. Dordrecht: Martinus Nijhoff.

Silverman, Hugh J, ed. 1989. *Derrida and Deconstruction*. New York: Routledge.

Smith, Paul. 1988. *Discerning the Subject*. Minneapolis: University of Minnesota Press.

Solomon, J. Fisher. 1988. *Discourse and Reference in the Nuclear Age.* Norman: University of Oklahoma Press.

Soja, Edward. 1989. *Postmodern Geographies: The Reassertion of Space in Critical Social Theory.* London: Verso Books.

Spivak, Gayatri Chakravorty. 1980. "Revolutions That As Yet Have No Model: Derrida's *Limited Inc.*" *Diacritics,* v.10, n.4 (December), 29–49.

————. 1983. "Displacement and the Discourse of Woman." in Mark Krupnick, ed., *Displacement: Derrida and After.* Bloomington: Indiana University Press, 169–95.

————. 1987. *In Other Worlds: Essays in Cultural Politics.* New York: Methuen.

Stalin, J. V. 1972. *Marxism and Problems of Linguistics.* Peking: Foreign Languages Press.

Stanton, Domna C., ed. 1986. *The Defiant Muse: French Feminist Poems from the Middle Ages to the Present.* New York: The Feminist Press.

Stanton, Harry. 1984. *Wittgenstein and Derrida.* Lincoln: University of Nebraska Press.

Steiner, George. 1982. *Language and Silence.* New York: Atheneum.

Stroud, Barry. 1977. *Hume.* London: Routledge and Kegan Paul.

*Taylor, Mark C. 1987. *Altarity.* Chicago: University of Chicago Press.

Theunissen, Michael. 1984. *The Other: Studies in the Social Ontology of Husserl, Heidegger, Sartre, and Buber.* Translated by Christopher Macann. Cambridge: MIT Press.

Theweleit, Klaus. 1987. *Male Fantasies.* Volume One. Translated by Stephen Conway. Minneapolis: University of Minnesota Press.

Tönnies, Ferdinand. 1988. *Community and Society.* Translated by Charles P. Loomis. New Brunswick, NJ: Transaction Books.

Trey, George S. 1989a. "The Philosophical Discourse of Modernity: Habermas's Postmodern Adventure." *Diacritics,* v.19, n.2 (Summer), 67–79.

————. 1989b. "Textualizing the Lifeworld: Critical Theory with a Difference." Unpublished manuscript.

Trotsky, Leon. 1960. *Literature and Revolution.* Translated by Rose Strunsky. Ann Arbor: University of Michigan Press.

————. 1970. *On Literature and Art.* Edited by Paul N. Siegel. New York: Pathfinder Press.

Ulmer, Gregory L. 1985. *Applied Grammatology: Post(e)-Pedagogy from Jacques Derrida to Joseph Beuys.* Baltimore: Johns Hopkins University Press.

————. 1989. *Teletheory: Grammatology in the Age of Video.* London: Routledge.

Voloshinov, V. N. 1973. *Marxism and the Philosophy of Language.* Translated by L. Matejka and I. R. Titunik. New York: Seminar Press.

Warren, Mark. 1988. *Nietzsche and Political Thought.* Cambridge: MIT Press.

Welch, Sharon D. 1985. *Communities of Resistance and Solidarity: A Feminist Theology of Liberation.* Maryknoll, NY: Orbis Books.

West, Cornell, and John Rajchman, eds. 1985. *Post-Analytic Philosophy.* New York: Columbia University Press.

Whitehead, Alfred North. 1978. *Process and Reality.* Corrected edition. Edited by David Ray Griffin and Donald W. Sherburne. New York: The Free Press.

Wittgenstein, Ludwig. 1974. *Tractatus Logico-Philosophicus.* Translated by D. F. Pears and B. F. McGuinness. New Jersey: Humanities Press.

Wolff, Lenny. 1983. *The Science of Revolution.* Chicago: RCP Publications.

Wood, Allen. 1981. *Karl Marx.* London: Routledge and Kegan Paul.

Wood, David. 1989. *The Deconstruction of Time.* Atlantic Highlands, NJ: Humanities Press.

*Wood, Ellen Meiksins. 1986. *The Retreat from Class: A New "True" Socialism.* London: Verso Press.

Wyschograd, Edith. 1985. *Spirit in Ashes: Hegel, Heidegger, and Man-Made Mass Death.* New Haven: Yale University Press.

*Zimmerman, Michael E. 1990. *Heidegger's Confrontation with Modernity: Technology, Politics, Art.* Bloomington: University of Indiana Press.

Zizek, Slavoj. 1989. *The Sublime Object of Ideology.* London: Verso Books.

Index of names

A page listing is given also in cases where the name of a particular figure is invoked but not expressly mentioned, in the case of a form of thought associated with that figure's name, e.g., Marxism, Heideggerianism, etc.